# Trade Policy in a
# Changing World Economy

Previous work by the author includes:

*Economic Development and Growth* (1966)
*Nontariff Distortions of International Trade* (1970)
*Foreign Trade Regimes and Economic Development: The Philippines* (1975)
*The Political Economy of US Import Policy* (1985)

# Trade Policy in a Changing World Economy

Robert E. Baldwin

*Hilldale Professor of Economics*

*University of Wisconsin-Madison*

HARVESTER · WHEATSHEAF

NEW YORK   LONDON   TORONTO   SYDNEY   TOKYO

First published 1988 by
Harvester · Wheatsheaf
66 Wood Lane End, Hemel Hempstead
Hertfordshire, HP2 4RG
A division of
Simon & Schuster International Group

Printed and bound in Great Britain by
A. Wheaton & Co. Ltd, Exeter

---

British Library Cataloguing in Publication Data

---

Baldwin, Robert E.
Trade policy in a changing world economy.
1. United States. Foreign trade. Policies
of government
I. Title
382'.3'0973

ISBN 0-7450-0419-9


1 2 3 4 5   92 91 90 89 88

# Contents

# Tables and Figures

# Preface

This volume contains a selection of my papers on various aspects of trade policy. While international economists have long been interested in trade policy from a welfare-theoretic viewpoint, too few, in my opinion, have devoted their attention to other important aspects of the subject. These include the relationship between the theoretical welfare conclusions of trade economists and the welfare implications of actual national laws and international rules governing international trade, the nature of changes in trade policies over time and the forces bringing about these changes, the political and economic factors that shape the nature of trade policy decisions by democratic governments, empirical analyses of the economic effects of government actions aimed at restraining imports or promoting exports, and realistic means by which policies and institutions could be modified to better achieve national objectives and improve international relations. I hope that these essays will not only add to readers' knowledge about these issues but serve to stimulate much-needed research in the trade policy field.

Part I is an autobiographical introduction, written at the request of the editors of Harvester · Wheatsheaf. It focuses on the various intellectual influences that have shaped my economic thinking. Part II outlines the history of US trade policy since the 1930s. The essay, 'The Changing Nature of US Trade Policy Since World War II', traces the remarkable shifts in the positions of the two major political parties and various pressure groups on trade policy issues and tries to relate these to underlying economic developments. 'The Political Economy of Postwar US Trade Policy' utilizes a political economy framework to analyse congressional voting patterns on the post-1945 bills that granted trade-liberalizing authority to the president. The last selection in this part, 'Trade Policies Under the Reagan Administration', explains the various factors accounting for the marked difference between the intended and actual performance of the Reagan administration on trade policy.

The papers in Part III consider various aspects of trade policy from a theoretical viewpoint. The first selection, 'The Political Economy of

Protectionism', surveys political economy theory as applied to trade policy and tries to integrate the analyses of various authors into an approach that is consistent with the results of empirical investigations of lobbying activities. 'Rent Seeking and Trade Policy: An Industry Approach' presents a short-run economic model that is consistent with the fact that labour and management in an industry generally adopt the same lobbying position on trade matters, in contrast to the antagonistic positions predicted by the Stolper—Samuelson theorem. 'The Economics of the GATT' analyses the basic rules of the General Agreement on Tariffs and Trade in terms of behaviour standards usually applied by economists and points out the producer bias and inconsistencies in these rules. In 'The Case against Infant-Industry Tariff Protection' I evaluate critically the theoretical arguments used to support protection for infant industries and conclude that the externality argument on which the case for protecting new industries rests does not hold up very well on close examination. The last paper in this section, 'The Inefficacy of Trade Policy', presents theoretical reasons why government measures to protect particular industries from import competition often do not bring about the increases in production, employment and profits expected from these policies.

The first of the two papers in Part IV, Multilateral Trade Negotiations: Employment Effects and Negotiating Techniques, describes the model I developed for the US Department of Labor to estimate the trade and employment effects in some 300 US industries of alternative tariff-cutting rules that were considered for adoption in the GATT-sponsored Tokyo Round of multilateral trade negotiations. The second essay, 'Toward More Efficient Procedures for Multilateral Trade Negotiations', compares the different tariff-reducing techniques followed in trade negotiations since the early 1930s and examines critically both the techniques followed by countries to achieve reciprocity and the efforts in the Tokyo Round to control so-called 'unfair' trade practices by negotiating new GATT behaviour codes.

The last part in the volume focuses on Policy Issues and Trade Strategies. The first essay, 'The New Protectionism: A Response to Shifts in National Economic Power', analyses the recent spread of import-protecting and export-promoting measures in terms of the rise of the United States to a position of economic dominance among non-communist countries, and then the gradual decline in US international influence and emergence of the European Community and Japan to positions of significant economic power. 'Responding to Trade-Distorting Policies of Other Countries' (co-authored with T. Scott Thompson), the second paper in Part V, describes and appraises various government actions being taken in response to allegedly unfair practices of other countries and considers changes in trading rules to reduce the inconsistency of these actions with present GATT rules. The next essay, 'GATT Reform: Selected Issues', further explores possible changes in GATT rules and procedures designed to strengthen the international trading system by considering such proposals as shifting from the unconditional to the conditional most-favoured-nation principle, extending GATT rules to cover trade in services, trade-related investment requirements and intellectual property rights, and modifying GATT procedures for settling trade disputes. The last paper in the volume, 'Alternative Liberalization Strategies', contrasts and evaluates the multilateral, bilateral and regional, and aggressive unilateral strategies that countries are pursuing in their efforts to shape the nature of the international trading system.

# PART I
Introduction

# 1 Autobiographical Introduction

As Joseph Schumpeter was fond of pointing out, the analyses of economists and other social scientists, and even the issues they study, are greatly influenced by the social and cultural environment in which they live and their personal experiences in this milieu. Consequently, to carry out the request of Harvester · Wheatsheaf, that I write an autobiographical introduction to this collection of essays, I think that what might best contribute as background for readers would be to point out the various intellectual influences and personal experiences that have shaped my economic thinking and to discuss some of the conclusions I have reached in my research.

I remember very well my first class in economics. After describing the topics to be covered in the course, the professor allowed the class to select the topic we would cover first, beginning that very day. Being fresh out of a highly structured course of studies in high school, this struck me as indicating both remarkable regard for the views of the students and extraordinary teaching ability. It was not until much later that Claude Puffer told me the students invariably picked money and banking as the beginning topic, and he had his notes and the course outline all prepared for that choice. Puffer also demonstrated his flair for getting students involved by cutting a dollar bill in half that first day and asking if he had destroyed wealth by so doing.

I did not start out at the University of Buffalo as an economics major. Business administration seemed to hold more promise for earning a living than a field in the social sciences or humanities, even though these fields were more appealing intellectually. (I had firmly rejected following the chemical engineering route of my father and brother because of my knowledge of factory life in my home town, Niagara Falls.) Fortunately, Harold Somers, a comparatively recent Berkeley Ph.D. and postdoctoral fellow at the University of Chicago, took me under his wing and allowed me to take a number of directed-study courses in economics in which he began to convey to me not only knowledge but the excitement of scholarly research. When he informed me there was an economics scholarship available in the college of arts and sciences, I jumped at the opportunity. Being able to pay the Buffalo tuition from the $400 the scholarship provided each semester meant a great deal, since I was financing my education from the funds I had saved working during high school and from summer jobs in the factories in Niagara Falls, plus the funds my mother could spare. My father had died in a plant explosion six months before I was born in 1924, and she and my brother and I lived mainly on the modest workmen's compensation she received.

Thus it evolved that I majored in economics as an undergraduate, and I began to focus on international economics at that time. I do not remember my reasoning but, like so many students who take trade courses, I suppose I thought it would help me get a job in which I could travel and see the world. I wrote my senior thesis in 1945 on the German reparations problem of the 1920s. In the process, I first became familiar with the controversy between Keynes and Ohlin over the role of income effects in bringing about the export surplus Germany needed to pay the reparations. I thought Ohlin had much the better of the argument, especially after reading, at Harold Somers' recommendation, Fritz Machlup's then-recent (1943) book *International Trade and the National Income Multiplier*. Machlup was a professor at the University of Buffalo but he was on leave during the war working at the Patent Office in Washington.

Fortunately, I did well in economics, graduating *summa cum laude*, and Somers, Puffer and Ralph Epstein, the chairman of the department who also helped me learn what economics was all about, encouraged me to go on to graduate school. I decided to try to get into Harvard, in part because Epstein had gone there but also because I had been visiting relatives in the Boston area for many years and was influenced by their (perhaps home-town-biased) regard for Harvard as the best educational institution in the country. But since I thought I wanted to work in the federal government after getting a Ph.D. rather than teach, during my senior year on my professors' advice, I applied for an internship in the federal government under a programme sponsored by the Rockefeller Foundation, and I was accepted in the one-year programme to begin in July 1945.

The programme provided a wonderful opportunity to learn about a career in the federal government and about life in Washington. For the first month or so, we visited various government offices to learn about their functions. I remember that Hubert Humphrey, then a congressman already establishing his reputation as a creative liberal, talked to us, as did Edward Stettinius Jr, who succeeded Cordell Hull as Secretary of State. We also visited one of the Supreme Court justices; I cannot remember which one. Washington was an exciting place during the closing days of the war, and I grew very fond of the city, despite the heat. The males in the program lived at the Brookings Institution, then on Jackson Place, across from the White House. I will always remember the crowds and excitement in Lafayette Park on V-J Day. In the evening President Truman came out of the White House and to the fence on Pennsylvania Avenue to shake hands with many in the crowd.

The Brookings staff worked in the front part of the building; the dormitories and dining facilities were in the rear. Later, in 1963 when I returned to Washington as the first chief economist of the Office of the US Trade Representative, I was temporarily given the office that had been occupied by Harold Moulton, who was president of Brookings when I was first there. By 1963 Brookings had moved up to Massachusetts Avenue and the government was preparing to tear down the old building to make way for the new Executive Office Building.

After our initial overall view of the government, each participant in the programme selected an agency in which to work as an intern. In keeping with my interest in trade, I selected the International Trade Commission (then called the Tariff Commission). It was not a very lively place, and I soon began to envy my colleagues who had selected more exciting jobs, such as in the State Department or in the office of a senator or representative. But Howard Piquet, chief economist at the Commission, was doing interesting work and I hoped eventually to work with him. I started in the statistical division, where I soon acquired a life-long scepticism about the exactness of government statistics. I specifically remember spending considerable time trying to track down an enormous discrepancy in two sets of government statistics on imports of sugar.

In the early part of September 1945, just as I was settling in nicely in my Tariff Commission position, I received a call from Ralph Epstein offering me an instructorship in the economics department at Buffalo. The postwar deluge of students was beginning and the university was desperate for teachers. At first I was going to turn down the offer, but the argument that a year of teaching would help me get into graduate school and the fact that my mother was in ill health changed my mind.

My nine-month salary was $2,400 and my twelve hours per week of teaching consisted of four elementary economics sections with about fifty students each. I recall asking Ralph Epstein how to grade exams. He told me to follow a percentage distribution curve but also to set an absolute standard as to what was acceptable. When I asked what I should do if everyone failed, he replied that this would be a failure for the instructor, not the student—a point I have always tried to keep in mind. At first, I did not enjoy teaching. Many of the students were older than I, others I had known as fellow undergraduates, and, as I told Epstein, I was not sure I was doing a good job. I was relieved when he reported he had surveyed some of the students and found that they thought I was doing well. As Harold Somers told me then, students never think you gave as good a lecture as you think you did, but they also don't think you gave as bad a lecture as you sometimes think. By the end of the year, I had come to enjoy teaching very much and was offered $3,000 if I would remain another year. But I turned down the offer, since I had been accepted at Harvard and received a non-teaching fellowship of $1,000 over and above tuition.

Harvard was an intellectually exciting place in the early postwar years. The first part of the three-semester theory sequence was taught by Edward Chamberlin, the second by Wassily Leontief, and the third by Joseph Schumpeter. Gottfried Haberler taught the graduate trade course and he and Seymour Harris ran the trade seminar. John Williams and Alvin Hansen shared the graduate money and banking course as well as the seminar. The department was weak in statistics and most of my fellow students and I felt we did not get good training in that subject.

Chamberlin gave a good, traditional macroeconomics course and also spent considerable time discussing monopolistic competition and how it differed from Mrs Robinson's imperfect competition. Few students chose Chamberlin as their major professor, in large part, I think, because he had such strong views on exactly what was and was not monopolistic competition. It seemed easy to suggest a line of inquiry that he shot down as rank heresy. He also showed little interest in directing empirical theses in the industrial organization field.

Leontief did not teach the second-semester theory course when I was ready to take it, and I took it from Haberler instead. But I later became Leontief's teaching assistant for the course and learned to appreciate his special talents. He spent little time developing economic tools; that was the teaching assistant's responsibility. He was, instead, trying to teach how one begins to theorize about or model a particular economic problem.

In contrast, Schumpeter took a topics approach in his course. I recall his spending a great deal of time on the Harrod–Domar growth model. He was a colourful lecturer. Occasionally he would pull a piece of yellow paper from his pocket and jot something down. We later found out that he would record what he had just said if he thought he had come up with an especially good thought or phrase. Unfortunately, he never talked about his own work and most of us never appreciated what a great thinker he was until we later read some of his writings.

Most of my fellow graduate students thought that money and banking, or what we now call macroeconomics, was the most exciting field. Alvin Hansen was presenting the Keynesian model as a major improvement over the neoclassical macroeconomic model. He was an excellent expositor and he conveyed the sense that Keynes's theory enabled us to understand the great depression of the 1930s and to take actions to prevent the recurrence of such an event. John Williams and most, if not all, of the older department members did not accept the Keynesian approach, but most of the students became Keynesians.

Pursuing my interest in trade, I took all of the available courses in the field. I wrote my first article while I was taking the trade seminar. Haberler, who was always generous with the time he would spend talking with me and reading my papers and whom I greatly admired as a scholar and later also as a friend, was a tough critic when it came to explaining theoretical matters clearly. I remember being frustrated when he kept telling me to rewrite certain sections of the first paper and my other early papers so that they would be more easily understood, but I learned the valuable lesson that it is not enough to come up with good ideas; they must also be expressed clearly and related to other relevant literature in the field.

An experience outside of the department from which I benefited greatly after I became a teaching fellow was my appointment as a resident tutor at Dunster House, one of the undergraduate resident houses at Harvard. Dunster was well known for its concentration of tutors in economics—Schumpeter, Leontief, Duesenberry, and Harris all being non-resident tutors there. Besides becoming better acquainted with these individuals, I got to know some of the economics tutors in other houses quite well, in particular Howard Hines and Jim Schlesinger. I also learned a great deal from the tutors in other fields, especially during the summers when we were the only persons living in the house, and came to realize how narrow my undergraduate education had been. I would never advise a would-be economist to major in economics as an undergraduate. Majoring in a broad field like history or literature and taking a good bit of maths serves one much better. Among the benefits I gained by interacting with students under many different social and academic circumstances over my four-and-a-half years as a resident tutor was a good understanding of what undergraduates were like. By getting a better appreciation of the total personality that is behind many types of classroom behaviour, I became a more effective teacher and more comfortable with the task of trying to convey knowledge and stimulate the minds of others.

After receiving my Ph.D. in 1950 I was very pleased to be offered an instructorship and later an assistant professorship at Harvard. It provided the opportunity to begin practising my skills as an economist in a highly stimulating environment where I could get first-rate feedback on my work. Jim Duesenberry, Carl Kaysen, Guy Orcutt, Bob Dorfman, Glenn Campbell and Jim McKie were among the young faculty with whom I had stimulating exchanges of ideas.

Arthur Smithies, whom I first got to know as his assistant in his graduate course in the public policy programme at Littauer and then much better later when he became chairperson of the economics department, was especially important in shaping my ideas of an economist's role. He was an excellent analytical economist with an active interest in public policy issues and a good understanding of the policy-making process, and he was committed to using his skills to promote the public welfare.

I also became acquainted with some of the economists in the MIT economics department, especially Charlie Kindleberger, Bob Bishop, and Paul Samuelson. I audited a trade seminar that Samuelson taught and he read drafts of some of my early papers and called my work to the attention of others. It was he who gave the name the Baldwin Envelope Curve to the construct I had developed to show the maximum range of goods a country could achieve through production and the use of its monopoly power in trade. Others with whom I became fairly well acquainted through their visits to Harvard and whom I particularly admired as scholars were Jacob Viner and John Hicks.

In 1954 I married Janice Murphy, who was working on her Ph.D. thesis at the Fletcher School of Law and Diplomacy at Tufts University and whom I had met when she was working for the Leontief input-output project one summer. We lived in an apartment on Linnean Street, a short distance from Littauer Center where the economics department was located. Two of our four children, Jean and Bob, were born while we lived in Cambridge.

During this period the trade seminar became the focal point of much of the research in economic development that was beginning to take place at Harvard, and I became very much interested in this subject. I taught the first undergraduate course in economic development at Harvard. There were also many graduate students since there was no graduate course in the field at that time. Gerald Meier and I wrote one of the first texts on the subject. I felt, and still feel, that the analytical part of any development course should cover the growth models of Smith, Ricardo, Marx, Schumpeter, the neoclassical writers, Keynes and the post-Keynesians, as well as recent theoretical analyses specifically having to do with developing countries. Furthermore, it seems to me that one should deal with the growth problems and policies of both developing and developed countries.

We left Harvard in the fall of 1957 to go to UCLA, where I took over the development field that was emerging there. Looking back, it is clear that the prospect of living in a sunny, warm climate played a not insignificant role in our choosing UCLA over other places from which I had offers. We liked the climate and lifestyle of Los Angeles very much, though we were not so sure we wanted our children to grow up there. Dick and Nancy were born while we were living there.

Soon after arriving at UCLA, I joined the African Studies Center, which was then ably headed by Jim Coleman. During this period the State Department was financing visits to the United States by a number of individuals who later held high political positions in their home countries in Africa. Several of those who visited UCLA became heads of state: Sekou Touré of Guinea, Julius Nyerere of Tanzania, and Kenneth Kaunda of Zambia. Others who played prominent political roles in their countries were Joshua Nkomo of Zimbabwe and Tom Mboya of Kenya.

Because of my interest in Africa, I applied for and was awarded a fellowship under the Ford Foundation's Foreign Area Training Program to spend the academic year 1960–1 in the Federation of Rhodesia and Nyasaland. During that year I completed the research for a book on the economic development of Zambia (then Northern Rhodesia) in which I emphasized the extent to which the technological nature of the production function for copper influenced the general pattern of development in the country. Though I visited the Copperbelt in Zambia fairly often, we actually lived in a university flat in Harare (then Salisbury) in Zimbabwe (then Southern Rhodesia) since the Federation's archives, university and the headquarters of the copper companies were all located in that city.

My experience in Africa began to convince me of the importance for development of government policies that provide economic incentives for workers and farmers to improve their living standards. The British officials who controlled the Zambian economy believed that African farmers were incapable of taking care of the soil and that the use of land should thus be tightly controlled. Yet, in instances when African farmers were given an opportunity to produce for a cash market, they responded by increasing their productivity remarkably and without bringing about the dire outcome of erosion and soil depletion predicted by government bureaucrats.

This view of the effectiveness of market incentives in bringing about economic growth was reinforced by discussions with colleagues at UCLA, such as Armen Alchian, Karl Brunner, Jack Hirshleifer, Harold Demetz, Bill Allen and Larry Miller. I realized that, up to that point, I had not really appreciated the operation of the private market system and how it is affected by government policies. The Harvard tradition in which I had been trained tended to view the price system and the effect of government policies on its operation in simple and limited mechanical terms. In contrast, many of my UCLA colleagues, who followed what was termed the Chicago tradition (though most were not trained at the University of Chicago), viewed the assumption of individual utility maximization in more personal and general terms. They asked themselves how individuals would respond to government interference, taking into account not just changes in how they would allocate a given income but changes in the magnitude and type of effort devoted to earning an income. Focusing at this more microeconomic level, one begins to appreciate why government interventions so often result in resource misallocation, a weakening of economic incentives and thus a slowdown in the growth rate, and a rise in rent-seeking activities.

I was also much influenced by Karl Brunner's views on the proper role of an economist in society. Unlike most of my colleagues at both Harvard and UCLA, Karl believes that one must not only develop hypotheses on public policy issues from careful model formulations but also test these hypotheses empirically, using econometrics or careful historical analysis.

After returning from Africa, I became increasingly disappointed with the field of development, mainly because most individuals in the field, especially area specialists who were not economists, were sceptical toward efforts to model the development process theoretically and conduct empirical tests of economic hypotheses. Thus when offered the chance, through the efforts of Guy Orcutt, to return to the trade field as the replacement at the University of Wisconsin for Paul (Blackie) Ellsworth who was planning to retire within a few years, I accepted. There was no possibility of moving into the trade area at UCLA, since there were already capable senior individuals in the field there.

When I was about to accept the Wisconsin offer, there was another development that greatly influenced my subsequent career. Carl Kaysen, who was working in the White House in the Kennedy administration, asked me if I would like to become the Chief Economist in the newly formed Office of the Special Trade Representative (now the US Trade Representative or USTR), an agency in the Executive Office of the President that was established to conduct the Kennedy Round of multilateral trade negotiations. After meeting with Christian Herter, the Special Trade Representative, and others, I was offered the job and I agreed to spend a year there. Fortunately, Wisconsin was willing to give me a year's leave so I accepted that position also.

My experience in Washington was both exhilarating and frustrating—exhilarating because I could actually influence the formation of the trade policies I had read about for so many years, and frustrating because of the scepticism (if not hostility) of many government officials—bureaucrats and political appointees alike—about the importance of economics in policy making, and from the inadequate data and resources to analyse the trade, employment and welfare effects of various patterns of tariff cuts. On the latter point, I was very grateful to Charlie Schultz, then an assistant director in the Budget Bureau, who lined up $360,000 from the old Exchange Stabilization Fund to begin a data bank and undertake some statistical analyses. Herter exemplified those who had little confidence in what economists had to say. I soon realized that he used the analysis I gave him only on those occasions when it served to bolster an argument he was making for entirely different purposes. One person who did respect the usefulness of economics was Mike Blumenthal, then a Deputy Special Trade Representative stationed in Geneva and later Secretary of the Treasury under President Carter. He was a masterful negotiator and is one of the brightest persons I have ever worked with.

Although I was under pressure to remain at USTR at least one more year, it was my judgement, which proved to be correct, that little progress would be made in the negotiations until shortly before the negotiating authority expired in July 1967. The differences between the negotiating positions of the United States and the European Community (EC) on agriculture and the so-called disparities issue, on which the Community wished to cut some high duties by a greater percentage than low duties, were so great that little was likely to be accomplished until pressure of the deadline for ending the negotiations was felt. The death of President Kennedy also meant the loss of much of the exciting feeling that the Kennedy Round was an important foreign policy initiative for the United States. So I moved to Wisconsin in the fall of 1964, though I continued to serve occasionally as a consultant to USTR.

The department at Wisconsin proved to be stimulating and compatible and I especially enjoyed being able to focus my teaching and research on international trade. Empirical work was strongly supported in the department and I devoted much of my early research there to testing the Heckscher–Ohlin theory. Continuing my interest in trade policy, I participated in committees dealing with this issue in the US Chamber of Commerce and the Atlantic Council. I also became a consultant for the international programme of the Committee for Economic Development (CED), a non-profit organization composed mainly of representatives from large US corporations who prepared position papers on various policy issues. This provided an opportunity to become better acquainted with the thinking of this group of business leaders and their counterparts in Europe and Japan, since we often developed joint position papers with these organizations. At this time, all these groups were strongly in favour of liberal trade policies.

I became particularly interested in non-tariff barriers (NTBs) to trade. USTR had the authority in the Kennedy Round to negotiate on non-tariff measures, but reaching agreement on the difficult tariff-reducing issue took almost all of the negotiators' time and NTBs received little attention. A visiting Rockefeller Research Professorship at the Brookings Institution for the academic year 1967–8 enabled me to write a book on the subject, and my connections in the government provided much more data than I otherwise would have been able to obtain.

Though most of my research time was devoted to trade issues, I did not give up my interest in development, especially its international aspects. In the early 1970s I joined a National Bureau of Economic Research project headed by Anne Krueger and Jagdish Bhagwati analysing the trade and exchange-rate regimes of several developing countries. The country I studied was the Philippines. The Wisconsin economics department directed a training programme at the University of the Philippines, and I already had fairly good contacts in the country.

It was remarkable how the conclusions of the authors of all nine country studies began to converge as the project proceeded. They agreed that a policy of extensive import substitution, after a short period of rapid growth, resulted in a slowdown in the rate of development as excess capacity and other inefficiencies emerged in import-competing sectors, export production declined and serious balance-of-payments problems developed. In contrast, growth rates generally accelerated when a country shifted to liberal trade and exchange-rate policies that permitted export activities to serve as an important engine of growth.

It was also apparent from cross-country comparisons that the economies of countries that consistently followed liberal policies grew considerably faster than those more closely tied to an import substitution strategy. Though many of us had been convinced early in our careers that considerable government intervention was necessary in both developed and developing countries to maintain adequate employment and growth levels, we gradually came to reject this view, especially as applied to developing countries, as we observed their experiences after World War II. The most powerful force that can be used to accelerate development seems to be the desire of individual workers, farmers, and business entrepreneurs to improve their economic lot. Governments can play an important role in maintaining the conditions necessary for this desire to flourish, but too often government actions stifle economic incentive and reduce growth rates below what is possible.

A tradition of the Wisconsin economics department that I liked very much was its encouraging faculty members to obtain hands-on experience in dealing with public policy problems. This tradition enabled me to go to Washington again for the academic year 1974–5 to work in the Office of Foreign Economic Research at the US Department of Labor in Washington, ably headed at that time by Bill Dewald. I constructed a detailed model that could be used to estimate the trade and employment effects in some 300 US industries of the various tariff-cutting rules proposed in the Tokyo Round negotiations. There had been an enormous change in how economic analysis was received by policy makers compared to ten years earlier. By this time, a large group of well-trained economists, many with Ph.D.s, were working throughout the government in top technical positions, and they, as well as most political appointees, were very interested in the results of the analysis that I and others working on the same subject did. It was clear that the analyses of economists could no longer be ignored by government officials, as they had often been in the early 1960s.

As I continued to study trade policy issues in both developed and developing countries, I became increasingly interested in the political economy of trade policy. It was apparent, especially as protectionist pressures grew in the late 1960s and 1970s, that the actual decision-making process often resulted in government actions that did not promote national welfare as defined by economists. To understand why and to be able to evaluate alternative policy options more realistically, I began reading in the political economy field and studying the factors that seemed to affect trade legislation. Part of my research at the Labor Department in 1974–5 was devoted to examining the congressional hearings on trade legislation since 1945. I also statistically tested the extent to which the House and Senate votes on the legislation authorizing the Kennedy Round were influenced by a member's political party, the contributions he or she received from protectionist labour unions, and the extent to which depressed import-competing industries and vigorous export-oriented industries were located in the members' districts or states.

After serving as chair of the Wisconsin economics department from 1975–8, I returned to Washington for the academic year 1978–9 on a research grant from the World Bank to study the political economy of US import policy. Helen Hughes and Bela Balassa were especially helpful to me in formulating the proposal. As I have discovered each time I have taken leave, one year is not long enough to complete the research for a book and write up the results. Because a heavy teaching schedule precluded my working on the manuscript except during summers, it was not until 1985 that my political economy book was published.

In the course of researching the formation of trade policy by Congress, the executive branch and the International Trade Commission (ITC), I became convinced that the widely accepted pressure group model of policy formation based on short-run economic self-interest, while often providing a good explanation of political-economic behaviour, should be broadened to include political behaviour based on social concerns. Of course, doing so makes rigorous modelling of political-economic behaviour more difficult, but economists must resist the temptation to sacrifice general explanations of behaviour for more rigorous but less complete descriptions of the relationships of interest to them.

For example, in the case of the Heckscher–Ohlin model a generation of trade economists, including myself, became overly fascinated with a formulation of trading relationships that yields such neat results as international factor-price equalization and the Stolper–Samuelson and Rybczynski theorems, and we tended to minimize the unreality of the assumptions needed for these results. The outcome has been a failure of trade theory until recently to keep up with the growing importance of imperfectly competitive markets in international trade and with analytical developments in other economic fields that can be used to understand and model the nature of trade under these conditions. Careful modelling is necessary for progress in the social sciences, but care must be taken to not be so captivated by the elegance of rigorous models that important economic relationships are ignored.

Through the efforts of Dick Cooper and Fred Bergsten, who were in the Carter administration, I was nominated by the president to be a member of the ITC just as I was completing my year at the World Bank. I did not want to spend a full nine-year term at the ITC, but the position for which I was nominated required my spending a year and a half there to complete the term of a commissioner who had resigned. I welcomed this opportunity, feeling that it would not only give me new insights into the political economy of policy making but would enable me to push for greater use of economic analysis in carrying out the provisions of US trade law. Though initially there was approval of my nomination by various labour and business organizations, some labour unions and business groups came to regard me as being too liberal in trade policy matters. Finally, Dick Cooper phoned me and said I had become a lightning rod for all the protectionists and they were going to have to withdraw my nomination.

During the period of the Tokyo Round trade negotiations, I was fortunate to participate in a series of meetings with the trade negotiators of various countries on issues that arose during the negotiations. In these meetings, which were arranged by Hugh Corbet, director of the Trade Policy Research Centre in London, I came to appreciate the respect most trade negotiators had for the General Agreement on Tariffs and Trade (GATT) and their reluctance to press for clear and specific trading rules for fear that the fragile consensus on which the GATT was based would be destroyed. But this experience and subsequent study convinced me that numerous opportunities for mutually agreeable liberalizing actions were being missed because the GATT Secretariat was not being permitted to play an active facilitator role.

Interest in trade policy issues has increased tremendously in the 1980s, stimulated largely by the huge US trade deficit. In 1982 I became a research associate of the National Bureau of Economic Research and director of the Bureau's Trade Relations project, which was funded first by the National Science Foundation and then by the Ford Foundation.

My Wisconsin colleagues, Dave Richardson and Rachel McCulloch, and I have tried to stimulate trade policy research at both the applied and theoretical levels and bring the results of this research to the attention of policy makers. One means that seems to have been quite successful is the holding of conferences for top technical staffers dealing with trade policy issues in executive branch agencies, in congressional committees and offices of members of Congress, and in various Washington-based private groups. We have also held conferences in which the participants and authors of papers are mainly academics and from which an NBER–University of Chicago volume results. We encourage our graduate students to specialize in trade policy issues as another means to inform the decision-making process better in the trade area.

I have continued to enjoy being an academic economist. Being able to convey to young people the knowledge we have acquired in the past, to make one's own search for new knowledge, and to participate in the process of utilizing this knowledge for improved public policy making has contributed to a full and rewarding professional life. My students have been interesting and stimulating, and I have become good friends with many of them. The willingness of my Wisconsin colleagues to exchange ideas on an informal basis has been especially appreciated. The University of Wisconsin has been generous to me. Much-appreciated actions were its awarding me named professorships in 1974 and in 1982, the latter one providing sufficient funds annually for me to hire a part-time secretary and no longer have to worry about obtaining sufficient travel funds for conferences or for collecting research data.

In 1971 Janice received her law degree from the University of Wisconsin and obtained a position with the Legislative Council of the Wisconsin legislature, which provides staff services to legislative committees and undertakes special studies. She had attended law school part-time after all the children had entered school.

We have been very fortunate that our children are pursuing satisfying careers. Two have become economists. Jean and Dick received Ph.D.s in economics from MIT, Jean in 1980 and Dick in 1986. Jean married an economist, Gene Grossman, who had been a fellow student at MIT. Bob and Nancy also did their graduate training at MIT, but in different fields: Nancy received an MA in urban planning in 1983, and Bob was granted a Ph.D. in computer science in 1987.

PART II
The Changing Nature of US Trade Policy

# 2 The Changing Nature of US Trade Policy since World War II*

## 1 INTRODUCTION

Future economic historians will undoubtedly stress trade liberalization as the most noteworthy feature of US commercial policy over the past fifty years. As Table 2.1 indicates, through a series of thirty bilateral agreements and eight multilateral negotiations, tariffs have been steadily cut to only about 20 per cent of their 1930 average level. [1] The increased use in recent years of nontariff protective measures modifies this liberalization picture somewhat, but the trend in protection over the period has clearly been downward.

Although tariff reduction has been the dominant theme of U.S. trade policy since the early 1930s, important changes have taken place in the nature and extent of US support for this trade liberalization. A consideration of these developments is helpful in better understanding American international economic policy over the period and in predicting possible significant shifts in future US trade policy. To further these objectives, this paper focuses on five closely related trends in or features of US trade policy since the end of World War II. They are: (1) the shift from the use of trade policy in the immediate postwar period as a means of promoting broad international political and national security goals of the United States to its greater use in recent years to advance national economic objectives and respond to domestic political pressures from particular economic interests; (2) the continuing efforts by Congress over the period to modify the trade powers of the president to make US international commercial policy more responsive to its wishes; (3) the changes in the positions of the Republican and Democratic parties on the issue of trade liberalization versus increased protectionism; (4) the shifts in the attitudes of business, labour and the farm sector on this issue; and

* From Robert E. Baldwin and Anne O. Krueger (eds) (1984), *The Structure and Evolution of Recent US Trade Policy*, Chicago: University of Chicago Press, pp. 5–27.

19

*Table 2.1:    Duty reductions since 1934 under the US Trade Agreements Program*

| GATT Conference | Proportion of Dutiable Imports Subjected to Reductions | Average Cut in Reduced Tariffs | Average Cut in All Duties | Remaining Duties as a Proportion of 1930 Tariffs[a] |
|---|---|---|---|---|
| 1. Pre-GATT, 1934–47 | 63.9% | 44.0% | 32.2% | 66.8% |
| 2. First Round, Geneva, 1947 | 53.6 | 35.0 | 21.1 | 52.7 |
| 3. Second Round, Annecy, 1949 | 5.6 | 35.1 | 1.9 | 51.7 |
| 4. Third Round, Torquay, 1950–1 | 11.7 | 26.0 | 3.0 | 50.1 |
| 5. Fourth Round, Geneva, 1955–6 | 16.0 | 15.6 | 3.5 | 48.9 |
| 6. Dillon Round, Geneva, 1961–2 | 20.0 | 12.0 | 2.4 | 47.7 |
| 7. Kennedy Round, Geneva, 1964–7 | 79.2 | 45.5 | 36.0 | 30.5 |
| 8. Tokyo Round, 1974–9 | n.a. | n.a. | 29.6 | 21.2 |

*Source*:    Real Phillipe Lavergne (1981), The political economy of US tariffs. Ph.D. thesis, University of Toronto.
[a] These percentages do not take account of the effects of either structural changes in trade or inflation on the average tariff level.

(5) the increased use of non-tariff measures to regulate international trade at the same time that tariffs were being significantly reduced.

Underlying the different shifts in postwar US trade policy outlined above are three more basic economic and political influences that help explain why these changes occurred and how they affected the US commitment toward a liberal trade policy. They are, first—and most important—the emergence and subsequent decline of the United States as a hegemonic power; second, the persistent pressure exerted over the entire period by a politically significant group of domestic industries (whose composition changed somewhat over time) against trade liberalization and in favour of increased import protection for themselves; and third, the efforts by Congress to reduce the greatly increased powers granted the president during the economic emergency of the 1930s and the military emergency of World War II.

## 2   US LEADERSHIP IN ESTABLISHING A LIBERAL INTERNATIONAL TRADING REGIME

Well before the end of World War II, the foreign policy leaders of the Democratic party had concluded that the lack of an open world economy during the 1930s was a major contributory cause of the war[2] and that the United States must, therefore, take the lead after the end of hostilities in establishing an open international trading system to make 'the economic foundations of peace ... as secure as the political foundations'.[3] Thus, even before the war had ended, the Roosevelt administration had not only drafted a proposal for a multilateral trade organization but had also requested substantial new tariff-reducing powers from Congress.

### 2.1   The Basis of Democratic Support for a Liberal International Regime

A desire on the part of political leaders for a new international regime is quite different from actually bringing about such a change, especially when—as in this case—there is a lack of strong direct pressure for the change from either the country's electorate or other governments. One factor that helped the Democratic leadership gain the support of members of their own party for the adoption of a liberal international economic order was the compatibility of such a regime with the trade policy position that the party had long supported. Since the late nineteenth century, the Democrats had associated high tariffs with monopoly profits for the rich and low tariffs with low prices for goods consumed by the average citizen.[4] Furthermore, they maintained that low US tariffs encouraged low foreign tariffs and thus indirectly stimulated increases in US exports, especially agricultural goods. This latter argument was crucial in obtaining passage of the Trade Agreements Act of 1934.[5] The gradual recovery during the 1930s in employment and exports as the trade agreements programme was implemented served to reinforce this ideological commitment of Democrats to liberal trade policies. Consequently, the greater emphasis in the postwar period by the party leadership on the foreign policy merits of a liberal trade policy, in addition to its domestic benefits, represented an extension of the party's recent position that was not difficult for most Democrats to accept. It was also consistent with the stance adopted by the Wilson administration at the end of World War I. Thus, over 80 per cent of the Democrats voting in the House of Representatives supported the party's position on extending the trade agreements program during the 1940s and 1950s.

The fact that implementing an open international trading system did not involve any significant new increase in the powers of the president also was important in gaining domestic support for the regime change.

As a consequence of what almost all regarded as the excessive use of logrolling during the enactment of the Smoot–Hawley Tariff of 1930, coupled with the sense of crisis created by the depression that followed shortly thereafter, the Congress in 1934 gave the president the authority to lower US tariffs by up to 50 per cent in negotiations with other countries in return for reciprocal cuts in their import duties. Consequently, the 1945 request for another 50 per cent duty-cutting power to enable the United States to take a leadership role in international trade liberalization did not entail any basic changes in existing presidential powers.

The most important reason, however, for the success of the Democratic leadership in first gaining and then maintaining support for the US leadership role in creating a liberal international economic regime was the hegemonic trade and payments position that the United States assumed in the immediate postwar period.[6] The United States emerged from World War II with its economic base greatly expanded, while the economic structures of both its enemies and industrial allies were in ruins. Except for Great Britain's position at the outset of the Industrial Revolution, economic dominance of this extent is unique in the history of the industrial nations. Even as late as 1952, the US share of total exports of the ten most important industrial countries was 35 per cent, whereas it had been only 26 and 28 per cent in 1938 and 1928 respectively (see Baldwin 1958). The 1952 US export share of manufactures was also 35 per cent in contrast to only 21 per cent in both 1938 and 1928. Furthermore, there was an export surplus in every major industrial group (e.g., machinery, vehicles, chemicals, textiles, and miscellaneous manufactures) except metals. These abnormally favourable export opportunities, together with the vigorous postwar domestic economic recovery, served both to mask protectionist pressures from industries whose underlying comparative cost position was deteriorating and to build support for liberal trade policies on the part of those sectors whose international competitive position was strong.

The ability of government leaders to obtain domestic support for trade liberalization was further enhanced by the emergence of the Cold War in the late 1940s. The public generally accepted the government view that the communist countries represented a serious economic and political threat to the United States, its allies, and the rest of the market-oriented economic world. The argument that the United States should mount a vigorous programme to offset the communist threat by providing not only military aid to friendly nations but also assistance in the form of economic grants and lower US tariffs, therefore, also received public support.

There was still considerable opposition to trade liberalization in the immediate postwar period, however. As in the 1930s, a long list of industries testified during the 1940s and 1950s against giving the president the power to cut duties on imports competing with domestically produced goods. The products covered included textiles and apparel, coal, petroleum, watches, bicycles, pottery and tiles, toys, cutlery, ball bearings, glass, cheese, lead and zinc, copper, leather, and umbrellas. The decision in this period not to apply a liberal trade policy to agriculture significantly weakened the sectoral opposition to liberalization and established a precedent that has been used several times since to offset protectionist opposition.

Pressures to halt further tariff cutting were also strengthened by the opposition of many Republicans to liberalization on doctrinaire grounds. The Republican advocacy for protectionism on the grounds that this policy promoted domestic economic development and high living standards had an even longer tradition than the Democratic position in favour of liberalization.

From the outset of the trade agreements programme, the Roosevelt administration assured Congress that no duty cuts would be made that seriously injured any domestic industry. But in 1945 the administration recognized the possibility that such injury might occur by agreeing to include in all future trade agreements an escape clause permitting the modification or withdrawal of tariff reductions if increased imports resulting from such a concession caused or threatened to cause serious injury to an industry.[7] Furthermore, under prodding from Republican members of Congress, President Truman in 1947 issued an executive order establishing formal procedures for escape clause actions whereby the ITC would advise the president whether such a modification was warranted.

The strength of the early opposition to across-the-board liberalization is further illustrated by the history of the peril-point provision that directed the president to submit to the ITC a list of all articles being considered for tariff negotiations and required the commission to determine the limits to which each duty could be reduced without causing or threatening serious injury to import-competing domestic industries. This provision was introduced in the 1948 extension of the trade agreements programme when both houses of Congress were controlled by the Republicans. It was repealed in 1949 when the Democrats regained control of the Congress but was then reintroduced in the 1951 extension act, even though the Democrats possessed a majority in both the House and the Senate. The escape clause was also made an explicit part of the law at that time.

These developments indicate that the US trade policy commitment at the beginning of the postwar period was to a policy of liberal trade rather than to a policy of free trade. It was recognized at the outset that protection of particular industries would be permitted if these sectors would otherwise be seriously injured by increased imports. Furthermore, as indicated by the provisions of the charter for an International Trade Organization (ITO) and GATT pertaining to such practices as dumping and export subsidization, the United States and the other major trading nations condemned so-called unfair trade.

The failure of the US Congress to ratify the ITO or even to approve the GATT as an executive agreement is another indication of the early concerns of domestic political interests for import-sensitive US indus-tries.[8] Among other concerns, Congress was fearful that establishing a strong international organization to deal with trade matters would lead to the destruction of many US industries as a result of increased imports. Numerous members of Congress and some of the groups they represented were also concerned about the increase in presidential power that the approval of such an organization might involve. They believed that the division of political powers among the legislative, executive, and judicial branches of government had shifted excessively in favour of the executive branch as a result of the unusual problems created by the depression and World War II and were, consequently, reluctant to extend new authority to the president, especially in an area specifically reserved for Congress under the constitution.

## 2.2   Gaining International Support for a Liberal Regime

As previously noted, the implementation of the change from an inward-looking to an open international trading regime required the support of other countries as well as of the US electorate. The hegemonic model is the major explanation put forth by political scientists to account for this support.[9] The reasoning behind this model is as follows.

An open international trading (and payments) system has elements of a public good. For example, adopting a mercantilistic viewpoint, if one country reduces its tariffs under the most-favoured-nation principle, other countries benefit from the improved export opportunities this action creates even if they do not make reciprocal duty cuts themselves. Consequently, any individual country has an incentive not to reduce its duties and to hope that it will benefit from the cuts made by other nations. This 'free-rider' problem may well result in the failure to secure a balanced, multilateral set of duty reductions even though they would benefit all participants. As Olson (1965) and other writers on collective goods have pointed out, it is less likely that the public good will be underproduced from a social viewpoint if one member of the concerned group is very large compared with the others. The dominant member is so large that the costs to it of free rides by other members tend to be small compared with its gains. Furthermore, the large member may be able to use its power to force smaller members to practice reciprocity. Thus, proponents of the hegemonic theory of regime change point to both the dominant trading position of Great Britain in the nineteenth century and the United States in the immediate post-World War II period to account for the creation of open world trading regimes in these periods.

More specifically, in the immediate postwar period the United States was willing and able to bear most of the costs of establishing a liberal international economic order. The other major industrial countries were plagued by balance-of-payments problems, and they rationed their meagre supplies of dollars to maximize their reconstruction efforts. Consequently, the tariff concessions they made in the early multilateral negotiations were not very meaningful in terms of increasing US exports. US negotiators were fully aware of this point, and they also offered greater tariff concessions than they received, even on the basis of the usual measures of reciprocity (see Meyer, 1978, p. 138). In effect, the United States redistributed to other countries part of the economic surplus reaped from its unusually favourable export opportunities to enable those countries to support the establishment of an open trading regime.

While the hegemonic model has considerable appeal, it should be noted that just as US domestic support for an open trading system was qualified in several ways (e.g., no industry should be seriously injured by duty cuts), so too was the support of other countries. The British insisted upon a provision in the GATT permitting the use of quantitative restrictions to safeguard a country's balance-of-payments position. Furthermore, they were successful in preventing the complete elimination of imperial preferences and in excluding customs unions and free-trade areas from the non-discriminatory provisions of the GATT. Other illustrations of the limited support of GATT signatories for free trade are the provisions permitting government purchasing policies, allowing (at the insistence of the United States) quantitative restrictions on primary products, and imposing almost no restraints on domestic subsidies.

## 3   SHIFTS IN DOMESTIC SUPPORT FOR LIBERALIZATION

The shifts in traditional party positions on trade policy that became evident in 1951, when the Democrats voted in favour of the peril-point provision and the escape clause, and when a surprisingly large proportion of Senate Republicans supported the administration's earlier efforts to establish a liberal trading system, continued over the next thirty years. They were the consequence of basic reassessments of attitudes toward liberalization versus import protection by the various economic groups making up the two major political parties. Congress also continued to restrict the president's ability to refuse to provide protection to industries judged by the ITC to be seriously injured by increased imports. At the same time, however, Congress granted significant new duty-cutting powers to the president.

## 3.1   Political Parties and Income Groups

When the Republicans gained both the presidency and control of Congress in 1952, some Republicans expected a return to traditional protectionist policies. However, President Eisenhower and his main advisors within the administration and in Congress believed—like earlier Democratic administrations—that trade liberalization was an important foreign policy instrument for strengthening the 'free world' against communism. As became apparent with the issuance of the report of a commission established in 1953 by the president to study foreign trade (the Randall Report), Republican business leaders—especially those in large corporations—also had concluded that a liberal trading order was desirable from their own economic viewpoint. Thus, after a stand-off period in 1953 and 1954 during which protectionist-oriented Republicans in the House blocked any further tariff cutting, the liberalization trend was renewed in 1955 when, with the help of a Democratic Congress, President Eisenhower succeeded in obtaining a further 15 per cent duty-cutting authority. In 1958 he was granted an additional 20 per cent tariff-reducing authority.

Just as more Republicans came to accept the desirability of a liberal trade policy as a general principle, more Democrats began to press for exceptions to this principle. In the late 1940s, the industries requesting import protection tended to be relatively small and not very influential politically. However, by the mid 1950s the politically powerful cotton textile, coal and domestic petroleum industries, whose employees tended to vote Democratic, were asking for protection. In 1955, the Eisenhower administration, as part of its efforts to obtain the support of the Democrats for its liberalization efforts, pressured the Japanese into voluntarily restricting their exports of cotton textiles to the United States. This did not fully satisfy the textile interests, however, and in 1962 President Kennedy agreed to negotiate an international agreement permitting quantitative import restrictions on cotton textiles as part of his efforts to gain the support of Southern Democrats from textile areas for the Trade Expansion Act of 1962.[10]

The coal and oil industries succeeded in obtaining a national security clause in the 1955 trade act that permitted quantitative import restrictions if imports of a product threatened 'to impair' the national security. Voluntary oil quotas were introduced on these grounds in 1958 and made mandatory in 1959.

The most significant change in the support for protectionism occurred in the late 1960s when the American Federation of Labour and Congress of Industrial Organizations (AFL-CIO) abandoned its long-held belief in the desirability of a liberal trade policy and supported a general quota bill. Basically, the shift in labour's position was related to the rapid rise in import penetration ratios (and thus to the increase in competitive pressures) that occurred in many manufacturing sectors in the late 1960s. These included wool and man-made textiles and apparel, footwear, automobiles, steel and electrical consumer goods, such as television sets, radios and phonographs (see US Congress, Committee on Ways and Means, 1973). Workers also believed that large numbers of domestic jobs were being lost because of extensive direct investment abroad by US manufacturing firms.

Still another reason for organized labour's change in view was its disappointment with the manner in which the Trade Adjustment Assistance (TAA) programme under the Trade Expansion Act of 1962 had operated. The AFL-CIO had supported passage of this act in considerable part because its leaders believed that the extended unemployment benefits and retraining provisions of the TAA programme would greatly ease not only any adverse employment effects of the Kennedy Round tariff cuts but also the job displacement effects of ongoing shifts in the structure of comparative advantage in the world economy. However, not a single decision providing adjustment assistance to workers was made under the programme until November 1969. Congressional modifications in the administration's original proposal on adjustment assistance that were not fully appreciated by labour or the Democratic leadership produced this unfortunate effect. As a result of the programme's disappointing performance, the AFL-CIO leadership became more and more disenchanted with a liberal trade policy, and in 1970 the organization testified in favour of protectionist legislation.

As would be expected, this change in organized labour's position was reflected in the trade policy votes of Democratic members of Congress. In 1970 Wilbur Mills, chairman of the Ways and Means Committee and long a strong supporter of liberal trade policies, yielded to the pressures of many of the members of his committee and sponsored a bill establishing import quotas for textiles and footwear and requiring the president to accept affirmative import-relief decisions of the ITC if certain conditions relating to the extent of import increases were fulfilled. In the House of Representatives, 137 Democrats voted in favour of the bill in contrast to only 82 against it. Republicans, on the other hand, opposed the bill 82 to 78. Further protectionist features, such as quotas on fresh, chilled, or frozen meats, were added in the Senate Finance Committee, but when the various trade provisions reached the Senate floor as an add-on to a social security benefits bill, the threat of a filibuster by a small group of Democratic senators who strongly supported liberal trade policies forced recommittal of the trade features of the bill to the Finance Committee, where they died.

The shift in the positions of the two parties was again demonstrated in the voting pattern on the Trade Act of 1974, which provided an additional 60 per cent duty-cutting authority to the president. In the final House vote, 121 Democrats voted against the bill whereas 112 supported it. Republicans favoured the bill 160 to 19. Part of the increased Republican support can be attributed to the significant surplus of agricultural exports that began to emerge in the early 1970s. The agricultural sector has become one of the most internationally competitive parts of the American economy, and most farmers, who tend to support Republicans as members of Congress, now press for trade liberalization to reduce foreign trade barriers against their own export products. At the same time, because the international competitive position of certain large-scale industries, such as steel and automobiles, began to deteriorate (and continued to do so in the late 1970s and early 1980s), some Republican members of Congress who rely heavily upon the support of big business began to adopt a more selective approach to liberalization.

It is doubtful, however, if the Trade Act of 1974 would have been approved had not the president made certain concessions both to organized labour and to particular industries subject to considerable import pressure. The criteria for obtaining adjustment assistance were made much easier to meet labour's objections, and the multilateral arrangement on textiles was extended to cover textile and apparel products manufactured from man-made material and wool as well as cotton. In addition, the voluntary export restraints agreed on in 1968 by Japanese and European steel producers were extended in the early 1970s. The shift to a flexible exchange-rate system in 1971 was also an important factor enabling the president to obtain new powers to reduce trade barriers.

Although the pattern of congressional voting on trade policy measures in the early 1970s shows that Republicans favoured and Democrats opposed liberalization, it is probably not correct to conclude that this represents a permanent shift in party positions. The fact that there was a Republican president at the time considerably influenced the nature of the voting by Republican and Democratic members of Congress. A more accurate description of what has happened is that liberalization versus protectionism is no longer a significant party position. The votes of individual members of Congress on trade policy are now more influenced by economic conditions in their districts or states and by the pressures on them from the president (if they are in the same party) than by their party affiliation. Regression analyses of the voting patterns on the Trade Expansion Act of 1962 and the Trade Act of 1974 (Baldwin, 1976, 1985) indicate that party affiliation was significant in 1962 but not in 1974.


## 3.2  Congressional Restraints on the President

From the outset of the trade agreements programme, many members of Congress felt that the president was too willing to reduce tariffs in import-sensitive sectors and—along with the ITC—too reluctant to raise them for import-injured industries. Furthermore, they believed that the executive branch was not sufficiently 'tough' in administering US laws dealing with the fairness of international trading practices. Consequently, Congress frequently took the occasion of the program's renewal to introduce provisions designed to force the president and the ITC to comply more closely with these congressional views. Much of the pressure for these provisions came from import-sensitive domestic industries and labour groups but part of the readiness of members of Congress to limit presidential authority on trade policy matters seemed to stem from a belief that Congress had given the president too much of its constitutional responsibility to 'regulate commerce with foreign nations' and to levy import duties.

Restricting the power of the president by introduction of the peril-point provision and a formal escape-clause provision in 1951 has already been mentioned. The peril-point provision was eliminated in the Trade Expansion Act of 1962, but the ITC was still charged with making a judgement as to 'the probable economic effect of modifications of duties'. More important, at congressional insistence, the chairmanship of the interagency committee established to recommend tariff cuts to the president was shifted from the State Department, long regarded by Congress as being insufficiently sensitive to the import-injury problems of US industry, to a new agency, the Office of the United States Trade Representative (USTR), which reports directly to the president.[11] The requirement of the 1974 law that an elaborate private advisory system be established has somewhat further restricted the degree of independence that the president has in selecting items on which cuts are to be made and in determining the depth of the cuts. The creation and subsequent strengthening of congressional delegations to trade meetings and negotiations under the 1962 and 1974 laws have had the same effect. Since 1954 the president has also been specifically directed not to decrease duties on any article if he finds that doing so would threaten to impair the national security. Also, in granting the president the authority in 1974 to permit duty-free imports from developing countries, Congress specifically excluded certain articles, such as watches and footwear, from preferential tariff treatment.

Congress first put pressure on the president to accept affirmative recommendations of the ITC on escape-clause cases when a provision was introduced into law in 1951 requiring the president to submit an explanatory report to Congress if these recommendations were rejected. Since this seemed to have little effect on the president, Congress included a provision in the 1958 renewal act that enabled the president's disapproval of any affirmative ITC finding to be overridden by a two-thirds vote of both the House and Senate. This was eased in 1962 to a majority of the authorized membership of both houses and then in 1974 to only a majority of members present and voting. [12]

Congress has also included numerous provisions in the trade laws passed since the end of World War II aimed at increasing the proportion of affirmative import-relief decisions by the ITC. The most obvious way to accomplish this has been to change the criteria for granting increased protection when an industry is threatened with or is actually being seriously injured by increased imports. For example, the Trade Agreements Extension Act of 1955 narrowed the definition of an industry and required an affirmative decision as long as increased imports contributed 'substantially' toward causing serious injury. The 1962 trade act sharply reversed this move toward easier injury criteria, as Congress apparently mistakenly believed that the new Trade Adjustment Assistance programme would ease the pressures for import protection, but in 1974 the language was again changed to resemble closely that of the 1955 law. Moreover, the requirement that the increased imports be related to a previously granted tariff concession was eliminated.

Less obvious ways that Congress used in trying to make the ITC more responsive to its views were utilizing its confirmation powers to try to ensure that commission members were sympathetic to its views and changing certain administrative arrangements relating to the agency. Beginning in the late 1960s, the chairman of the Senate Finance Committee, Senator Russell Long, and his committee colleagues began to argue forcefully that 'it is to the Congress, not the Executive, that the Tariff Commission is expected to be responsive', [13] and they began to be critical of nominees whose professional background was largely in the executive branch of the federal government. In the period between 1953 and 1967, five of the thirteen commissioners appointed had extensive employment experience in the executive branch and another two in the commission itself. Between 1968 and 1980, none of the twelve newly appointed commissioners had either of these backgrounds. Instead, seven of the approved nominees had significant congressional experience, either as a member of Congress (one person) or as congressional staffers. In a further effort to weaken the influence of the president over the commission, Congress in 1974 removed all controls of the executive branch over the commission's budget and eliminated the power of the president to appoint the chairperson of the commission. This latter change was modified in 1977, but the president cannot appoint either of his two most recent appointees as chairperson.

Similar steps were taken by Congress to try to ensure stricter enforcement of US trade laws relating to unfair foreign practices. Many members of Congress long felt that the Treasury Department was too lax in administering US antidumping and countervailing duty legislation. One step designed to change this was to transfer in 1954 the determination of injury (but not the determination of dumping) from the Treasury Department to the ITC. Furthermore, under pressure from Congress, the president in 1980 transferred the authority to determine both dumping and subsidization from the Treasury to the Commerce Department—an agency that Congress believed would more closely carry out its intent in these areas.

The 1974 change in the manner of administering US legislation pertaining to unfair import practices (sec. 337 of the Tariff Act of 1930) is another illustration of the decline in presidential authority over trade matters. Prior to 1974, the ITC conducted the investigations into alleged violations of this law and then transmitted its findings to the president. If the president was satisfied that unfair import methods had been established, he could ban the importation of the relevant products. In 1974 Congress gave the ITC this authority to ban imports of the affected products or to issue a cease and desist order to the person practising the violation. The only power the president retains under this law is the ability to set aside the actions of the ITC within sixty days 'for policy reasons'.

Perhaps the most significant reduction in the president's authority over trade policy concerns the ability to negotiate agreements with other countries covering non-tariff measures. When Congress directed the president to seek such agreements under the Trade Act of 1974, it stipulated—unlike its provision on tariffs—that any agreements must be approved by a majority vote in both the House and Senate. This provision was extended in the Trade Agreements Act of 1979, giving Congress much greater control over the nature of any agreement and increasing its control over the pattern of tariff cuts undertaken by the president in a multilateral trade negotiation, since the tariff and non-tariff concessions made by the participants are closely linked.

## 4   THE INCREASING IMPORTANCE OF NON-TARIFF TRADE-DISTORTING MEASURES

As tariff reductions by the industrial countries continued during the 1950s and 1960s, greater attention began to be given to non-tariff trade-distorting measures, not only because they became more obvious as tariff rates declined but because they were increasingly used. During the 1960s, the extension in the use of quantitative restrictions from primary product sectors, such as agriculture and petroleum, to manufacturing activities, such as cotton textiles and steel; the greater use of export-rebate and import-deposit schemes to improve a country's balance-of-payments position; and the introduction of many new domestic subsidies to stimulate growth in depressed areas, ease structural adjustments, and promote high-technology industries, all served to direct attention to the fact that the benefits of tariff liberalization could be offset by NTBs.

As the above illustrations indicate, the increased use of NTBs, particularly beginning in the 1960s, stemmed both from the efforts of particular sectors to secure protection or special export assistance through these measures and from the concerns of governments with balance-of-payments problems and with various social and economic policy objectives. In the case of the United States, for example, the sharp increase in the lending and guaranteeing authorizations of the Export–Import Bank in the late 1960s and early 1970s and the approval of the Domestic International Sales Corporation (DISC) in 1971 represented efforts to increase the country's exports within the constraints of the then-fixed exchange-rate system. While the United States followed other industrial nations during the 1960s in greatly expanding domestic programmes to improve social and economic conditions for disadvantaged income groups and depressed sectors, most American programmes had little direct or indirect effect on the pattern of trade. Such did not appear to be the case in a number of other industrial countries. Substantial financial assistance by other governments to specific industries and particular economic activities appeared to public and private officials in the United States to represent a serious threat to US trade competitiveness and to the liberal international order in general. Consequently, widespread support developed for a new GATT-sponsored effort to provide more detailed NTB codes that would reduce the injurious effects on others of such measures as a country's domestic subsidies or its rules pertaining to product standards.

US officials did have the authority to undertake negotiations on NTBs during the Kennedy Round of trade negotiations, and a GATT committee was established to deal with this subject. Agreement on an antidumping code was reached, as well as on eliminating a number of particular non-tariff measures, such as the American selling price (ASP) system of customs valuation and European discriminatory road-use taxes. But reaching agreement on tariff issues proved to be so difficult and time consuming that negotiations in the non-tariff field were not very extensive. Moreover, Congress felt that the president had exceeded his authority by trying to implement the new antidumping code as an executive agreement rather than submitting it to Congress for approval, and passed a law directing the ITC to ignore the new code when making its injury determinations. Congress also rejected the proposal to eliminate ASP.

In the markup sessions on the Trade Act of 1974, key members of the Senate were adamant about the necessity of submitting international agreements reached on non-tariff matters to Congress for final approval, and, as noted earlier, such a requirement was included in the act. Once this matter was settled, Congress fully supported the efforts of the president to negotiate new NTB codes in the Tokyo Round, and approved without difficulty the set of codes eventually agreed on.

At the same time, efforts were made to negotiate new agreements that would mitigate the adverse effects of foreign NTBs. US producers were pressuring government officials for stricter enforcement of existing US 'fair trade' legislation, such as the antidumping and countervailing laws, and were seeking import protection under these laws to a greater extent than in the past.[14] They also were demanding the greater use of quantitative restrictions (as compared with import duties) to protect their industries against injurious import increases.

One factor accounting for the greater number of less-than-fair-value cases has been the difficulty of obtaining protection through the traditional provisions pertaining to injury caused by import competition. Despite the 1974 easing of the criteria for determining whether import relief should be granted, only forty-seven cases were decided by the ITC between 1975 and 1982, and in all but twenty-four of these a negative decision was reached. Furthermore, the president rejected import protection in all but ten of the twenty-four cases. The likelihood that routine acceptance of affirmative ITC decisions would be interpreted by foreign governments as US abandonment of its international economic leadership role appears to have made the president reluctant to accept more than a small proportion of these decisions. Even Congress has been hesitant, on similar grounds, to weaken the import-relief criteria much beyond what they were in the 1950s.

Providing protection to offset alleged unfair trade practices is much less likely to be interpreted as representing a basic shift in policy, either by other governments or domestic interests supporting a liberal trading order. Thus, within reasonable bounds a president can support efforts to achieve 'fair trade' through measures that protect domestic producers while still being regarded as a proponent of liberal trade policies.

Not only has a better understanding of this point led domestic industries to utilize US fair trade legislation more extensively in seeking import protection, but legislative and administrative changes relating to these laws have facilitated this shift. Congress, though diluting the president's power to reduce trade barriers and to set aside ITC decisions, has at the same time given him new authority to limit imports on fairness grounds. For example, the 1922 and 1930 tariff acts granted the president the authority to impose new or additional duties on imports or even to exclude imports from countries that impose unreasonable regulations on US products or discriminate against US commerce. The 1962 Trade Act further directs the president to take all appropriate and feasible steps to eliminate 'unjustifiable' foreign import restrictions (including the imposition of duties and other import restrictions) and to suspend or withdraw previously granted concessions where other countries maintain trade restrictions that 'substantially burden' US commerce, engage in discriminating acts, or maintain unreasonable import restrictions. The Trade Act of 1974 restates these provisions and in section 301 also gives the president the authority to take similar actions in response to 'subsidies (or other incentives having the effect of subsidies) on its [a foreign country's] exports ... to the United States or to other foreign markets which have the effect of substantially reducing sales of the competitive United States product or products in the United States or in foreign markets' and 'unjustifiable or unreasonable restrictions on access to supplies of food, raw materials, or manufactured or semimanufactured products which burden or restrict United States commerce'. However, Congress could veto any actions taken by the president. In amending this provision, the 1979 Trade Act stressed the president's responsibility for enforcing US rights under any trade agreement and simplified the list of foreign practices against which he is directed to take action. Interestingly, this act also eliminated the authority of Congress to nullify presidential actions taken under this provision by a majority vote of both houses within ninety days.

The extension of the definition of dumping in the Trade Act of 1974 to cover not only sales abroad at lower prices than charged at home but to include sales of substantial quantities at below cost over an extended period (even if domestic and foreign prices are the same) is another legislative change that encouraged the use of fair trade legislation to gain protection. Under this provision, the steel industry filed dumping charges in 1977 covering nearly $1 billion of steel imports from Japan, all the major European producers and India. However, as Finger, Hall and Nelson (1982) point out, cases of this magnitude in key sectors attract so much political opposition, both domestic and foreign, that they cannot be disposed of at a technical, bureaucratic level and spill over into the political route for gaining import protection. In this instance, the domestic industry was successful in convincing President Carter that its claims were justified, and the so-called trigger-price mechanism (TPM) for steel evolved as an alternative to pursuing the antidumping charges to the final stage.

A similar political solution was reached in 1982 when the steel industry filed charges that European steel producers were receiving extensive subsidies and should be subject to countervailing duties. The possibility of countervailing duties had such significant economic and political implications that the governments of the parties involved did not wish the matter to be settled on technical grounds and sought a solution at the political level. Eventually the Europeans agreed to quantitative export limits on a wide range of steel products to the United States.

Other important sectors that have been protected in recent years by non-tariff barriers are the footwear, television and auto industries. Voluntary export restraints were negotiated by the president in the first two sectors after affirmative injury findings by the ITC, but the ITC rejected the auto industry's petition for import relief. Nevertheless, the industry was successful in persuading the administration of the need for import controls, and the Japanese eventually agreed to restrict their sales of cars to the United States.

The increased use of non-tariff trade-distorting measures obviously has weakened the liberal international trading regime, not simply because they represent a move toward protectionism but because many of them have been applied in a discriminatory manner and are negotiated outside the GATT framework. Some of the political decisions reached at the presidential level have also occurred without the opportunity for all interested parties to be heard, as would be the case if a technical route such as an import-injury petition before the ITC were being followed, or even a political route at the congressional level.

Several of the most important non-tariff measures utilized by the US government to restrain imports or promote exports are analysed in greater detail in other chapters of this volume. Their purpose is to explain more fully how these measures operate and to appraise their effects on trade and economic welfare.

## 5   DECLINING US HEGEMONY AND THE LIBERAL INTERNATIONAL ECONOMIC ORDER

The hegemonic model of regime change predicts openness in world trading arrangements when a hegemonic state is in its ascendancy and a shift toward a closed system as this nation declines in power and is not replaced by another dominant state. Though this theory is consistent with the early part of the postwar period, there is general agreement (Krasner 1976; Goldstein 1981; Lipson 1982) that the model does not perform well as an explanation of regime change for more recent years.

Most writers (e.g., Whitman 1975; Kindleberger 1981) date the US decline as beginning in the 1960s. The decline in relative economic power is evident, for example, from the fact that the US share of merchandise exports of the fifteen largest industrial countries fell from 25.2 per cent in 1960 to 20.5 per cent in 1970, and then to 18.3 per cent in 1979.[15] The percentages for exports of manufactures for the same years are 22.8, 18.4, and 15.5. The US share of the GNP of these countries was 57.1 per cent in 1960, 50.2 per cent in 1970, and only 38.1 per cent in 1979. It became clear during the long difficult Kennedy Round negotiations on a tariff-cutting rule that other industrial countries, especially the European Community, were no longer prepared to continue to accept routinely the US leadership role.[16] As the reduction in cold war tensions during the 1970s reduced the perceived need for US military protection against the Soviet Union, the decline in American economic and political influence became even more evident.

Despite a shift in power from a situation in which one country dominated the economic scene to one with three major economic blocs (the United States, the European Community and Japan), most observers agree that the trade and payments regime continues to be essentially an open and liberal one. As Table 2.1 shows, the tariff cuts made in the 1960s and 1970s were actually much deeper than those made in the 1940s and 1950s. Furthermore, the new non-tariff codes negotiated during the Tokyo Round, though often very general in their wording, do represent a significant accomplishment in providing the basis for preventing non-tariff measures from undermining the liberalization benefits from the postwar tariff cuts. While the GATT ministerial meeting in November 1982 again demonstrated the inability of the United States to dominate international deliberations on trade policy issues, it did reconfirm the continued commitment of the major industrial nations to a liberal economic order. The increased use of non-tariff trade-distorting measures described in the last section represents derogation from this order, but the trading regime remains essentially an open one.

A consideration of either the economic theory of market behaviour or the production of collective goods suggests that the failure of the hegemonic model to predict the continuation of an open system should not be surprising. A single firm that dominates a particular market is likely to stabilize the price of the product at a monopolistic level while still tolerating some price-cutting by the smaller firms that make up the rest of the industry. Oligopolistic market theory suggests that the same result is likely if two or three firms dominate an industry. Similarly, as Olson (1965) pointed out, the free-rider problem associated with collective action by an industry can be overcome if a small number of firms (as well as just one firm) produce a significant share of the industry's output. Thus, the continued support for a stable, open trading order as the distribution of power changed from an almost monopolistic situation to an oligopolistic one is quite consistent with market behaviour theory.

The shift from a hegemonic position to one in which the country shares its economic and political power with a small number of other nations is likely to alter the country's international behaviour somewhat, just as the change in the status of a firm from a monopolist to an oligopolist is likely to change the firm's market behaviour. In the US case, the change has been the initiation of trade negotiations mainly to achieve economic benefits for the country rather than to further general US foreign policy and national security goals.[17] This shift in emphasis first became apparent in the Dillon and Kennedy Rounds of negotiations when government leaders stressed to the public the economic gains that would be achieved by lowering the European Community's tariff level, thereby reducing the trade diversion resulting from the formation of this customs union. The usual arguments about the need to strengthen the free world to meet the threat of communist expansion were also presented, but with less vigour than in the past.

Support for a multilateral trade negotiation based on the view that it was in the economic interest of the United States to participate in such a negotiation was even more evident in the Tokyo Round. In early 1973 President Nixon sent a generally worded bill to Congress that provided the president with the authority to modify tariffs as he thought appropriate and to conclude agreements with other nations on non-tariff issues. Congress took the opportunity of a proposed negotiation to reshape the bill so that it dealt with many of its concerns about the nature of the international trading system. It soon became apparent that business, labour and agricultural interests were very fearful that the increasing use of the non-tariff measures by other countries would significantly curtail US export opportunities and lead to injurious increases in imports. Congress reacted in part by strengthening US fair trade legislation, but its main response was to give the president detailed directions about negotiating new international codes aimed at reducing non-tariff trade-distorting measures. In other words, both Congress and the president agreed that strengthening the liberal international economic order was in the economic interest of the United States, quite aside from its political and national security implications.

As might be expected, the less altruistic behaviour of the United States in its international economic relations has resulted in an increased number of trade disputes between the United States and other countries.[18] Many who support a liberal trading order are concerned that these disputes will become so numerous and difficult to solve that the system will collapse, with each of the major trading powers pursuing inward-looking trade policies. This is, of course, a possibility. However, most of the trading frictions do not arise because of disagreements on the principles involved in the commitment to an open trading system but on matters of interpretation within these principles. For example, as pointed out earlier, the key parties in the system have always agreed that it was proper to shield an industry from injurious increases in imports. When the United States protects the auto and steel industries from import competition or the Europeans subsidize industries as a means of retaining their domestic market shares, this is not regarded by most countries as a departure from the basic liberal trading rules. Disagreements sometimes arise, however, over whether a country is going beyond the intent of the rules and engaging in what, in effect, are beggar-they-neighbour policies. The settlement of major disputes at a high political level and the continuing efforts to improve the GATT dispute settlement mechanism are a recognition by the major trading nations of the damage to the system that could occur from such disagreements.

Krasner (1976) argues in his amendment to the hegemonic model that abandonment of the commitment to a liberal trading order by the United States (or the other major trading nations) is likely to occur only when some major external crisis forces policy leaders to pursue a dramatic new policy initiative that they believe to be in their country's interest. It may be that the existing power-sharing arrangement between the United States, the European Community and Japan reduces the likelihood of this outcome compared with the case of a declining hegemony in the midst of many smaller states. In this latter situation, the dominant power is tempted in a crisis to take advantage of its monopoly power over the terms of trade. But when power is shared, the recognition that a country's market power is limited and that retaliation is likely to be swift and significant tends to discourage such adventurism. Of greater concern than the possibility of a dramatic abandonment of the liberal international economic order is the likelihood of continuing gradual erosion in the openness of international trade because of the inability of the major industrial powers to agree on international measures that take into account the interrelationships between trade policies and policies in the exchange rate, monetary, fiscal and social areas.

## NOTES

1. If the effects of structural shifts in trade and of inflation on specific duties are included along with the negotiated tariff cuts, the average tariff on dutiable imports drops from a 1931 level of 53 per cent to about 5 per cent after completion of the Tokyo Round cuts.
2. Gardner (1980, p. 9) documents this point and describes the planning activities of the administration for the postwar period.
3. Statement by President Roosevelt to Congress on 26 March 1945.
4. Hull (1948, vol. 1, p. 81) and Dobson (1976, pp. 56–66) describe the traditional Democratic and Republican positions on trade policy.
5. *See* Wilkinson (1960, chs. 1 and 5) for an elaboration of this point and a discussion of the subsequent postwar shift in emphasis toward foreign policy considerations.
6. Authors who developed this explanation for the postwar establishment of a liberal international economic order under US leadership include Kindleberger (1973, 1981), Gilpin (1975), and Krasner (1976).
7. *See* Leddy and Norwood (1963) for a detailed discussion of the escape clause as well as the peril-point provisions.
8. Diebold (1952) analyses the reasons why the ITO failed to gain US support.
9. *See* Lipson (1982) for a succinct statement and analysis of the hegemonic model.
10. For a description of the protectionist pressures from the cotton textile industry and the oil and coal industries during the 1950s and early 1960s, *see* Bauer, Pool, and Dexter (1963, ch. 25).
11. In response to complaints from Congress and the private sector on the lack of a unified US trade policy strategy, President Reagan in the spring of 1983 proposed merging USTR and parts of the Commerce Department into a new Department of International Trade and Industry.
12. The June 1983 Supreme Court decision declaring the congressional veto to be unconstitutional presumably means that this provision will no longer apply.
13. Hearings before the Senate Committee on Finance, 23 June 1971. In these hearings, Senator Long explained the actions of the committee during the late 1960s on various presidential nominees to the commission.
14. Between 1955 and 1972, the average number of antidumping reports issued by the ITC averaged less than six per year, whereas this rate increased to thirteen between 1974 and 1979. Similarly, the number of countervailing duty investigations completed by the ITC between 1962 and 1973 was twelve, while the number rose to thirty-seven between 1974 and the end of 1978.
15. These and the following figures are from the Office of Foreign Economic Research, US Department of Labor (1980, ch. 3).
16. This was due in part to the fact that the United States was no longer willing to provide the necessary compensation to these other countries to gain their acceptance of US proposals.
17. Krasner (1979) also makes this point.

18.  Cooper (1973) discusses the increase in trade disputes after the mid 1960s and the implications for foreign policy.


# REFERENCES

Baldwin, Robert E. (1958), The commodity composition of trade: selected industrial countries, 1900–1954, *Review of Economics and Statistics* 40:50–68, supplement.
——. (1976), The political economy of postwar US trade policy, *The Bulletin* 1976:4.
——. (1985), *The Political Economy of US Import Policy*, Cambridge, Mass.: MIT Press.
Bale, M. D. (1973), Adjustment to free trade: an analysis of the adjustment assistance provisions of the Trade Expansion Act of 1962, Ph.D. thesis, University of Wisconsin, and Report no. DLMA 91-55-73-05-1 of the National Technical Information Service, Springfield, Virginia.
Bauer, R. A., J. Pool and L. Dexter. (1963), *American Business and Public Policy: The Politics of Foreign Trade*, Chicago: Aldine-Atherton, Inc.
Caves, Richard E. (1976), Economic models of political choice: Canada's tariff structure, *Canadian Journal of Economics* 9:278–300.
Cooper, Richard N. (1973), Trade policy is foreign policy, *Foreign Policy* 9:18–37.
Diebold, William, Jr (1952), *The End of the ITO*, Essays in International Finance, no. 16, Princeton: Princeton University.
Dobson, J. M. (1976), *Two Centuries of Tariffs: The Background and Emergence of the US International Trade Commission*, Washington, DC: US International Trade Commission.
Finger, J. Michael, H. K. Hall and D. R. Nelson (1982), The political economy of administered protection, *American Economic Review* 72:452–66.
Gardner, Richard N. (1980) '*Sterling-Dollar Diplomacy in Current Perspective*, New York: Columbia University Press.
Gilpin, Robert (1975), *US Power and the Multinational Corporation: The Political Economy of Foreign Direct Investment*, New York: Basic Books.
Goldstein, J. L. (1981), The state, industrial interests and foreign economic policy: American commercial policy in the postwar period. Paper prepared for the National Science Foundation Conference on the Politics and Economics of Trade Policy, Minneapolis, 29–31 October 1981.
Hull, Cordell (1948), *The Memoirs of Cordell Hull*, 2 volumes, New York: Macmillan.
Kindleberger, Charles P. (1973), *The World in Depression, 1929–1939*, Berkeley: University of California Press.
——. (1981), Dominance and leadership in the international economy: Exploitation, public goods, and free rides, *International Studies Quarterly* 25:242–54.
Krasner, Stephen D. (1976), State power and the structure of international trade, *World Politics* 28:317–47.
——. (1979), The Tokyo Round: particularistic interests and prospects for stability in the global trading system, *International Studies Quarterly* 23:491–531.

Leddy, J. M. and J. Norwood (1963), The escape clause and peril points under the trade agreements program, In *Studies in United States Commercial Policy*, ed. W. B. Kelley, Jr, Chapel Hill: University of North Carolina Press.

Lipson, C. (1982), The transformation of trade: the sources and effects of regime changes, *International Organization* 36:417–55.

Meyer, F. V. (1978), *International Trade Policy*, New York: St. Martin's.

Olson, Mancur (1965), *The Logic of Collective Action*, Cambridge, Mass.: Harvard University Press.

US Congress. House Committee on Ways and Means, prepared by the staff of the US Tariff Commission (1973), *Comparison of Ratios of Imports to Apparent Consumption, 1968–72*, Washington, DC: Government Printing Office.

US Congress. Senate Committee on Finance (1968) Hearings on the nominations of Will E. Leonard Jr, of Louisiana, and Herschel D. Newsom of Indiana to be members of the US Tariff Commission, Ninetieth Congress, Second Session, 9 October, Washington, DC: Government Printing Office.

US Department of Labor, Office of Foreign Economic Research (1980), *Report to the President on US Competitiveness*, Washington, DC: Government Printing Office.

Whitman, Marina V. N. (1975), The decline in American hegemony, *Foreign Policy* 20:138–60.

Wilkinson, Joe R. (1960), *Politics and Trade Policy*, Washington, DC: Public Affairs Press.

# 3   The Political Economy of Postwar US Trade Policy*

## INTRODUCTION

Postwar commercial policy in the United States has been characterized by major compromises between the political forces favouring trade liberalization versus protectionism and by significant shifts in the congressional voting patterns of the two major parties on trade matters. For example, while the president has been authorized over the years to reduce most tariffs by as much as 93 per cent of their 1945 levels, quantitative restrictions on imports of textiles and apparel, petroleum, steel and several agricultural products have also been introduced during the period. The change in voting behaviour is illustrated by the fact that in 1945 an overwhelming majority of Democrats in the House of Representatives voted for extending the trade agreements programme with an additional 50 per cent tariff-cutting authority, whereas in 1973 most House Democrats opposed a trade bill that granted the president new significant duty-reducing powers. On the other hand, Republicans in the House opposed further tariff cutting in 1945 by a very large majority but supported the 1973 trade bill. This paper attempts to explain why US trade policy has emerged in its particular compromised form as well as why realignments in party support have occurred. Particular attention is devoted to the role of pressures from groups with common economic interests as a determinant of trade policies.

Traditional economic theory is not very useful in explaining actual US trade policies. Except when a country can influence its terms of trade by its own action, this theory concludes that a unilateral shift to free trade is a desirable policy. Even when several countries with monopolistic power participate in multilateral tariff-cutting negotiations, economic analysis suggests that such exercises are likely to be in the best interest of all participants since the trading terms of none of the countries are likely to

* From *The Bulletin*, New York University, Graduate School of Business Administration (1976-4), pp. 5-37.

shift appreciably. Economists have tended to assume that by explaining the advantages of trade liberalization, governments will eventually realize these benefits and introduce policies directed toward this end. In fact, however, actual trade policies in most industrial countries have consisted in recent years of a mixture of protectionism and liberalization. Moreover, it is not clear that the liberalizing actions that have occurred have been influenced to any significant extent by arguments employed by economists.

## A MODEL OF TRADE POLICY BEHAVIOUR

Fortunately, within recent years economists have become increasingly concerned with the manner in which public policies are actually determined and have attempted to formulate a theory of public choice.[1] Essentially they have adapted economic theories of private market behaviour to political situations in which decisions are determined by majority voting. The following framework for making public decisions represents an effort to apply the theory developed by writers in this new field to the determination of commercial policies in the United States.

### A Simple Model
To keep the model as simple as possible initially, suppose the following conditions hold: (1) voters directly determine by majority voting whether a particular public policy is put into effect; (2) there is only one policy issue to be decided within voters' time horizons; (3) the tastes of all voters are identical and homothetic and do not change in the period under consideration; and (4) there is perfect knowledge and there are no costs involved in acquiring or providing information, in voting, and in providing compensation or bribes to any individuals. The objective of each individual is to maximize his welfare, which depends upon the goods and services that he consumes.

The policy under consideration is whether to provide tariff-cutting authority for the purpose of engaging in a multilateral tariff-reducing exercise with other countries.[2] Assume that the terms of trade of the country under consideration do not change as a result of the tariff negotiations. Furthermore, suppose there are no market inefficiencies in the economy other than the existence of tariffs.[3] On the basis of the standard Heckscher–Ohlin–Samuelson model of international trade it follows that those productive factors intensively used in the production of export goods benefit when tariffs are reduced under these circumstances, whereas those utilized relatively intensively in the production of import-competing goods suffer a decline in real income. However, it can also be shown that the gainers under free trade are capable of fully compensating the losers for their income reduction with the gainers still being better off than before the change.[4]

Under the voting framework assumed up to this point the tariff proposal will be acted on favourably whether the gainers are in the majority or not. However, when they are a minority, it is necessary to tie the tariff-cutting exercise to a redistribution scheme that provides net gains to a majority of the electorate.

**Modifying the Simple Model**
When various assumptions of the model are eased in order to increase the degree of its correspondence with real world conditions, the conclusion that tariff liberalization will always take place under a system of majority voting no longer holds. Suppose that there are costs involved in compensating losers for their injury and that these costs are borne by the gainers. If the gainers are in a minority and the costs of compensating enough losers to achieve a majority voting bloc are greater than the gains to the majority, the liberalization proposal will fail. The existence of voting costs and costs of acquiring information can also serve to thwart tariff liberalization. The gains from duty reductions may be so small to some voters that they are more than offset by the costs of voting. These individuals, consequently, will not vote. Similarly, if the costs of voting exceed the losses incurred by some who are adversely affected by the duty cuts, it will not be worthwhile for these citizens to vote. Consequently, the voting outcome will be determined by the larger gainers and losers, a majority of whom may not support the trade-liberalization proposal.

Probably the best-known reasons for divergences between what is economically desirable and politically feasible are the existence of information costs and the fact that attitudes can be changed by freely supplying certain types of information. Just as it does not pay some voters to incur the costs of voting, it is not rational for many voters to pay the costs of acquiring detailed information about the effects of a particular tariff liberalization.[5] Voters usually are able to acquire some information about most policy proposals at very low cost either as a by-product of their income-earning activities or as consumers of such communication services as newspapers and television. Unless this information indicates that a voter's real income position is likely to be significantly affected by the policy, he generally will not seek out any further information. On the other hand, if his initial information suggests that he may be greatly affected, then it will pay him to invest further to determine more exactly the possible impact of the policy. As Downs points out, this is the reason why producers generally are better informed about tariff policy than consumers.[6] Producers, consequently, are likely to have more importance in the voting outcome than their numerical importance would suggest, since the poorly informed voters are likely to vote in a somewhat random fashion.

Not only do those who are significantly affected by the tariff liberalization invest time and money to determine in more detail the possible outcome of the policy but they supply information to other voters in an effort to influence their votes. As William Brock and Stephen Magee have pointed out, producers can be viewed as attempting to maximize their net benefits (or minimize their net losses) from a proposed tariff change by spending an appropriate sum to influence other voters.[7] If those who would lose significantly with duty reductions are unable to bribe the majority gainers into rejecting the liberalization proposal, they still may be able to achieve their objective by spending funds to influence the majority. It would not pay the losers to spend more than the present value of their losses but within this constraint they will spend enough to obtain a majority voting position. When uncertainty is introduced, influencers can be viewed as spending—subject to the above constraint—up to the point where additional outlays equal the resulting increase (decrease) in the expected welfare gain (loss) to them.[8]

Another factor affecting the extent of efforts to influence others is the size of the group sharing a gain or loss of a given magnitude.[9] The smaller the group and thus the greater the gain or loss to any individual member, the more likely will it be rational for an individual to spend enough money to affect the voting outcome. With large groups the minimum outlay needed to have any effect at all is likely to be greater than the gain or loss to the individual. He will hope that others in his group contribute funds to influence other voters but in this case it is not worthwhile for him to do so. Sometimes group pressures (costs) and rewards can be used to force individuals in large groups to provide resources for persuading others to vote in a particular manner. Generally, however, a large group with an aggregate gain or loss that amounts to only a small gain or loss on an individual basis is at a serious disadvantage compared with smaller groups with a smaller total gain or loss yet larger individual gains or losses. This is why consumers and industries consisting of many small firms do not organize to influence tariff policy as extensively as producers in oligopolistic industries and labour unions that dominate particular industries.

So far it has been assumed that there is only one policy matter under consideration, namely, tariff liberalization. However, in practice, voters or their representatives are called upon to decide a series of issues over time. This situation opens up the possibility of logrolling. With vote trading it is possible, for example, for two policies to be defeated even though they would each result in a rise in the community's real income.

This could occur if compensation is ruled out on cost grounds and if there is a net loss to a majority of voters when the two policies are combined. But if compensation is costless, the gainers will be able to offset this unfavourable vote by overcompensating enough losers to obtain a majority. As in the case of a single policy, the lack of the compensation possibility due to high costs is necessary for defeating a series of policies in the public interest. The existence of a number of policy issues also tends to increase the volume of lobbying activity. While it may not pay a group of individuals to establish a lobbying organization on any one issue, it is more likely to pay them to do so if they share common views on a number of the issues.

Another assumption that should be dropped concerns the direct voting procedure of citizens. Most policies are decided by the elected representatives of the voters rather than directly by the voters themselves. In this framework it can be assumed that the elected officials, like other individuals, try to maximize their welfare. To do this as representatives of the voters, they must take actions that will first enable them to be elected and then retain their positions. In a world characterized by the assumptions initially made, competition forces political officials and parties to attempt to maximize the number of votes from the electorate. Unless politicians follow this practice, they will not long stay in office since others can unseat them by doing so. Consequently, the results obtained in the simple, direct voting model will also hold, even though voters express their preferences indirectly. When, however, the various assumptions of the simple model are modified, additional possibilities emerge as to why the tariff-cutting proposal may not be accepted. For example, when there are information costs, it is much easier to set up vote-swapping arrangements when only a small number (rather than the entire electorate) are voting on specific proposals. The existence of political parties, which are associated with representative government, also opens up possibilities for the defeat of such income-raising proposals as a tariff reduction. Party leaders (including elected officials) are primarily concerned with gaining and retaining political power rather than maximizing voter strength. The maximizing behaviour is forced upon them when there is a high degree of political competition. But if it is costly to provide information to voters and if there are substantial economies of scale in providing this information, the costs of entering the political marketplace become high for potential challengers. Incumbents have an advantage in this regard in that they usually can utilize their party's resources to help meet the high costs of campaigning. Because they wish to minimize their costs of being elected rather than maximize the vote, they will try to satisfy the preferences of enough voters to prevent others within their own party or in other parties from being able to secure the funds needed to make a successful challenge. One rational means of carrying out this objective is to satisfy the preferences of minority groups who gain or lose significantly while the majority only gains or loses to a moderate degree. Those greatly affected are more likely to provide funds needed to persuade other voters of the candidates' merits and ensure their election.

Another situation in which the majority's wishes can be thwarted under representative government is when, as in the US Senate, the representation is not proportional to the population size. Consequently, the majority of the population favouring trade liberalization, for example, may be in states that do not have a majority in the Senate.

One of the important political advantages of cutting tariffs on a reciprocal basis is that it does not just bring adverse adjustment problems to some industries but, unlike a unilateral tariff reduction, it also opens up improved profit opportunities to selected sectors. Consequently, there will be both business and labour groups who actively oppose tariff cuts and those who favour the reduction. However, if—as seems reasonable—a short-run change in a given amount of income results in a greater change in an individual's utility if it is negative rather than positive, the possibility of serious market losses is likely to provoke more lobbying activities than the chance of large market gains. Therefore, if the large gains and losses from the cut are about equal, politicians are likely to be helped more by opponents to the reductions than proponents of the cuts and, as a result, to oppose tariff liberalization.

Besides introducing into a voting model the fact that citizens express their views on most policy issues only indirectly, it is also important to recognize the existence of an executive branch. The president possesses great power in being able to influence the nature of legislation. Through sympathetic legislators he can introduce specific legislation, and, more importantly, obtain through the press and the information activities of the government, wide dissemination of his views as to the merits of the proposed legislation. The patronage powers of the president also can be used effectively to influence the voting actions of legislators.

One of the main functions of the president is to conduct the country's foreign policy, and in judging his performance, many voters put considerable weight on his success in this field. Presidents also find that foreign policy is one of the policy areas over which they can exercise the greatest direct control and most easily pursue their goals. Since it has been the accepted wisdom among most political leaders for many years that closer trading ties among nations improve the chances for harmonious political relations, tariff liberalization provides greater opportunities for a president to gain personal satisfaction by enhancing his international reputation than does a policy of protectionism. But a president may sometimes find it necessary to offer import protection to particular industries in order to obtain general tariff-reducing authority from the Congress. The general public has also adhered to the view that closer trading ties promote peace, and voters who are affected economically in only a minimal way by tariff liberalization have also tended—though not strongly—to favour a reciprocal duty-reduction policy.

A final set of modifications to the simple model that should be made is to drop the assumptions of identical homothetic tastes and fixed terms of trade. When different taste patterns are permitted (but the fixed trading terms assumption still maintained) it is no longer possible to say that the actual collection of goods rendered under tariff liberalization is sufficient to compensate the losers by appropriate redistribution.[10] What can be said is that under tariff liberalization it would be *possible* to obtain a collection of goods under which the losers could be compensated for their loss in the move to the tariff-liberalization policy.[11] As the wide acceptance of the use of changes in consumer and producer surplus as a measure of changes in a community's welfare indicates, many people are willing to accept the *possibility of compensation* as the appropriate welfare criterion.

When the possibility of adverse movements in the country's trading terms in response to tariff liberalization is introduced into the model, tariff cutting cannot be judged as always desirable even under this welfare criterion. The real income loss associated with the deterioration in the country's trading terms may swamp the consumption and production gains related to the improvement in allocative efficiency. Whether this is so in a particular case could be determined by the measurement of consumer and producer surplus changes, given appropriate parameters such as demand and supply elasticities for exports and imports. If tariff levels among the major trading nations are equal among countries (as they roughly are today for industrial products) and these levels are simultaneously reduced by the same percentage, then a country's terms of trade will improve if the absolute sum of the demand elasticity for the country's exports divided by the sum of its elasticity of export supply and the demand elasticity for its exports is greater than its elasticity of demand for imports divided by the sum of the supply elasticity of imports it faces plus its elasticity of demand for imports.[12] Empirical studies have generally indicated a higher elasticity of demand for US exports than the US demand elasticity for imports but the evidence on supply elasticities is inconclusive.[13] As one investigator notes, reciprocal elimination of tariffs by the United States and her trading partners would involve a net terms-of-trade effect for the United States that could be either positive or negative but in either case very small.[14] Thus, until more evidence is available it seems reasonable to assume that, for the United States at least, terms-of-trade shifts are not important enough to negate the welfare benefits of a multilateral tariff-liberalization policy under which the countries involved reduce duties approximately the same degree.

The main conclusions of the preceding analysis can be summarized into several simple hypotheses describing the voting behaviour of legislators on the issue of granting the president new tariff-cutting authority. First, constituent pressures to vote in a particular manner are not likely to be a decisive factor in determining a representative's voting behaviour unless there are politically important economic groups in his or her district who believe they will be significantly hurt or helped by tariff liberalization. By 'important' is meant that either the number of voters in the group or the profits and losses at stake with the tariff change are relatively large. In the United States where imports and exports are a relatively small fraction of GNP, most individual citizens are not likely to exert any pressure on their representative in this matter. Multipurpose pressure groups with general consumer or foreign policy concerns, such as the League of Women Voters and the International Chamber of Commerce, will apply some pressure in support of trade liberalization, whereas similar organizations like the AFL-CIO will apply general pressures in the opposite direction. But since trade policy is only one of many issues on which these groups have views, under these circumstances, a legislator's response on other issues is likely to be more important in determining whether the members of these organizations actively support or oppose a congressional candidate.

Legislators operating in a situation where there are no strong political pressures either in favour of or against trade liberalization are apt to be influenced heavily by the position of their party on the issue. As with individual voters the costs of acquiring reliable information are high for the individual legislator. Consequently, it is sensible for him or her to follow the recommendations either of fellow party members who have become knowledgeable about the subject through membership on the relevant congressional committee or of the president, if he is a member of the same party.[15]

In districts where economic interests that represent large numbers of voters or that pay substantial local and national taxes strongly oppose or support trade liberalization, members of Congress are more likely to adopt the views of these economic pressure groups than those of their party or some other lobbying organization. They can less afford to ignore the loss of votes and campaign contributions that failure to respect these parochial pressures will bring. Industries that are depressed economically and those that have had to contend with rapid increases in imports will tend to be especially energetic in attempting to secure a negative vote on trade liberalization.

Given the sometimes conflicting pressures exerted on members of

Congress from various lobbying groups, the leadership groups in Congress and the president, an optimal solution for legislators is to seek a compromise among the various interests. For example, faced with a desire on the part of an administration of their own political persuasion for new tariff-cutting authority yet faced also with pressures from certain industries in their districts that claim injury from imports, they are likely to seek legislation combining protective measures for the industries alleging injury and tariff-cutting authority for all other industries. In this way, they can minimize vote losses as well as any punitive actions taken by the president or the congressional leadership. The nature of the compromises actually emerging from Congress thus depends mainly on four factors: (1) the extent of pressures from economic groups favouring trade liberalization or protectionism; (2) the party positions of Republicans and Democrats on trade issues; (3) the relative strength of the two parties in Congress; and (4) the political affiliation of the president and how vigorously he urges that the Congress pass a particular trade policy. Of course, on a more fundamental level the determinants of each of the factors could also be analysed, but the viewpoint of this study will be mainly short run with these various factors being taken as given.


## AN ANALYSIS OF POSTWAR TRADE POLICY

This section is devoted to illustrating the significance of the four factors just enumerated in shaping the nature of the trade policies enacted by the Congress since 1945. The analysis is qualitative in this section, but in the next part of the paper, quantitative techniques will be employed to test, in particular, the role of economic pressures in shaping congressional voting patterns on the Trade Act of 1974. The entire period can usefully be divided into four sub-periods: (1) 1945–50; (2) 1951–61; (3) 1962–7; and (4) 1968–75.


### The 1945–50 Period

The first period, in which the reciprocal trade agreements programme was renewed three times (1945, 1948 and 1949), illustrates the importance of traditional party positions in the trade field as well as the relative strength of Democrats versus Republicans in Congress in determining the content of the trade legislation enacted by Congress. The party position of Democrats at this time was to continue to support the reciprocal-trade programme initiated by President Roosevelt and Secretary of State Cordell Hull in 1934. The key argument used by the executive branch and the Democratic leadership in Congress tied trade liberalization to US foreign-policy interests. A statement by President Roosevelt to Congress on 26 March 1945 typifies the position of the Democratic Party: 'If the economic foundations of peace are to be as secure as the political foundations, it is clear that this effort [the liberalization associated with the reciprocal-trade-agreements program] must be continued vigorously.'

During this period administration spokesmen also maintained (as they had since the beginning of the trade-agreements programme) that no injury would be imposed on any important domestic industry. Furthermore, they testified that tariff liberalization would actually increase total employment and stimulate agricultural exports. The fact that the major labour unions supported the president's 1945 request for a three-year extension of the trade-agreements programme and for an additional 50 per cent tariff-cutting authority was a key reason for the widespread support of this proposal by Democratic members of Congress. A few small unions (e.g., the Amalgamated Lace Operatives, the Flint glass workers and the Watchmakers Union) argued against passage of the bill, but such unions as the United Auto and Aircraft Workers, the Textile Workers of America, the International Brotherhood of Teamsters and the United Electrical, Radio and Machine Workers, who formed an important political base for the Democratic party at that time, favoured trade liberalization.

Republicans in the House generally voted against trade legislation sponsored by the Democrats. They stated that they did not oppose tariff liberalization *per se*, but rather objected to the depth of the tariff reductions in many product lines that competed with the products of domestic industries. In the Senate, on the other hand, the Republicans opposing trade bills sponsored by Democrats outnumbered those favouring them by only a small margin. Republican Senators who voted for the legislation fashioned by Democrats did so mainly on the basis of the foreign-policy arguments for trade liberalization.[16]

The highly partisan nature of voting patterns in the 1945–50 period is indicated by the fact that in the House no less than 94 per cent of those Democrats voting and 92 per cent of voting Republicans supported their traditional party positions on the three trade bills passed during these years.[17] Since Democrats controlled both the House and Senate during the 1945 and 1949 renewals of the trade programme, a liberal trade bill was easily passed. Conversely, when in 1948 both branches of Congress were controlled by Republicans, a bill considered to be protectionist at that time was adopted. The main protectionist proviso in the 1948 bill was a peril-point clause whereby the Tariff Commission would establish minimal tariff rates below which domestic producers of the product would be seriously injured. When the Democrats regained control of both congressional branches in 1949, the 1948 legislation was promptly repealed in favour of a bill that did not include a peril-point clause.

## The 1951–61 Period

The solidarity of Democrats in Congress behind an unencumbered program of trade liberalization and of Republicans in opposition to such a policy began to break down in the 1950s. To an increasing extent, the voting patterns of Democrats reflected the economic interests of constituents who feared that extensive trade liberalization would have a large adverse economic impact on their industries. The absence of a Democrat in the White House throughout most of the period 1953–60, and less aggressive liberalization pressures on the part of the executive branch during President Truman's last few years in office also contributed to this increase in protectionist votes by Democrats. Among Republicans a conflict arose between those who wished to respond positively to the mildly protectionist proposals put forth by the Eisenhower administration and those Republicans who, now they finally had a majority in both congressional houses as well as a Republican in the White House, wanted to implement the traditional, more protectionist position of their party. As the decade wore on, more Republican members of the House also accepted the argument that trade liberalization was an important means of contributing to world peace.

The 1951 extension of the reciprocal trade programme illustrates the move towards a more protectionist position by Democrats. Even though the president was a Democrat and both the House and Senate were controlled by Democrats, the pro-liberal trade bill reported out by the Ways and Means Committee ran into difficulty on the floor of the House. A peril-point provision and an explicit escape clause were finally adopted by the House when 42 out of 247 (i.e., 17 per cent) Democrats joined 183 (out of 187) Republicans in favouring these measures. Democratic support for these provisions was concentrated in textile, oil and coal-producing areas. The importance at this time of the size of a party's control in Congress can be illustrated by noting that if 42 Democrats had voted along protectionist lines in 1945, a liberal bill would still have been passed in the House.

The one-year renewals of the reciprocal trade programme in 1953 and 1954 are best described as holding operations while the new Republican administration could determine its trade policy and establish a working relationship with the new Republican majority in Congress. In 1953, the president asked for a simple one-year extension during which time a seventeen-member bipartisan commission (to be established under the bill) would study foreign trade and recommend appropriate policies. The bill finally passed by the House included these provisions but also increased the Tariff Commission membership to seven (to eliminate tie votes) and shortened the reporting time for the commission on escape-clause actions.

Many Republicans wanted a much more protectionist bill, and an amendment imposing import quotas on petroleum and tariff quotas on lead and zinc was recommitted to the Ways and Means Committee only by a vote of 242 to 161. Without any restraining pressures from a Democratic president, a protectionist swing among Democrats also became more evident. 56 Democrats and 105 Republicans opposed recommittal (thus favouring consideration of the bill on the floor of the House) and 137 Democrats and 104 Republicans supported the motion, in effect, killing the bill. Democratic support was centered in oil and coal-producing states (e.g., Louisiana, Oklahoma, Texas and West Virginia) and in lead and zinc areas (e.g., Colorado, New Mexico and Idaho). Republican opposition to the quotas was fairly widespread but especially heavy in New England, New York, and New Jersey where oil imports were significant.

By 1954 the report of the Commission of Foreign Trade (the Randall Report) was completed, and the president recommended a trade bill to Congress that was consistent with the report's recommendations. Essentially, the proposal called for a three-year extension of the trade programme and a new 15 per cent (5 per cent per year) tariff-cutting authority. The peril-point and escape clauses were to remain intact. Representative Reed, the new Republican Chairman of the Ways and Means Committee and a long-time strong opponent of tariff reductions, delayed scheduling hearings on the administration's bill with the explanation that a heavy workload facing the committee prevented sufficient time for the public hearings obviously required for the Randall Commission recommendations. President Eisenhower finally agreed to accept a one-year extension of the existing law, and the committee then reported out such a bill without holding any hearings. Both parties accepted the one-year extension by large majorities.

In 1955 President Eisenhower asked for essentially the same trade bill he did in 1954, a three-year extension with a 5 per cent per year tariff-cutting authority and retention of the escape-clause and peril-point provisions. One important difference from 1953 and 1954, however, was that the Democrats had again gained control of both the House and Senate. A bill containing most of the features desired by the president was reported out by the Ways and Means Committee early in the congressional session, but an amendment disclaiming congressional approval or disapproval of GATT was again added, as well as one stating that no provision in a trade agreement could be inconsistent with existing US legislation covering import restrictions on agricultural commodities.

The extent of the opposition to the bill on the floor of the House was surprising. In the absence of party pressures from the White House and faced with extensive labour and business opposition from textile, .

coal–oil, and lead–zinc interests, a substantial number of Democrats voted along protectionist lines. On a motion to recommit the bill with instructions to amend it so that the president would be required to comply with Tariff Commission recommendations on escape-clause actions, 80 Democrats voted in the affirmative, 140 in the negative. In the three southern textile states of Georgia, North Carolina and South Carolina, 18 of the 27 voting Democrats from these states favoured the recommital motion. A massive letter-writing campaign by textile employers in these states, who were concerned about imports from Japan, apparently had a profound effect in changing the traditionally liberal-trade voting pattern of these and other southern representatives. [18] All six Democratic representatives from West Virginia, where protectionist pressures from the coal industry, the coal-carrying railroads and the glass and pottery industries were strong, voted in favour of the motion, as did a large proportion of Democratic Representatives in such oil-producing states as Louisiana and Texas. All in all, 50 of the 80 Democratic votes came from the south. Democrats representing textile and coal interests in the north (Massachusetts and Pennsylvania) and lead–zinc interests in the west (Colorado, New Mexico and Idaho) supplied the bulk of the remaining affirmative Democratic votes.

The Republicans were even more deeply divided. A majority of those voting (109 out of 185) favoured the motion to recommit. There seems to be no special economic interest or regional voting pattern in the Republican vote. Apparently, it was a test of strength between loyalty to the president and traditional dissatisfaction with the way the programme had been carried out by the executive branch. After the motion was rejected and the bill reached a final vote, 109 out of 185 Republicans voted for passage, as did 186 out of 191 Democrats.

The bill was passed by the Senate and when accepted by the House included additions that made it easier to obtain favourable action under the escape clause and permitted the president to impose import quotas on any product that threatened the national security. The national security clause represented an important victory for the oil and coal interests. They had pushed for a quota limiting oil imports to 10 per cent of domestic consumption but accepted the national security provision as a compromise with the understanding that the administration would restrict imports of oil. [19] Protectionist pressures in Congress continued to be strong during the 1958 renewal effort, but the administration was more successful in dealing with them. This was partly due to more active support for a liberal trade policy by the executive branch. The president spoke at a bipartisan conference on trade that also included Secretary of State Dulles, Adlai Stevenson and House Speaker, Sam Rayburn, and directed the Department of Commerce to undertake detailed industry studies of the benefits of exports to each state and more than 100 congressional districts. In addition to exploiting fully the Cold War arguments for greater trade among non-communist nations, administration spokesmen used effectively a new economic argument: the need for new tariff-cutting authority over an extended period to negotiate with the newly created European Economic Community.

Another factor strengthening the administration's position was the weakening of opposition from oil and coal interests because of the existence of voluntary import quotas.[20] Twenty-nine Representatives from the oil–coal states of Louisiana, Oklahoma, Texas, West Virginia and Pennsylvania voted yea on the motion to recommit the bill as reported by the Ways and Means Committee. This bill provided for a five-year extension, a further 25 per cent duty-cutting authority, and also for the right of Congress to override the president's disregard of Tariff Commission decisions for escape-clause action by a two-thirds vote. The 1955 recommital motion was supported by forty-four Representatives from these states. This technique of weakening opposition from the congressional group representing a particular industry by making a specific concession to the industry has been used on several occasions since 1955.

The number of Democrats voting for recommital dropped from 80 in 1955 to 61 in 1958, largely because of the change in the oil–coal vote, but the number of Democrats in the southern textile-producing states of Georgia, North Carolina and South Carolina who voted affirmatively rose from 18 to 20, even though the Japanese agreed to voluntary export quotas in 1955. The greater support given to the president by House Republicans is indicated by the fact that 141 out of 187 voted against the motion to return the bill to the Ways and Means Committee in contrast to only 66 out of 185 in 1955. The vote on the final bill was, in favour, 184 Democrats and 133 Republicans; opposed, 39 Democrats and 59 Republicans.

As in 1955, the Senate Finance Committee amended the House bill to make it more protectionist. The reciprocal trade programme was extended only three years rather than five; a concurring majority vote in both the House and Senate was required on presidential decisions to override an affirmative escape-clause finding by the Tariff Commission; the national security clause was amended to make it easier for industries to obtain protectionist treatment under the provision; and the tariff-cutting authority was put at only 15 per cent. In floor action, however, the provisions on vetoing escape-clause actions by the president and on dealing with the votes in the Tariff Commission were eliminated. The Senate bill was passed 72 to 16 with 6 out of 42 Democrats and 10 out of 46 Republicans opposing it.

The Act that finally passed, after resolving differences in the House and Senate bills, provided for a four-year renewal, a 20 per cent tariff-cutting authority, and the veto procedure of escape-clause actions by the president that the House bill contained. The other major feature of the Act was the adoption of the Senate's broadening of the national security provision.

## The Period 1962–7

The passage of the Trade Expansion Act of 1962 represents in many ways a halt and partial reversal of the protectionist trend of the 1950s: the 50 per cent tariff-reducing authority was the deepest given to a president since 1945; the time period within which this power could be used (five years) was longer than under any previous trade bill,[21] non-tariff trade barriers as well as tariffs were to be covered in the proposed negotiations; the peril-point provision was considerably weakened;[22] and the criteria for qualifying for escape-clause action were strengthened somewhat by requiring increased imports to be 'the major factor' causing serious injury rather than to have 'contributed substantially' towards causing injury. By providing for financial assistance to firms and groups of workers injured, the Act also in effect modified the long-defended notion that no group should be seriously injured by duty reductions except possibly for short periods. Previously, if firms in an industry were significantly injured, the prescribed remedy was to raise the duty again. Now such firms might receive assistance that could enable their adjustment to take the form of moving into new production lines.

Following President Eisenhower's example with respect to the oil industry, President Kennedy did, however, make an important concession to a politically powerful industrial group. A voluntary quota system was established for cotton-textile imports in 1961, and a formal international marketing agreement for cotton textiles permitting the use of quotas to prevent 'market disruption' was negotiated in 1962. Quotas on oil imports were also continued under the national security clause, which was essentially unchanged in the new trade act. Two senators (Long of Louisiana and Kerr of Oklahoma) indicated after the trade bill was passed that an understanding to maintain oil quotas had been reached with the administration.[23] Two other steps taken by President Kennedy prior to final passage of the trade bill were the announcement of a six-point programme to assist the north west lumber industry and the acceptance of a Tariff Commission recommendation to raise duties on carpets and glass under the escape-clause provision of the 1958 trade act.

Not only did the administration weaken opposition to its trade proposals with key concessions to special economic interests but it conducted an unparalleled public campaign to sell its ideas. President

Kennedy made the trade bill a key part of his legislative programme and led the fight for it. In his message to Congress on the proposed bill, he concluded with the following statement:

At rare moments in the life of this nation an opportunity comes along to fashion out of the confusion of current events a clear bold action to show the world what it is we stand for. Such an opportunity is before us now. This bill, by enabling us to strike a bargain with the Common Market, will 'strike a blow' for freedom. [24]

This combining of the traditionally claimed foreign-policy benefits from a liberal trade policy with hardheaded economic arguments on the advantages of negotiating with the European Economic Community (EEC) proved effective in selling the new proposals. The economic case for the negotiation was simply that the United States would suffer large export losses to the EEC countries as they reduced duties to zero among themselves (and the prospective admission of the United Kingdom to the group made the losses even larger) unless we bargained down their common external tariffs.

The success of the efforts to sell the trade bill is indicated by the small number of congressional changes in the initial proposal and the ease with which it passed in both the House and Senate. The usual motion in the House to recommit the bill reported by the Ways and Means Committee with instructions to substitute a one-year extension of the existing act was rejected 253 to 171. The Democratic vote was 44 for recommital and 210 against, while the Republican alignment was 127 for and 44 against. The increased Democratic majority compared to the 1950s explains part of the large vote against recommital, but it is interesting to note that in the southern textile states of Georgia, North Carolina and South Carolina only ten legislators cast affirmative votes as compared with 21 in 1958. The yea vote of representatives from the oil states of Louisiana, Oklahoma and Texas was larger than in 1958 (17, up from 11), but only one Democrat in the coal-producing states of Pennsylvania and West Virginia voted yea, compared with 10 in 1958.

In the Senate, where the rules make it much easier to introduce amendments from the floor, the closest margin of victory of adminis-tration forces came on an amendment to restore the old peril point procedure. This was defeated by 40 to 38, with 13 of the 53 voting Democrats joining all 25 Republicans to vote in favour of peril points. Southern senators in textile-producing states, Georgia, Mississippi, North Carolina and South Carolina, supplied 10 of the 13 affirmative Democratic votes. But after this and several other amendments were defeated, the bill passed the Senate 78 to 8. Only one Democrat opposed passage while 22 of 29 Republicans supported the bill.

## The Period 1968–75

At the conclusion of the Kennedy Round of GATT-sponsored trade negotiations in 1967, protectionist pressures again increased to levels even higher than during the 1950s. The economic foundations for this development were a rapid rise in the ratio of imports to domestic consumption in many important industries and the large-scale investment activities abroad by many US manufacturing firms. The list of tariff items for which the import-penetration ratio increased sharply includes such major product lines as wool and man-made textile products, footwear, automobiles, steel and electrical consumer goods (e.g., T.V. sets, radios and phonographs).[25] The fundamental factor leading to the improved competitive ability of foreign producers in US manufacturing markets seems to have been the narrowing of the technological gap between the United States and other industrial nations. In part this came about through greater US direct foreign investment that combined American technology and managerial skills with lower-wage foreign labour. But the US adjustment to this underlying trend was made much more severe than necessary by the reluctance of the United States and the other major trading nations to correct a growing overvaluation of the US dollar by depreciating the dollar. Thus, the brunt of the adjustment pressures fell on US import-competing and export-oriented industries.

The alleged job displacement through foreign investment and a rapid rise in imports of certain products have been important factors in the change in attitude towards trade policy by the AFL-CIO. Until the late sixties this organization had always strongly supported a liberal trade policy. An appreciable number of unions in selected import-sensitive sectors (e.g., glass, pottery, coal and textiles) had begun actively opposing tariff reductions in the 1950s but the AFL-CIO remained in favour of liberalization through the passage of the Trade Expansion Act of 1962. By 1970, the organization testified before the Ways and Means Committee that it favoured a bill that would impose quotas whenever a significant share of a domestic market was captured by foreign producers.[26] It was claimed that 700,000 jobs had been lost from 1966–9 because of rising imports.

Another cause of the shift in the views of the AFL-CIO was disappointment with the manner in which the adjustment assistance programme for workers under the 1962 Trade Act had worked. Not a single favourable decision for labour was made until November 1969. Since the very active support of labour for the 1962 bill was largely based upon the inclusion of the adjustment assistance programme, the AFL-CIO felt it had been badly misled when the adjustment assistance did not materialize.[27] Unfortunately, modifications by Congress in the administration's bill with respect to the adjustment assistance provisions made the conditions for securing help for workers so stringent that a literal interpretation of the Act ruled out aid in most instances.

The management in many industries joined labour in actively seeking quantitative restrictions in the late 1960s. An important new member to the protectionist ranks at that time was the steel industry. Beginning in 1967, both management and labour leaders began pushing for import quotas on steel, and a bill to that effect was introduced by Senator Hartke, a Democrat from Indiana, and cosponsored by twenty-four other senators.[28] In 1968 the industry was successful in its efforts when a voluntary export restraint programme was accepted by Japanese and European steel producers. This programme was renewed for three more years in 1971 but with the permitted annual growth rate of imports into the United States cut from 5 per cent to 2.5 per cent.

There were, however, some firms and industries that began to take a more active role in promoting a liberal trade policy. Most of the rapidly growing number of multinational firms favoured a minimum of restrictions on trade, since these barriers impede the most profitable combinations of resources and flow of goods among their producing units and markets. Thus, while in the 1940s and 1950s export interests were content, with only a few exceptions, to express their support for liberal trade policies through such multipurpose organizations as the US Chamber of Commerce and the Committee for Economic Development, by the 1970s several firms and industry groups testified in favour of further tariff reductions. These included manufacturers of computers and business equipment, aircraft and other aerospace products, machinery and machine tools, scientific apparatus, electronic and electrical products and paper products. On the other hand, labour unions in most of these industries vigorously opposed trade liberalization. The rise of the multinational firm has had as one of its by-products the development of sharp differences in views between labour and management in a number of industries on trade policy. Business, the traditional bastion of protectionist attitudes, has become more liberal-trade oriented, while labour, the strong supporter of liberal trade for many years, has become protectionist.

The first indication of the strength of protectionist forces came in 1968 when President Johnson proposed a new trade bill. He requested that the authority to cut tariffs under the limits given in the 1962 Trade Act be extended until 1970 and the ASP system be abolished as part of the tentative agreement reached by US negotiators during the Kennedy Round. Not only did the chemical industry lobby strongly against eliminating ASP, but such industries as textiles (wool and man-made), dairy products, steel, leather and oil used the occasion to press for import quotas. (The domestic oil industry wanted the existing administrative quotas to be made statutory.) Although a strongly negative reaction to the quota bills by the administration (including the threat of a presidential veto) succeeded in preventing the passage of these bills, the president's proposal never got beyond the hearings stage in the House. Moreover, as already noted, the administration yielded to the steel industry's views by helping to negotiate voluntary export restraints for Japanese and European steel producers.

It was in 1970, however, that the strongest pressures for protectionism emerged. In late 1969, President Nixon requested an additional 20 per cent duty-cutting authority (to extend until mid 1973), the elimination of ASP, favourable tax treatment for firms qualifying as DISC and liberalization of the adjustment assistance provisions of the 1962 Trade Act. The Ways and Means Committee did not begin hearings on this proposal until May of the following year, when it also considered a quota bill introduced by its chairman, Wilbur Mills. Mills had long been a strong supporter of liberal trade policies but he now sponsored a bill to establish import quotas for textiles and footwear. During the twenty days of committee hearings, a long list of industries and unions (including the AFL-CIO) called for greater protection against imports and fifty-two representatives and senators personally testified in favour of protection for some special industry.

The bill finally approved by the committee combined the administration and Mills proposals and added a few more protectionist features. For example, a trigger mechanism was established by which the president, unless he determined such action was not in the national interest, was required to impose the import restrictions (e.g., quotas) recommended by the Tariff Commission when increased imports not only caused serious injury but also met certain other conditions relating to the extent of the import increases or their effects on domestic production, profits and wages and to the price and unit costs of domestic goods compared with imports. A provision establishing a tariff quota on imports of mink fur also was included. The repeal of the ASP system for the relevant chemical products was covered in the bill but rubber-soled footwear, another item on which ASP applied, was excluded. Furthermore, the president was prohibited from adjusting oil imports through tariff changes rather than quota changes.

The bill as recommended by the Ways and Means Committee passed in the House by a vote of 215 to 165. The usual motion to recommit failed by 172 to 207. The Republican vote on the final bill was 78 in favour and 82 against, whereas the Democratic tally was 137 in favour and 83 against. Every voting Democrat from Alabama, Georgia, Kentucky, Louisiana, Massachusetts, North Carolina, Oklahoma, Rhode Island, South Carolina, Tennessee and West Virginia voted for the bill. The main centres of Democratic opposition were California, Michigan, New Jersey and New York. The nearly evenly divided Republican vote was partly due to the ambivalent position of the president; he favoured quotas on textiles but opposed them on other products. States with a high proportion of Republicans supporting the bill were characterized, as in the Democratic case, by economies in which the production of textiles, footwear, mink, oil or coal was significant: Alabama, Georgia, Massachusetts, New Hampshire, North Carolina, Pennsylvania, Tennessee, Virginia and Wisconsin. Republicans in areas other than New England and the South generally voted against adoption of the bill.

The Senate Finance Committee added a few more protectionist features to the House-passed bill. For example, the escape-clause criterion was eased and quarterly quotas on fresh, chilled or frozen meats were established. Moreover, rather than sending the various provisions to the Senate as a separate bill, they were added on to a bill in which social security benefits were being increased by 10 per cent. The plan was to utilize the broad support for the social security measure to ensure passage of the trade provisions, but after the small group of hard-core liberal traders such as Senator Javits refused to go along with this strategy and were prepared to filibuster, the trade features of the bill were recommitted to the Finance Committee where they died.

The passage of a fairly liberal trade bill by the House in 1973 (and the Senate in 1974) demonstrates once again the potent effects of aggressive actions by the president and making a few key concessions to protectionist forces. In late 1973, the Watergate Affair had not yet become a major issue, and President Nixon's prestige among Republicans on the Hill was high in view of his overwhelming election victory and success at détente with China and the USSR. The administration had also renewed the quota arrangement on steel in 1971, and even more important, had first negotiated a series of bilateral agreements limiting imports of non-cotton textiles and then a new multilateral agreement, which went into effect in 1974, covering all textile products manufactured from man-made materials, wool and cotton. Thus, almost the entire textile industry, including apparel, was protected by quotas.

While more vigorous efforts by the president, coupled with a few key compromises, seem to have been important in offsetting broad protectionist pressures at this time, the passage of a liberal trade bill would probably not have been possible without the depreciation of the dollar in 1971 and 1973 and the eventual adoption of a floating exchange system for the major trading nations. These changes increased the cost of foreign imports and alleviated the import pressures on many import-competing US industries.

In 1973 the president asked Congress for the right to lower or raise duties over a five-year period to any level he wished (with a few statutory exceptions). The two other main features sought by the administration involved: (1) authority to put into effect automatically agreements reached on non-tariff trade barriers, unless new legislation was required or a majority of members of either the House or Senate voted against the agreement within 90 days of the president's delivering a copy to Congress, and (2) modifications in the criteria for import relief that would make it much easier to obtain assistance. Among the other aspects of the bill was the authority to provide duty-free treatment for imports of manufactured and semimanufactured products from the developing nations, but in his message to Congress the president stated that certain import-sensitive products such as textiles, footwear, watches and steel would be excluded from this preference scheme.

The final bill passed by Congress (the Trade Act of 1974) narrowed the powers asked for by the president, but these changes seemed moderate in view of the apparent protectionist mood of the House and Senate. The modifications included the following: (1) the president's tariff-reducing powers were limited to 60 per cent for duties above 5 per cent and 100 per cent below this level; (2) agreements covering non-tariff trade barriers required explicit affirmative action by the Congress; (3) the criteria for import relief were further eased so that increased imports (not necessarily a result of previous tariff concessions) only needed to be a 'substantial' rather than a 'primary' cause of serious injury to a firm, industry, or worker group; (4) various products, such as textiles, watches, certain electronic products, certain steel articles, footwear and certain glass products, were specifically excluded from the preference arrangement; and (5) the ability of the president to retaliate against unfair trade practices was increased. Another politically significant rider to the president's bill was a section that excluded non-market economies, such as the USSR, from US export credits or investment guarantees and from most-favoured-nation tariff treatment until they permit free emigration of their citizens.

In attempting to persuade Congress that a new trade bill was necessary, government witnesses emphasized, as the Kennedy administration had done in 1962, that further negotiating authority was needed to improve the US international economic position and ease adjustment problems for US industries. For example, it is a widely held view in Congress that our main trading partners use non-tariff measures to curtail or promote trade artificially much more extensively than the United States does. Thus, the request to negotiate in this field was well received. Similarly, the administration argued that the oil crisis pointed up the necessity of negotiating for adequate commitments from foreign suppliers on the availability of key raw materials. The portions of the bill that permit firms and workers to obtain adjustment assistance more easily and that provide for an enhanced ability to retaliate against unfair practices made the granting of authority to negotiate in the tariff and non-tariff areas even more palatable. The standard claim that international peace and harmony are promoted by greater trade was made, but not as a central point. Instead, the selfish economic interests of the United States were stressed as the major reason why additional negotiating authority was needed.

The final vote on the House bill was 272 in favour and 140 opposed—a margin nearly as impressive as in 1962. Republicans supported the bill 160 to 19, while Democrats opposed it 112 to 121. The impact of the new textile agreement on the voting pattern was apparent. In Alabama, Georgia, Mississippi, North Carolina, South Carolina, Tennessee and Virginia, every Republican and all but 2 Democrats voted in favour of the bill. Democratic opposition was centred in the northern states (only 17 out of 149 Democrats in these states favoured the bill) where many of the other import-sensitive industries, such as footwear, were located and where the influence of the AFL-CIO was greater. The AFL-CIO favoured a general quota bill jointly sponsored by Representative Burke, a Democrat from Massachusetts, and Senator Hartke, a Democrat from Indiana. The small Republican opposition consisted of a few hard-core protectionists and of representatives of districts in which import-sensitive industries were located. The size of the hard-core group had greatly decreased since the 1950s as more and more protectionist features were introduced in US trade policy. As a result, by 1973 the Republicans in Congress could be termed more liberal on trade matters than the Democrats.

After a long wrangle over the emigration rider, the Senate finally passed a trade bill in late 1974.[29] The final vote was 77 to 4, with 3 Democrats and 1 Republican casting negative ballots. A better indication of the relative strengths of liberal-trade versus protectionist forces in the Senate was given in an amendment to prohibit the president from cutting duties on manufactures for which imports exceeded one-third of domestic consumption for three of the last five years. This amendment failed 35 to 49, with 26 Democrats and 9 Republicans favouring it and 23 Democrats and 26 Republicans opposing it. The states in which both senators favoured the amendment were Alabama, Alaska, Indiana,

Maine, Massachusetts, Missouri, Pennsylvania, Rhode Island, Virginia and Washington. Such industries as textiles, shoes, steel, glass and forestry are important in these states.

## A STATISTICAL ANALYSIS OF VOTING ON THE TRADE ACT OF 1974

Although a non-statistical analysis of voting patterns seems to give ample evidence that economic factors influence the voting behaviour of legislators on trade issues, it is possible to test this hypothesis in a more formal manner. For this purpose, the voting pattern of the House and Senate on the 1974 Trade Act was selected. To discover whether economic pressures influenced legislators' voting on this bill, a list of import-sensitive and export-oriented industries was determined on the basis of testimony before the Ways and Means Committee. If workers or management in any industry opposed the liberalizing features of the bill, the industry was regarded as import-sensitive; if members of the industry supported its key provisions, the industry was termed export-oriented. Table 3.1 lists the import-sensitive sectors. Only two industries, office and computing equipment (SIC 357) and aircraft (SIC 372), were selected as export-oriented industries.[30]

Obviously, such a list depends in part on the judgement of the investigator. For example, management in the electronic sector (SIC 365–367) generally supported the bill whereas the labour unions in this sector opposed it, but it was felt that the workers would exercise more influence on Congress than would management. Two notable exclusions from the list are textile mill products (SIC 22) and apparel and other textile products (SIC 23). These two sectors combined not only exceed in size any other two-digit SIC manufacturing sector, but these industries are much more widely dispersed than other manufacturing industry. When representatives from the textile and apparel unions representing the two industries testified in the House in June 1973, they opposed the trade bill and urged the adoption of the system of quotas contained in the Burke–Hartke bill. At the time of the hearings, however, the US government was attempting to negotiate a multilateral textile agreement covering all major textile and apparel products. These negotiations were successful and, as previously noted, the new agreement went into operation in 1974. That this agreement met the objections of the textile industry is indicated by the fact that they did not testify at all before the Senate Finance Committee when the bill was before the Senate in 1974. Moreover, by the time the House voted on its bill in the fall of 1973, it appeared that the success of the new marketing agreement was assured.

Thus, legislators sensitive to textile interests did not oppose the bill and, indeed, on the whole supported it.

Another problem with a list such as this is that the strength of the opposition to the trade bill varied considerably among the groups on the

Table 3.1:   *Import-sensitive industries, 1973 House and 1974 Senate hearings*

| Standard Industrial Classification (SIC) Number | Industry |
|---|---|
| 103 | Lead and zinc ores |
| 11 | Anthracite coal |
| 12 | Bituminous coal and lignite mining |
| 131 | Crude petroleum and natural gas |
| 141 | Dimension stone |
| 145 | Clay, ceramic and refractory materials |
| 2022 | Cheese |
| 3084 | Wines, brandy and brandy spirits |
| 2085 | Distilled, rectified and blended liquors |
| 2432 | Veneer and plywood |
| 26 | Paper and allied products |
| 2615 | Cyclic intermediates, dyes, organic pigments and cyclic products |
| 282 | Plastic materials and synthetic resins |
| 302 | Rubber footwear |
| 31 | Leather and leather products (includes non-rubber footwear) |
| 321 | Flat glass |
| 325 | Structural clay products |
| 3262 | Vitreous china |
| 3263 | Fine earthenware |
| 331 | Blast furnaces and basic steel products |
| 3321 | Gray iron foundries |
| 3332 | Primary smelting and refining of lead |
| 3333 | Primary smelting and refining of zinc |
| 342 | Hand and edge tools, excluding machine tools |
| 345 | Screw machine products |
| 3554 | Paper industries machinery |
| 3562 | Ball and roller bearings |
| 365 | Radio and television sets |
| 366 | Communications equipment |
| 367 | Electronic components and accessories |
| 371 | Motor vehicles |
| 375 | Motorcycles, bicycles and parts |
| 387 | Watches, clocks and parts |
| 391 | Silverware, plated ware, stainless steel ware |
| 3941 | Games and toys |
| 3942 | Dolls |
| 3964 | Needles, pins, hooks and eyes, etc. |

list. For example, the automotive workers seemed to oppose the bill less strongly than the electronic workers. Lumping the various industries together clouds the varying degrees of political pressure exerted by the different industries. For that reason, information on the industries was collected separately as well as on an aggregate basis.

Having selected a list of import-sensitive and export-oriented industries, the next step was to determine the proportion of workers represented by these industries in each congressional district in each state. The first of these allocations was accomplished by obtaining employment in the industries by county for each state and then aggregating these figures to a congressional-district basis. For this purpose, two Bureau of the Census, Department of Commerce publications, *County Business Patterns, 1973* and *Congressional District Data Book, 93rd Congress*, were utilized.[31] State figures were given directly in *County Business Patterns*.

The dependent variable used in testing the importance of economic factors in the House voting pattern is whether a legislator voted for the 1973 Trade Bill (a liberal trade vote) or against the bill (a protectionist vote). The independent variables are the political party to which a legislator belongs, the proportions of workers in import-sensitive and export-oriented industries and, finally, the campaign contributions from certain unions received during the year 1974 by legislators who voted on the 1973 trade bill and who chose to run for office again in 1974. The unions are the International Brotherhood of Electrical Workers, the Communications Workers of America, and the United Steelworkers of America,[32] which actively opposed the trade bill, and presumably their campaign contributions in 1974 were highly correlated with their financial aid to these legislators in earlier periods.

There are several problems with trying to separate out the effects of economic pressures on a particular vote. Logrolling raises one obvious difficulty. Members of Congress who do not have significant numbers of import-sensitive or export-oriented industries in their districts may vote in a particular way in return for a sympathetic vote on other issues of interest to them by members representing districts where economic interest in the trade bill is considerable. If these votes are distributed in the same proportions as those where economic pressure groups are strong, the results will not be biased. While it seems reasonable to expect this, one cannot be sure of this outcome, and, therefore, logrolling may distort the correlation results. A more serious problem would seem to arise with regard to campaign contributions. Trade is just one of many issues that interest labour unions. Legislators may still receive substantial financial help even though they oppose labour's position on trade simply because they support enough of labour's other positions. Again, one would expect this factor to weaken any relationship between campaign contributions and voting patterns rather than to reverse the expected direction of the relationship. Clearly, there are also many other variables besides the ones included in the analysis that affect voting patterns. If these are systematically correlated with the variables used, the results will be biased. The assumption here is that this is not true.

The directions of the expected relationships between the dependent and independent variables in the analysis are as follows. Since a Republican president proposed the trade legislation, presumably after consultations with congressional leaders in his party, one would expect Republicans generally to support the bill. In contrast, a larger proportion of Democrats could be expected to oppose the bill, partly because the AFL-CIO—a major force in the Democratic Party—opposed it and partly because of the absence of White House pressure to vote in a particular manner. The higher the proportion of import-sensitive industries in a congressional district, the more one would expect a negative vote on the trade bill. Similarly, legislators from districts with export-oriented industries should tend to vote in favour of the bill. Finally, the higher the level of political contributions legislators receive from the three protectionist unions selected, the greater the likelihood that they will vote against the bill.

In the results of the probit analysis reported below, a 'yes' (liberal trade) vote for the bill was assigned the number '0' while a negative (protectionist) vote was assigned a '1'. Republican legislators were assigned a '1' and Democrats a '0'. Therefore, since Republicans should tend to favour the bill and Democrats oppose it, the sign of the coefficient on political status should be negative, in other words, the higher the number representing the political party, the lower this number representing the position of a legislator on the bill. In addition, the relationships between both the proportion of import-sensitive industries and the size of campaign contributions and the vote on the bill should be positive, in other words, the higher the proportion of sensitive industries and the size of campaign contributions, the higher is the expected number assigned to depict voting behaviour. The relationship between export-oriented industries and the voting pattern should, on the other hand, be negative. Equations 1–3 in Table 3.2 present the probit analysis.[33] Equation 1 aggregates the import-sensitive and export-oriented industries. The variables for party affiliation, union contributions, and proportion of import-sensitive industries all have the expected sign and are significant at the 1 per cent level. The two export-oriented industries do not show up as significant or with the expected sign. Equation 2 differs from equation 1 in that the textile and apparel industries are added. The fact that the coefficient on this term is

*Table 3.2:   1973 House vote on the trade bill related to various economic and political factors*

| Variable | Equation 1 | | Equation 2 | | Equation 3 | |
|---|---|---|---|---|---|---|
| Constant | − 0.40 | (2.78)** | − 0.25 | (1.50) | − 0.23 | (1.17) |
| Party affiliation | − 1.20 | (6.79)** | − 1.24 | (6.95)** | − 1.45 | (6.95)** |
| Union contributions | 0.0004 | (3.22)** | 0.0004 | (2.89)** | 0.0003 | (2.11)** |
| Import-sensitive industries | 3.49 | (2.62)** | 3.28 | (2.45)** | — | — |
| Export-sensitive industries | 1.16 | (1.28) | − 0.11 | (0.03) | 0.76 | (0.17) |
| Textiles and apparel | — | — | − 2.46 | (1.64) | − 3.38 | (1.92)* |
| Oil−coal | — | — | — | — | 16.51 | (2.35)** |
| Screw machine products | — | — | — | — | 112.08 | (3.19)** |
| Watches, silverware, games, dolls and needles | — | — | — | — | 44.87 | (2.11)* |
| Hand tools | — | — | — | — | − 62.62 | (2.15)* |
| Coal-tar products | — | — | — | — | 102.47 | (1.75) |
| Lead and zinc | — | — | — | — | 32.45 | (0.177) |
| Ceramic materials | — | — | — | — | − 3604.58 | (0.22) |
| Cheese | — | — | — | — | 42.57 | (0.73) |
| Wines and liquors | — | — | — | — | − 76.30 | (0.67) |
| Veneer and plywood | — | — | — | — | − 58.22 | (0.13) |
| Paper | — | — | — | — | 5.09 | (0.64) |
| Plastics | — | — | — | — | − 15.97 | (0.92) |
| Rubber footwear | — | — | — | — | − 66.15 | (1.06) |
| Leather products | — | — | — | — | 13.51 | (1.21) |
| Flat glass | — | — | — | — | 26.45 | (0.61) |
| Clay and china products | — | — | — | — | 9.15 | (0.24) |
| Basic steel and iron | — | — | — | — | 2.29 | (0.73) |
| Paper machinery | — | — | — | — | 25.74 | (0.20) |
| Ball bearings | — | — | — | — | 59.40 | (0.88) |
| Electrical equipment | — | — | — | — | 1.13 | (0.21) |
| Motorcycles and bicycles | — | — | — | — | 1.06 | (0.46) |
| Motor vehicles | — | — | — | — | − 95.03 | (0.99) |

*Notes:* The $t$ statistics are in parentheses in the columns next to the maximum likelihood estimates of the coefficients. By the Chi-square test, equations 1 and 2 are significant at the 1% level and equation 3 at the 5% level.
\* Significant at the 5% level.
\*\* Significant at the 1% level.

negative (and significant at the 10% level) represents further evidence that the traditionally protectionist textile industry was 'bought off' by the successful negotiation of a multilateral marketing agreement covering all major textile products.

When the various industries were entered separately (equation 3), the coefficients generally were not significant. Besides textiles and apparel, other industries that enter as significant at levels of 5 per cent or less are oil and coal, screw machine products, hand tools and a miscellaneous industry group representing watches, games and toys, silverware and stainless steel ware, and needles and fasteners. Of these, the significance of the oil–coal group is not surprising, since this coalition has in the past proved to be very effective in opposing trade liberalization. The industry that produces cyclic intermediates, dyes and pigments and coal-tar products also has proved to be successful in past lobbying efforts, as the rejection of the proposed ASP agreement during the Kennedy Round indicates. The high significance level for screw machine products and hand tools is surprising and probably arises because of its correlation from some omitted variable in the model. The significance of the opposition in areas represented by watches, stainless steel flatware, games, dolls, etc. is an expected result, since these industries have long vigorously opposed liberalization.

For the Senate, the vote selected to test the influence of economic factors was on an amendment by Senator McIntyre, a Democrat from New Hampshire, to the Trade Bill of 1974 that prohibited the president from reducing tariffs or duties on manufactured goods for which imports exceed one-third of domestic consumption during three of the last five years. Data on campaign contributions by the three unions were not collected for the Senate so that the independent variables were party status and the proportions of sensitive import-competing and export-oriented industries in each state. As before, a '0' represented a vote for liberalizing trade (in this case, a 'no' on the amendment) and a '1' represented a protectionist vote. Also, as in the previous equations, Democrats were entered as a '0' and Republicans as a '1'. Consequently, the expected signs are: negative on political party (Republicans vote for trade liberalization and Democrats against it); positive on the proportion of import-sensitive industries; and negative on the proportion of export-oriented industries.

Table 3.3 includes the first two of the same three probit equations used in testing the House vote, except that union contributions are omitted as an independent variable.[34] As in the case of the House vote, political party and proportion of import-sensitive industries have the expected sign and are significant at the 5 per cent level. The variable representing export-oriented industries again has the wrong sign and is not significant. Textiles and apparel also appear with the wrong sign but the coefficient is not significant.

In summary, the statistical analysis does give support for the hypotheses developed from the model set forth in the early parts of the paper. In particular, workers and management who think they are being adversely affected by imports are apparently able collectively to persuade their members of Congress to vote against trade liberalization. Export-oriented industries are not similarly successful. The problem with a statistical analysis of these industries is that relatively few testify strongly in favour of liberalization. Interestingly, the example where a group was able to exert pressure in favour of the bill represents an industry (textiles)

*Table 3.3:  1974 Senate vote on the trade bill related to various economic and political factors*

| Variable | Equation 1 | Equation 2 | |
|---|---|---|---|
| Constant | $-0.72(2.18)^{*}$ | $-0.90$ | $(2.51)^{**}$ |
| Party | $-0.66(2.21)^{*}$ | $-0.66$ | $(2.18)^{*}$ |
| Import-sensitive industries | $9.71(2.85)^{*}$ | $9.62$ | $(2.82)^{**}$ |
| Export-sensitive industries | $10.44(0.91)$ | $13.71$ | $(1.15)$ |
| Textiles and apparel | $-$ $-$ | $3.92$ | $(1.40)$ |

*Notes:* The $t$ statistics are in parentheses next to the maximum likelihood estimates of the coefficients. By the chi-square test, equations 1 and 2 are significant at the 5% level.
[*] Significant at the 5% level,
[**] Significant at the 1% level.

that had often in the past successfully opposed liberalization. Campaign contributions by protectionist unions are also correlated with voting behaviour in the expected direction. In this case, however, the probable correlation of voting on trade issues with voting on other issues not included in the analysis but of greater concern to the unions weakens any conclusion about causality that one might draw from this result.

## NOTES

1. Probably the two best-known works in this area are: Anthony Downs (1957), *An Economic Theory of Democracy*, New York: Harper, and Brothers and James M. Buchanan and Gordon Tullock (1962), *The Calculus of Consent*, Ann Arbor: University of Michigan Press.
2. Most of the recent investigations of tariffs by economists have not been directed at this issue but rather at explaining the structure of a country's tariffs or changes in this structure. *See*, for example, Norman S. Fieleke (1974), Determinants of the US tariff structure, mimeographed 20 February; J. H. Cheh, United States concessions in the Kennedy Round and short-run labor adjustment costs, *Journal of International Economics* 4, No. 4, November; Richard E. Caves (1975), The political economy of tariff structures, Institute for Economic Research, Queens University, Kingston, Ontario, January; and J. Pincus (1975), Pressure groups and the pattern of tariffs, *Journal of Political Economy* 83, No. 4, August.
3. It is assumed that any purely redistributive changes that would obtain majority support have already been undertaken.
4. Because the assumption of identical, homothetic tastes yields a unique set of non-intersecting community indifference curves, the consumption point for

the country after the relative price of imports has fallen due to the tariff liberalization must represent a higher collective income level even if the consumption point does not represent more of all goods.

5. For an extensive analysis of the subject, *see* Anthony Downs, *op. cit.*, ch. 13. It is interesting that Downs illustrates his points with the tariff example.

6. Downs, *op. cit.*, pp. 255–6.

7. William A. Brock and Stephen P. Magee, An economic theory of politics: the case of tariffs (mimeographed).

8. It is assumed that given increments in expenditures eventually result in fewer and fewer favourable votes.

9. For an extensive discussion of this subject, *see* Mancur Olson Jr (1968), *The Logic of Collective Action*, New York: Schocken Books.

10. It does follow, however, that the losers will be unable (without becoming worse off than after the change) to bribe the gainers into not making the change.

11. The standard measurement of net changes in consumer and producer surplus is directed at determining if this type of compensation is possible. As is well known, with fixed international prices, these calculations always yield a net gain as tariffs are lowered.

12. Specifically a country's terms of trade will improve if

$$\frac{t_x d_x}{(t_x + 1)s_x + d_x} > \frac{t_m d_m}{(t_m + 1)s_m + d_m}$$

where $t_x$ and $t_m$ are its duty rates against the country exports and on its imports, respectively; $d_x$ and $d_m$ are the elasticities of demand for its exports and imports, respectively; and $s_x$ and $s_m$ are its supply elasticities of exports and imports.

13. See Stephen P. Magee (1975), Prices, incomes and foreign trade, in *International Trade and Finance*, ed. Peter Kenen, New York: Cambridge University Press, for a survey of the empirical results on import and export demand elasticities. In his work on supply elasticities, Magee obtained a higher US supply elasticity for total exports than import supply elasticity for finished manufactures into the United States, *op. cit.*, p. 183. However, a widely used set of estimates by John Floyd (1965), The overvaluation of the dollar: a note on the international price mechanism, *American Economic Review*, March, places both the demand elasticity for US exports higher than the US demand for imports and the US supply elasticity of exports lower than the supply elasticity of imports for the United States.

14. Giorgio Basevi (1968), The restrictive effect of the US tariff and its welfare effect, *American Economic Review* LVIII, No. 4, September: p. 851.

15. These will not always be the same, but usually the president first checks with his fellow party members in Congress to make sure his recommendations will receive their support.

16. Joe R. Wilkinson (1960), *Politics and Trade Policy*, Washington: Public Affairs Press, p. 34. This excellent study surveys US trade policy during the years 1934–58.

17. *Congressional Quarterly*, 1945, 1948 and 1949.

18. For an interesting discussion of this lobbying effort, *see* Raymond A. Bauer, Ithiel De Sola Pool and Lewis Anthony Dexter (1972), *American Business and Public Policy*, 2nd ed., Chicago: Aldine-Atherton, Inc., pp. 359–62.

19. *Congressional Quarterly*, 1955, p. 298.

20. Mandatory quotas were put into effect in 1959.
21. The new Act finally replaced the initial Reciprocal Trade Agreements Act and obviated the need to keep renewing the trade agreements programme in the future.
22. The Tariff Commission merely had to provide its judgement as to the probable economic effects of duty modifications rather than come up with actual duties below which an industry would be imperiled.
23. *Congressional Quarterly* (1962), p. 289.
24. *Public Papers of the President* (1962).
25. Committee on Ways and Means, prepared by the staff of the US Tariff Commission (1973), *Comparison of Ratios of Imports to Apparent Consumption*, 1968–72, Washington: US Government Printing Office.
26. Andrew J. Biemiller (1970), *Tariff and Trade Proposals*, Hearings before the Committee on Ways and Means, House of Representatives, 19 May, p. 1008.
27. The proposal for government assistance to workers in case of injury due to tariff changes was first made in 1954 by the president of the United Steelworkers of America when he was a member of the Randall Commission.
28. *Congressional Record*, p. 812.
29. The sections prohibiting export credits and most-favoured-nation treatment to certain countries remained in the bill.
30. The proportion of the employment in import-competing and export-oriented industries to the total labour force is 0.077 and 0.012, respectively.
31. For some industries in some counties, employment data is not given in *County Business Patterns* because of disclosure problems. However, in most of these cases, it is possible to determine a reasonable figure by taking the midpoint of the employment-size classes that are given in the tables. When employment in a particular industry is in the open-ended size-class, 500 or more, a figure is determined either by subtracting the sum of all other industries from an appropriate sub-total for manufacturing or by utilizing the employment-size classes given by state for reporting units with 500 or more employees. Combining counties into congressional districts required the use of even more personal judgement, since counties are often not contiguous with congressional districts. The use of tables in the *Congressional District Data Book* that list the division of cities into the various congressional districts was helpful in allocating a given county into more than one congressional district.
32. The information on contributions was obtained from records on file at the National Information Center on Political Finance (Citizen's Research Foundation), Washington, DC.
33. Since the independent variables are not continuous, probit analysis was employed rather than ordinary least-squares regressions. However, for comparison purposes ordinary least-squares regressions (not reported) were also run. They gave essentially the same results as the probit analysis.
34. The third equation is omitted, since the log of the likelihood function fails to approach zero smoothly.

# 4 Trade Policies under the Reagan Administration[1]*

## 1 INTRODUCTION

An administration's trade policies are the consequence of a complex interactive process involving its own foreign and domestic policy goals, pressures from various domestic interest groups, the Congress, and foreign governments, and basic economic and political developments over which it has little control. President Reagan took office with an unusually well-defined set of domestic and international policy objectives, and his vigorous efforts to implement them have significantly affected certain aspects of US trade policy over the last two and a half years. Three policy aims of the president have been especially important in shaping trade policy: (1) to curtail the role of the government in economic affairs and instead rely to a greater degree upon the private free-market mechanism to allocate economic resources and distribute income; (2) to restore non-inflationary growth; and (3) to increase the military strength of the United States relative to the Soviet Union. As typically happens, however, various conflicts and unexpected interactions among policy goals, difficult-to-resist domestic and international political pressures and unforeseen economic and political events have combined to produce a set of actual trade policies over this period that only imperfectly reflect the Reagan administration's initial objectives.

The purpose of this paper is to analyse the Reagan administration's major trade policy actions and initiatives in terms of the varied economic and political factors that have influenced them. Following this introductory section, the president's main trade policy objectives are summarized together with their expected interrelationships with his non-inflationary growth and national security goals. In the third section, the failure of the administration's macroeconomic policies to reduce interest rates and the international value of the dollar as much as expected is analysed along

* From Robert E. Baldwin (ed.) (1984), *Recent Issues and Initiatives in US Trade Policy*, Conference Report, Cambridge, MA: National Bureau of Economic Research, pp. 10–32.

with the resultant adverse effects on trade-oriented domestic sectors. Exporters have been especially hard-hit by the high value of the dollar, and the way in which this factor and others have influenced the administration's attitude toward promoting exports is then considered. The fifth section is an analysis of how security objectives have played an important role in determining trade policies.

The sixth section examines the administration's import relief policies and discusses the ways in which various interactions between the president's goals, different political pressures and exogenous events have shaped these policies. Next is a review of the Reagan administration's efforts to enforce existing laws and codes on 'fair trade' more vigorously and also to eliminate certain unfair trading practices on the part of the European Community and Japan. The paper concludes with a discussion of the policy-making limitations and opportunities faced by a president in the trade field.

## 2   THE ADMINISTRATION'S TRADE POLICY OBJECTIVES AND THEIR RELATION TO ITS OTHER GOALS

Although all post-World War II presidents have supported the free-market system, none has been as firm in his belief in the economic efficacy of this approach as President Reagan. Believing that the government's intervention in social and economic matters has been excessive, he has vigorously worked to curtail the growth rate of federal spending for non-defense purposes, lower personal tax rates and accelerate cost recovery for business, and reduce levels of government regulation. In the trade field his free-market philosophy takes the form of a strong ideological commitment to freer trade.

The administration's stance on trade issues was officially set forth by the United States Trade Representative, William Brock, before the Senate Finance Committee in July 1981. In this 'Statement on US Trade Policy' Ambassador Brock maintained that free trade is essential to the pursuit of a strong US economy. At the same time, he emphasized that the Reagan administration would strictly enforce US laws and international agreements relating to such unfair practices as foreign dumping and government subsidization. With respect to export-credit subsidies, the international objective was 'to substantially reduce, if not eliminate, the subsidy element, and to conform credit rates to market rates' (Brock, 1981, 5).

Along with cutting back on measures that artificially stimulate exports, the administration pledged to reduce or eliminate laws and regulations that needlessly retard exports. Three types of policies with export-disincentive effects were singled out: the taxation of Americans employed abroad, the Foreign Corrupt Practices Act, and export regulations and controls.

An important import implication of the free-market approach is that when other nations 'have a natural competitive advantage, US industry must either find a way of upgrading its own capabilities or shift its resources to other activities' (Brock, 1981, 5). As the statement noted, primary reliance was to be placed on market forces rather than on adjustment assistance or safeguard measures to facilitate adjustment in affected industries.

Several negotiating initiatives were outlined in the paper. Most significant were those aimed at reducing government barriers and subsidies to services that are internationally traded and at negotiating new international rules dealing with both trade-related investment issues, such as export performance, and local-content requirements and government interventions that affect trade in high-technology products. With regard to developing countries, the stated goal was to ensure that the more advanced ones undertake greater trade obligations and that the benefits of differential trade treatment go increasingly to the poorer members of this group. Efforts to encourage greater conformity on the part of non-market economies with accepted principles of the international trading system were also promised.

The administration believed that greater reliance on the free-market mechanism would give consumers greater freedom of choice and restore strong non-inflationary growth. It was the president's belief that reducing government expenditures and regulatory activity and lowering tax rates would provide the private sector with the resources and incentive to significantly expand the output of goods and services. This supply-side response, coupled with constraints on the growth of the money supply, was expected to both reduce inflation and raise real growth rates. Benefits to trade-oriented sectors would take the form of higher export levels and enhanced ability to compete with foreign producers for domestic markets and to adjust to changing international market conditions.

The national security field was one area where some conflicts among goals were foreseen. The perceived need to increase defence expenditures obviously implies fewer resources available for private goods and services and thus, greater pressures on consumer prices. But it was the president's view that government reductions in social spending and the productivity-enhancing effects of tax cuts and deregulation would provide sufficient resources to ensure both non-inflationary growth and increased defence expenditures. The adverse export effects of a tightening of trade with the Soviets, especially in high-technology items, also was minimized.

## 3   THE IMPACT OF THE ADMINISTRATION'S MACROECONOMIC POLICIES ON TRADE-ORIENTED SECTORS

Although the Reagan administration expected its macroeconomic policies to facilitate the implementation of its trade policies, the reverse was in fact the case. The basic reason was the failure to stimulate strong real rates of growth and at the same time reduce inflation. Significant progress was achieved in reducing the rate of increase in prices, but double-digit unemployment rates replaced double-digit inflation rates and until early 1983, growth was modest or negative.

The sequence of repercussions of the government's macroeconomic policies on export and import-competing sectors can be summarized as follows. When the new administration took office in 1981, both interest rates and inflation rates were at very high levels. The continuation of tight monetary policies by the Federal Reserve System finally produced a significant slackening in the pace of inflation by the last quarter of 1981, but an additional consequence was the onset of an unexpectedly severe recession that started in July 1981.

The Fed's tight monetary policies also initiated a strong upward movement in the international value of the dollar, beginning near the end of 1980. As real rates of interest in the United States relative to those in other industrial countries remained high throughout 1981 and much of 1982, the demand for US assets continued strong, and by the end of 1982 the real value of the dollar had increased by 26 per cent compared with the first quarter of 1981.

The administration expected interest rates to decline quickly once inflation was under control and vigorous non-inflationary growth to ensue, fuelled by the favourable impact on investment of lower interest rates, by the stimulus to exports of a return of the dollar's value to lower levels, and by the incentive effects resulting from lower tax rates and regulatory reform. Unfortunately, interest rates declined much less than expected, the dollar remained unusually strong, and there was a significant reduction in real GNP coupled with a sharp rise in unemployment. The small drop in interest rates is usually attributed to high current and prospective government deficits due to high defence spending, the inability to control spending on social programmes, and the relatively lower tax revenues associated with the cut in tax rates. Not only did interest rates fall less than expected but the value of the dollar did not change to reflect fully the actual interest rate decline. Apparently, political and economic uncertainties in many countries have increased the dollar's attractiveness for safe-keeping purposes.

The appreciation of the dollar has had a very adverse effect on both US export and import-competing industries. Exporters have found it increasingly difficult to compete abroad with foreign producers, and import-sensitive sectors have had to contend with both the sales-depressing effects of the recession and increased import pressures as US purchasers shift to cheaper foreign products. By the third quarter of 1982, the US trade deficit significantly worsened and has continued to be highly unfavourable.

Export industries have not only been hurt by what they regard as a significantly overvalued dollar but by the effects of the debt crisis in a number of developing countries. As the recession spread abroad and the volume of world trade declined, those countries that had borrowed heavily abroad in the latter 1970s found that their exports were falling at the same time that their debt burden had risen because of high international interest rates. The restrictive monetary and fiscal policies imposed on them by the IMF, as the price for agreeing to a rescheduling of their debt payments, then had the effect of curtailing their imports and thus further compounding the export problems of US industries.

## 4  EXPORT-PROMOTING POLICIES

The adverse effect of the overvalued dollar and the debt crisis problem on US exporters appear to have been important factors in causing the Reagan administration to modify its views on certain export-promoting policies. As noted earlier, initially the administration favoured a cutback in export-credit subsidies on the grounds that they were an inefficient intervention in the free-market mechanism and, therefore, the president proposed to Congress that the lending and guarantee activities of the Export–Import Bank be significantly reduced. For the same reasons, some of the president's advisors favoured repeal of the export-related tax benefits in the DISC legislation, particularly since the GATT had ruled DISCs to be inconsistent with GATT's rules on export subsidies. But the opposition of export interests to these proposals intensified as their market positions abroad deteriorated, due in part to the appreciation of the dollar. The Reagan administration also discovered, as had earlier administrations, that most other industrial countries were reluctant to reduce their own credit subsidies and special tax benefits for exporters. These and other forms of subsidization by foreign governments increased the competitive pressures on certain US export industries. Thus, exporters pressed for the continuation of Export–Import Bank credits and the DISC both for 'fairness' reasons and for strategic behaviour purposes.

Under considerable prodding from Congress, the administration began to respond favourably to these arguments. For example, in 1983 it asked Congress to increase the loan guarantee authority of the Export–Import Bank and also to provide the Bank with a sizable standby fund to match the export-financing activities of other countries. Furthermore, instead of scrapping DISCs, the executive branch has drafted new legislation that will provide the same tax benefits for exporters, yet be consistent with GATT rules.

The administration has delivered on most of its promises to reduce self-imposed export disincentives. The 1981 Tax Act eased the US tax burden on Americans residing abroad for at least eleven out of the twelve months. They are now able to exempt the first $75,000 in foreign earned income and to deduct housing expenses above a base amount. In the fall of 1982 Congress passed and the president signed the Export Trading Company Act. This important legislation permits bank holding companies and certain types of banks to take an equity interest in export-trading companies and permits a partial exemption from the antitrust laws for specified export activities that do not substantially lessen competition with the United States. The expectation is that, by being able to tap an important source of financing and being given greater assurance of exemption from antitrust action, US exporters will be able to compete with foreign companies more effectively.

Another export-promoting measure proposed by the administration is the Business Accounting and Foreign Trade Simplification Act, modifying certain provisions in the Foreign Corrupt Practices Act of 1977, which advocates of the changes claim is too vague in its meaning and enforcement provisions and has resulted in American business often not bothering to compete abroad for contracts for fear that certain payments regarded as legal and customary in foreign countries will be regarded as illegal under US law.

One example of the type of change being proposed is the stipulation that a US firm would be liable under the law only if it 'directs or authorizes, expressly or by course of conduct' that an illegal payment be made by its foreign agent instead of being liable, as under the 1979 act, simply because it had 'reason to know' such a payment was being made. The revised measure also explicitly permits payments to officials of foreign governments that are lawful under the local law and payments aimed at expediting or securing the performance of routine official action. The Senate passed the bill in 1982 but thus far in 1983 has not acted on the measure and opposition to it has developed in the House.


## 5   NATIONAL SECURITY AND TRADE POLICIES

The administration's trade policies have not only been significantly influenced by the macroeconomic measures it has pursued but also by its national security policies. The most important instance where national security considerations affected trade policy was when the president, in December 1981, used the occasion of the Polish government's imposing restrictive policies to tighten economic sanctions against the Soviet Union. Exports of gas and oil equipment for the construction of pipelines and other high-technology items were banned. Moreover, after earlier lifting the embargo on grain sales to the Soviet Union imposed by the Carter administration, President Reagan postponed negotiations on a new long-term grain agreement. Then in June 1982, he extended the sanctions on the export of gas and oil equipment to include equipment produced abroad by US subsidiaries and by foreign companies using licensed US technology.

West Germany, France, the United Kingdom, Italy and other European countries raised strong objections to the December sanctions and angrily interpreted the June extensions as a threat to their sovereignty. The situation was exacerbated when some foreign companies that used technology licensed from US firms were directed by their own governments to export equipment to the Soviets and then found themselves the object of retaliatory US action in the form of banned access to any US technology or equipment.

There was strong pressure to lift the sanctions because of the deterioration in US–European economic relations and the export-market losses of US companies to foreign firms. Finally, in November 1982, the president eliminated the regulations imposed in both June and December. Also, in the spring of 1983, the administration began negotiations with the Soviet Union on a new long-term grain agreement and in late July, signed an agreement committing the Soviets to buy at least nine million metric tons in each of the next five years.

The pipeline episode illustrates the type of government intervention in the trade field to which exporters most object, on the grounds that it was both poor policymaking in economic terms and damaging to the administration's foreign policy. As a number of earlier incidents have shown, sanctions of this sort are not effective unless most of the other non-Soviet bloc countries agree to enforce the same restrictions. Yet in this case, it was clear from preliminary talks with US allies that they did not favour the initial sanctions and would actually resent the June extensions. The result was that US firms lost short-term sales to European and Japanese companies and the US long-term competitive position in the affected items was weakened because of this demonstration of its unreliability as a supplier.

Apparently the president extended the sanctions to US affiliates abroad and foreign firms utilizing US-licensed technology because of his failure to secure meaningful agreement about restricting East–West trade at the Versailles meeting of the heads of state of the major allied industrial powers earlier in June. The subsequent events were a humiliating lesson in the decline of the United States as a hegemonic power. Even when the president finally lifted the sanctions in November with the statement that a cohesive alliance strategy on East–West trade had been worked out, France publicly disavowed the agreement. The issue was not settled until Secretary of State George Schultz went to France in December 1982 and, with his French counterpart, held a joint news conference in which a series of studies on East–West issues were outlined.

Despite the unfavourable experience in the pipeline episode, it is clear that there is still strong support within the administration for a tough stance on export controls. The legislation proposed by the president to replace the Export Administration Act of 1979, a measure that permits export controls for reasons of national security, domestic short supplies and foreign policy and which expires this year, gives the government increased powers to enforce restrictions on exports of strategically sensitive goods and technology. Particularly offensive to foreign governments is the continuation of the authority to impose export controls on foreign-based US companies and on foreign-owned firms using US-licensed technology. The one concession made to US exporters in the proposal is allowing sales under existing contracts to continue for 270 days after restrictions are imposed.

The administration's national security concerns have influenced import as well as export policies. A recent example is the reduction in May of the annual US import quota for sugar from Nicaragua from 58,800 tons to 6,000 tons. The difference is to be distributed to El Salvador, Honduras and Costa Rica—countries regarded by the administration as more friendly toward the United States.

The fear that Central America will come under the influence of the Soviet Union also prompted President Reagan's Caribbean Basin Initiative (CBI) in February of 1982. Under the program about two dozen countries in the area will receive duty-free treatment on exports to the United States. About 87 per cent of all items exported from the area were already receiving duty-free treatment under the General System of Preferences (GSP), but according to the president, the remaining 13 per cent offered significant export opportunities for the countries of the region. But he excluded textiles and apparel and sugar from the free exportation status. His proposal also included $350 million of immediate economic aid and the extension for five years of the 10 per cent domestic tax credit to investments in the Caribbean countries. The former was accepted quickly, but the free-trade portion of the plan was not approved by Congress until the summer of 1983. Furthermore, the list of exclusions from duty-free status was expanded to include footwear, leather products, petroleum products and tuna fish. In the end, duty-free treatment was extended from the initial 87 per cent to 94 per cent of all exports from the area.

The administration's trade policies toward other developing countries are shaped primarily by its free-market philosophy coupled with a desire to prevent disruptive import increases in vulnerable US industries. For example, the president has urged the developing countries to follow liberal trade policies, and he has used the occasion of the annual review of the GSP to eliminate GSP treatment on a product-specific basis for many of the most rapidly growing less developed countries (LDCs). Furthermore, the administration's proposal for extending GSP after it expires at the beginning of 1985 provides for graduation.

National security considerations can also affect import policy through Section 232 of the Trade Expansion Act of 1962, which permits the president to restrict imports if they 'threaten to impair the national security'. The industrial fasteners industry sought import protection under this provision but it was rejected by the Commerce Department in March 1983.

## 6   IMPORT RELIEF POLICY

Most of the Reagan administration's policies aimed at providing relief from injury caused by import competition have been shaped by a complex mixture of free-trade ideology, practical politics and unanticipated events. On the basis of its Statement of Trade Policy, one would have expected the administration to take a very tough stance against import protection. As Ambassador Brock stated in response to a question on this 'white paper', import relief was not to be ruled out but the case 'has to be good' to win approval. The administration's actual performance in granting import relief does not seem to differ significantly from the varied record of other recent administrations, at least on the surface.

In 1981, for example, the administration pursued the Japanese to voluntarily limit their export of autos to the United States, even though the ITC had earlier rejected the auto industry petition for import relief. In the same year the president reintroduced sugar quotas and supported an extension and tightening of the Multifiber Arrangement (MFA). More recently, he accepted the affirmative import-injury determinations of the ITC in the motorcycle and specialty steel cases. Duties were raised sharply on certain imported motorcycles and a combination of increased import duties and quotas was used to restrict imports of specialty steel items.

In contrast, on the side of liberal trade policy actions, the president permitted the Orderly Marketing Agreements on non-rubber footwear with Korea and Taiwan to expire in 1981, despite an ITC recommendation that the Taiwanese agreement be extended for another two years. Furthermore, he has actively opposed 'domestic-content' legislation for the automotive industry.

One policy to deal with increased competition on which there is a clear difference in performance between this and other recent administrations is trade adjustment assistance for workers. Prompted by a desire to reduce government intervention in the adjustment process and to reduce inflationary pressures by cutting government expenditures, the administration secured new legislation in 1981 that sharply curtailed the Trade Adjustment Assistance (TAA) programme by introducing more stringent qualifying requirements and by reducing financial benefits. Legislation in 1982 restored the qualifying requirements of the 1974 Trade Act, but the Labour Department has interpreted the criteria strictly so that the programme remains small. The administration has proposed a 'voucher' system whereby workers displaced for whatever reason would search for suitable education or training and use vouchers issued to them by the government to pay their employer for on-the-job training or for the costs of training at various schools.

Given the political constraints within which a president operates and the strong protectionist pressures produced by the recession, the overvalued dollar and the increased incidence of subsidizing by foreign governments, it can be argued that the Reagan administration's overall import-relief record is a fairly liberal one. In speculating about what another administration might have done under similar circumstances, it should be stressed that today a president shares policy-making powers in the trade field with Congress.[2] Moreover, Congress is much more responsive than the executive branch to the immediate economic problems of industries and groups.

Consider, for example, the auto case. In early 1981 Congress held hearings to publicize the plight of the industry, and Senator Danforth, Chairman of the Subcommittee on International Trade of the Senate Finance Committee, introduced a bill that would impose quantitative restrictions on Japanese auto imports. He and his colleagues preferred the president to negotiate a voluntary export restraint agreement with Japan, but apparently were prepared to push the bill through Congress (with little opposition expected) if such an agreement was reached. Faced with this prospect and the fact that he had made a campaign speech arguing for a cutback in Japanese exports, the president eventually put pressure on the Japanese government for voluntary export restraints. But, as Cohen and Meltzer (1982, 82–5) note, this pressure was relatively modest and did not include a request for a cutback to a specific level. The president might have held to a strong free-trade position and threatened to veto any restrictive bill emerging from Congress, but it would have been politically difficult to do so in view of his own stated position and the generally recognized fact that increased Japanese imports were an important cause of injury in the politically powerful auto industry.

The failure to follow the ITC's recommendation to extend footwear quotas against Taiwan was probably a consequence of the president's decision on autos, as Cohen and Meltzer (1982, 111) also point out. The administration feared that approval of the ITC recommendation would send an undesirable protectionist signal to the rest of the world, and, from a domestic political viewpoint, the fact that the footwear industry has less political clout than the auto, steel or textile industries and has already been given five years of import protection made it easier to reject the recommendation.

The proposed domestic-content legislation for the auto industry presents still a different set of circumstances for the president. This legislation is clearly inconsistent with the trading rules of the GATT and is likely to lead to an outpouring of protectionist charges by other countries and retaliation against US exports. The United States would jeopardize its traditional role as the leader of a liberal international trading order. Domestic political support—even within the auto industry—is also not nearly as strong as in the Japanese voluntary export-restraint case, especially as auto sales pick up in response to economic recovery. Thus, the president is able to adopt a much stronger free-trade position without high political costs.

Finally, the administration's policy position during the international negotiations in the fall of 1981 on the renewal of the MFA further illustrates the complexity of trade policy decisions. The president had previously expressed sympathy for the view that textile imports should only expand at the same rate as the domestic market. He also needed the support of members of Congress from southern textile districts to pass the budgetary changes he proposed, which he viewed as more important than import policy with regard to textiles. Moreover, the EC strongly favoured a more restrictive international agreement, and it would have been difficult to oppose their position.


# 7   IN PURSUIT OF 'FAIR TRADE'

While there is room for disagreement on just how liberal the Reagan administration's import-relief record is compared with that of other administrations, the record suggests that the current administration has pursued the goal of 'fair trade' more vigorously than any previous administration. Three efforts in this regard are especially noteworthy: (1) the enforcement of existing US fair trade laws; (2) the attempted reduction in the agricultural export subsidies of the EC; and (3) the opening of the Japanese market to a greater extent.

The main push for stricter enforcement of US laws relating to such practices by foreigners as dumping, subsidization, patent infringements and unjustifiable, unreasonable or discriminatory trade actions has come from Congress over the last several years, and it was at the instigation of this body that enforcement of the fair trade laws was transferred in 1979 from the Treasury Department to the Commerce Department. It has been under the Reagan administration, however, that the fair trade laws have been most strongly enforced.

The Commerce Department's initiation of a countervailing duty investigation into the subsidization of exports of certain steel products by six European countries is a good example of the administration's aggressive stance toward unfair trade practices. The case was significant not only for the volume of trade involved and the fact that it was the first time that the government had initiated such an investigation, but for the careful manner in which the Commerce Department tried to measure the extent of the subsidies.

The case was settled, however, not by imposing countervailing duties equal to the subsidies, as provided by the law, but by an agreement with the subsidizing EC countries that quantitatively limited the majority of EC steel mill exports to the United States for a three-year period. Specifically, the permitted shares of the US market established for ten key steel mill products are as follows: hot rolled carbon and alloy sheet and strip, 6.81 per cent; cold rolled carbon and alloy sheet, 5.11 per cent; carbon and alloy plate, 5.36 per cent; structurals, 9.91 per cent; wire rod, 4.29 per cent; hot rolled bars, 2.38 per cent; coated sheet, 3.27 per cent; tin plate, 2.2 per cent; rail, 8.9 per cent; and sheet piling, 21.85 per cent. Consultation must take place if imports of EC pipe and tube exceed 5.9 per cent. It is surprising that an administration committed to free but fair trade settled its major fair trade case with an arrangement that was not carefully designed to just offset the alleged subsidies and is regarded as the worst form of protection by free traders.

There has also been greater use of section 301 of the Trade Act of 1974, which deals with unjustifiable, unreasonable or discriminatory trade practices by foreign countries, under the Reagan administration. Prior to 1981, only three presidential determinations supporting the petitions had been made, whereas in 1981 and 1982, there were five such determinations. The products and countries involved in the five cases were sugar, poultry meat, pasta, canned peaches, canned pears, and raisins (the EC), and specialty steel (Austria, France, Italy, Sweden, the United Kingdom and Belgium). In the last case, the president requested an import-injury determination from the ITC. This was affirmative, and, as noted earlier, he imposed import quotas and raised tariffs.

Not only has the Reagan administration supported the greater use of section 301, but, at the urging of Congress, has agreed to a strengthening of its provisions. Specifically, the administration supports an amendment that would explicitly extend the president's authority to retaliate against unfair practices affecting trade in services and direct foreign investment. This so-called 'reciprocity' bill also requires an annual report of foreign trade barriers and what is being done to reduce them. Congress actually preferred a considerably stronger version of the bill but accepted this compromise at the urging of the administration.

A case brought by Houdaille Industries in May 1982 under section 103 of the Revenue Act of 1971 further illustrates the increased concern with unfair trade practices. This law permits the president to deny investment tax credit on imported goods if the exporting country 'engages in discriminatory or other acts (including tolerance of international cartels) or policies unjustifiably restricting United States commerce'. Houdaille requested indefinite suspension of the investment tax credit on certain numerically controlled machines imported from Japan, on the grounds that the Japanese government had for many years fostered a cartel among its domestic machine tool manufacturers that had given them an unfair advantage. Although the Senate passed a resolution urging prompt retaliation, after a ten-month investigation the administration denied the request. At the same time, it announced that the US and Japanese governments would hold talks on the issue and that there may be future action on the matter.

As the section 301 cases dealing with agricultural products indicate, the present government has made a major effort to limit the EC's subsidizing exports of agricultural products. The United States contends that the Community's subsidies have significantly reduced the US export share of agricultural goods in third markets. At the November 1982 GATT ministerial meeting, the United States sought an agreement that would gradually phase out such subsidies. The EC rejected the US proposal, arguing that agricultural export subsidies are permitted under GATT rules provided they do not result in the subsidizing country's obtaining 'more than an equitable share in world export trade in that product' (Article 16). The most they would agree to was the establishment of a committee that would study 'subsidies affecting agriculture, especially export subsidies, with a view to examining its [the GATT's] effectiveness, in the light of actual experience, in promoting the objectives of the General Agreement and avoiding subsidization seriously prejudicial to the trade or interests of contacting parties' (Ministerial Declaration, 9). Shortly after the GATT ministerial meeting the EC also agreed to hold bilateral talks with the United States on agricultural issues. Thus far, little progress has been made in these talks.

The administration took other steps to pressure the Community into reducing their export subsidies. In the 301 case involving pasta that was mentioned earlier and another one involving wheat flour, the United States requested that a GATT panel decide whether the Community's export subsidies were inconsistent with GATT rules. In the meantime, the United States itself subsidized the export of 1.1 million tons of wheat flour to Egypt. The panel on wheat flour determined that there was insufficient evidence to support US charges that its export subsidies had enabled the Community to obtain more than an equitable share of world markets. The panel dealing with the pasta case did find in favour of the US position.

A third area where administration officials have vigorously pushed the notion of fairness relates to US–Japanese trade. No other trade topic generates more heated discussion in Congress and within the administration than the US trade deficit with Japan. This deficit increased from $7 billion to $18 billion between 1979 and 1982. It has become standard doctrine in many parts of the government to attribute much of the deficit to unfair trading practices by the Japanese. On the export side, these allegedly take the form of industrial targeting—a practice whereby the Japanese government selects certain product lines for export emphasis and facilitates their development by coordinating and helping to finance research, by helping particular private firms secure low-cost finance, by encouraging specialization among potential competitors, by providing marketing assistance and so forth. On the import side, it is claimed that the unfair use of such non-tariff measures as standards certification procedures, customs procedures, preferential government purchasing policies and discriminatory distribution arrangements exclude a significant volume of US goods from the Japanese market.[3]

Since the fall of 1981, top administration officials, including the president himself, have pressed the Japanese to remove these unfair barriers, as well as to enlarge agricultural quotas and lower tariff rates still further. Some success has been achieved along these lines, but there is still widespread dissatisfaction with Japan's response thus far. The reciprocity bill Congress insisted on is largely a manifestation of this dissatisfaction. Recently, trade officials have begun to focus more closely on the industrial targeting practices of Japan, and the United States may take some trade policy actions to offset the effects of these practices.

The soundness of the case against Japan is difficult to determine. On the one hand, US firms have documented numerous instances of practices that seem to restrict unfairly US exports to Japan. More is becoming known about the export-promoting policies of the Japanese government. On the other hand, writers such as Saxonhouse (1982) and even the president's own Council of Economic Advisers (1983) argue that Japan's trade pattern of a significant trade surplus for manufactured goods, more than balanced by a significant trade deficit for primary products, is consistent with the country's human and physical resource endowments. While the Council of Economic Advisers believes that major trade liberalization by Japan would do much to relieve the political strains between the two countries, they state that 'Japanese trade policy does not play a central role in causing bilateral imbalance with the United States' (Council of Economic Advisers, 1983, p. 56).

## 8 TRADE POLICYMAKING BY THE PRESIDENT: LIMITATIONS AND LIBERTIES

An analysis of the Reagan administration's performance to date on trade policy matters serves to reinforce a number of points about presidential behaviour in this area. One is the difficulty from a political viewpoint for any modern president of promoting openly a general policy of import protection. The United States is still viewed by the other major industrial nations as the leader of the liberal international trading order that developed after World War II. They still basically support this regime and believe that if the United States adopts general protectionism it will rapidly spread throughout the trading world, along with beggar-thy-neighbour exchange-rate policies. It is widely accepted in these countries, as well as in the United States, that if the existing trade and financial order collapsed, extensive job losses in export sectors and massive financial losses in industries with export and foreign direct investment interests would result. Because of the great political and economic power of these sectors, together with the considerable pressures foreign governments can bring to bear, a president would run significant political risk if he openly pursued a policy of general protectionism.

At the same time, it is difficult politically for a president to resist granting protection to specific industries that are politically significant in voting and/or financial terms and that also seem to have a good case in terms of US and international import relief or fair trade laws and regulations. If, for example, the ITC had rendered an affirmative decision in the auto case and the president had rejected this decision, it seems highly likely that the Congress would have vetoed this action, as it could have at that time with a simple majority vote, and probably would have blocked other legislation desired by the president in retaliation for his decision. Even without the congressional veto, a president runs this risk when he takes actions against a strongly held congressional view. Thus, unless a president regards resistance to import relief for a politically powerful industry considered to be deserving of relief by many members of Congress to be so important to his political goals as to accept these high costs, it is not politically rational to turn down 'good' cases for protection.

There is, of course, room for considerable differences in behaviour that are consistent with these two positions. Clearly the differences in actual behaviour depend upon such factors as a president's political strength among voters, his economic and political goals, his effectiveness in dealing with Congress and the public, the extent to which his own party controls Congress, and so on. President Reagan thus far has not exhibited special interest in international economic matters. His policy decisions in this area have been mainly reactive, and, while he has been guided by a strong preference for the free-market mechanism, he has also shown a willingness to compromise in the face of strong domestic or international opposition to a clear-cut free-market solution. As noted earlier, although this administration's trade policy decisions over the last two and a half years are more similar to those of other recent administrations than would be expected from its initial statement on the subject, it seems likely that the Reagan administration will be regarded from a historical perspective as fairly liberal.

Where a president can make a significant difference in the nature of trade policy is when he does not simply react to events and pressures but, instead, when he initiates major trade policy actions himself. In this way he is often able to transcend the narrow, short-run concerns that dominate most political decision making and gain support among legislators and the public based on their concerns for the long-run economic and political welfare of the country. In considering major initiatives that might have been proposed by other administrations faced with the same set of circumstances, two come to mind: a well-defined 'industrial policy' for the country and an international effort to achieve greater coordination among the industrial nations of their international and domestic economic policies.

Industrial policy means different things to different people, but it basically involves the active participation of the state in shaping the pattern of industrial development. Management, labour and the governments make coordinated efforts to expand certain sectors and contract others. The means employed involve not only financial aid from the government but may include agreements among the affected parties concerning wages, prices and production levels.

Most European countries, as well as Japan, have adopted elements of industrial policy in recent years. The more aggressive enforcement of US countervailing duty and antidumping laws, typified by the European steel case, has in part been a response to this trend toward industrial policy abroad. While the Reagan administration clearly favours this fair trade approach, another strategy is to embrace the industrial policy concept ourselves as a means of offsetting foreign subsidization. Given the imperfectly competitive nature of industrial markets, a number of the measures involved in industrial policy can also be supported on national economic efficiency grounds, but the problem of coordinating the policies of different nations would remain. A possible outcome is that vigorous enforcement by each nation of countervailing duty and anti-dumping rules, coupled with the subsidization of declining domestic industries, produces the same effect as general protection.

Industrial policy on an extensive basis is anathema to the Reagan administration on ideological grounds, but a small step in this direction is the president's recent proposal to create a cabinet-level Department of International Trade and Industry by merging the Office of the USTR, which is in the Executive Office of the President, and parts of the Commerce Department. The new department would 'provide a strong, unified voice for trade and industrial matters'. There are sound arguments both for and against such a merger. With the 1979 transfer to the Commerce Department of the responsibility for administering the basic fair trade laws and the greater emphasis under the Reagan administration on the enforcement of these laws, significant parts of trade policy administration are divided between USTR and the Commerce Department. Conflicts between the two agencies that weaken our effectiveness in international trade disputes and sometimes send conflicting signals to domestic producers are inevitable under the present arrangements. Deficiencies in the present arrangements would presumably be reduced with the new agency. Bringing together the economic staff of the Commerce Department and the trade officials of USTR would also stimulate the kind of in-depth economic studies that are so badly needed to prepare US negotiators adequately and to undertake long-range trade policy planning.

A possible drawback of the new department is that the interagency aspect of trade policy formation, which has existed since the 1930s, will be lost or seriously weakened. Trade policies affect matters over which most of the major federal departments have some control, and decisions on most issues are now reached through interagency meetings chaired by USTR and involving such agencies as State, Treasury, Commerce, Labor, Agriculture, Interior, ITC and Defence. Some fear that the current process of balancing the diverse views of representatives from these agencies would be lost and replaced by a process in which the

business-oriented views of the Commerce Department become dominant. There is also some concern that trade policy may end up being
downgraded in importance, since it will no longer be directed from the
Executive Office of the President.

The merger issue is not likely to be resolved soon, since there is
significant opposition to it in Congress. In the meantime, planning and
manoeuvring within the administration and in Congress may weaken the
effectiveness of existing US trade policy.

An alternative to industrial policy that President Reagan might have
followed was to propose an international negotiation, as Presidents
Kennedy and Nixon had done earlier. Actually, at the GATT ministerial
meeting in November 1982 the administration did propose a significant
policy agenda, but the president did not play a major planning or
implementing role, and the conference did not turn out as well as the
United States had hoped.

The United States proposed actions on several issues. First, US
negotiators pressed for a moratorium on new protectionist measures,
coupled with an agreement to begin dismantling existing trade barriers.
But the EC did not support such a commitment, and it did not appear in
the final declaration. Interestingly, however, the declaration issued after
the Williamsburg Summit meeting in late May 1983 states that the leaders
of the seven industrial countries 'commit ourselves to halt protectionism,
and as recovery proceeds to reverse it by dismantling trade barriers'.

With respect to specific current issues, the US aims were: (1) to reach
agreement on a new safeguards code—a matter left over from the Tokyo
Round negotiations on non-tariff matters; (2) to obtain GATT authori-
zation for a study of agricultural subsidies that would lead to the eventual
elimination of such subsidies; (3) to improve the dispute-settlement
procedures by reducing long delays in reaching decisions and preventing
an aggrieved party from blocking an adverse judgement; and (4) to
secure endorsement for a new round of North–South trade negotiations
directed at gaining the adherence of these countries to existing GATT
rules and codes.

The United States largely failed to achieve these objectives. On the
safeguards issue there was some preliminary agreement on 'consensual
selectivity', an arrangement by which an importing country applies trade
barriers selectively, that is, on a non-most-favoured-nation basis, against
an exporting country but with this country's consent, and also taking
account of the possible adverse effects on third countries. The procedures
would be temporary, open, and transparent with a committee meeting
every six months to monitor the agreement. Because the EC wanted to
use the selectivity principle more aggressively and the developing countries opposed the entire concept, the ministers could only agree on the

desirability of expeditiously reaching a safeguards agreement and some general principles to follow in doing so.

Agricultural export subsidies generated the most heat at the conference. The EC maintained that its export subsidies were perfectly acceptable under the GATT and, while not objecting to a study in the area, adamantly refused to agree to any statement implying that these subsidies should eventually be phased out. A series of press conferences on the subject held by members of the US congressional delegation attending the meeting as well as by some EC ministers also seemed to polarize the two sides. As noted earlier, the establishment of a Committee on Trade in Agriculture was finally agreed upon for the purpose of simply studying the issues involved.

There was more progress on the dispute-settlement issue than on most other matters. The Director-General and his staff were given a greater role in the dispute-settlement process, provisions were established to utilize more qualified experts on panels, delays in decisions were reduced, and parties to a dispute 'agreed that obstruction in the process of dispute settlement shall be avoided' (Ministerial Declaration, 8).

The section of the Ministerial Declaration covering the developing countries made no mention of their assuming greater GATT responsibilities; in fact, the thrust of the statement is that developed countries should make greater efforts to assist the developing nations.

In addition to these four current issues, the United States also pushed for commitments by the contracting parties on three other new topics: (1) trade in services; (2) trade-related investment issues; and (3) trade in high-technology products. With respect to trade in services, the administration wanted a GATT study programme to determine both the types of government actions that create the most important barriers to this type of trade and the applicability of existing GATT rules in dealing with them. In addition, the United States pressed for a statement that, in effect, would commit the participants to future negotiations in the area. The objective with regard to the other two topics was to set up work programmes to ascertain the extent of trade-distorting practices and their economic effects. In the investment field there is concern over the trade-impairing effects of the export incentives and performance requirements that many host countries have introduced. In the high-technology field the practices that most bother US negtiators are industry targeting, government-financed R and D programmes and general public programmes to foster innovation.

The GATT ministers were not very receptive to the US proposals. For example, the developing countries vigorously opposed the US proposal on services, and the ministers merely recommended that members with an interest in services undertake national examination of the issues involved, exchange information and review the results at the 1984 GATT session in order to consider whether any multilateral action is desirable. The other two subjects were not even mentioned in the final declaration.

In retrospect, there are several reasons why the United States failed to achieve many of its objectives in the GATT ministerial meeting. One widely accepted view is that poor planning and inadequate preparation contributed to disappointing results. For example, it is alleged that the agenda included too many items. Furthermore, the document presented to the ministers contained some tentative agreements by representatives preparing for the conference but also included a list of unresolved issues with little guidance on how to proceed. The outcome was that the ministers fell to bickering over these issues. Previous experience with such short meetings demonstrates that they should not be held without enough prior agreement on the issues involved to guarantee what can be termed a successful outcome. Direct White House involvement is important in gaining such agreement.

There also seems to have been a misperception of what was feasible. The best illustration of this is the agricultural export subsidy issue. Given the importance of the Common Agricultural Policy (CAP) in the EC and the great difficulty US negotiators have had since the early 1960s in extracting concessions that would reduce its adverse effects on this country, it is surprising that the conference planners would expect the EC to agree to an eventual phasing out of its export subsidies during a three-day conference. For any progress to be achieved on this subject, the top political leaders of the United States and the EC must be involved, and the negotiations will be long and complex.

The incident again illustrates the influence of Congress in current trade policy formulation. The congressional leaders attending the conference were primarily interested in the agricultural issue, and they helped bring it to the foreground by issuing strong warnings about possible congressional reactions should the EC fail to agree to our proposals. This approach failed as a negotiating procedure, and the Community hardened its position. It may pay off in the long run, since the message came across clearly concerning the willingness of the United States to engage itself in agricultural export subsidization to eventually force an agreement to phase out such subsidies.

If one regards the reaffirmation by members of their commitment to the GATT trading system and the agreement on a work programme as major objectives of the ministerial meeting, the conference can be interpreted as having resulted in a reasonable outcome that may serve as the basis for moving toward future negotiations. Besides establishing a committee on trade in agricultural products and inviting members to exchange information on services trade, the final declaration committed GATT members to new or continuing studies of: (1) world trade in textiles and clothing; (2) structural adjustment and trade policy; (3) existing quantitative restrictions; (4) the prospects for increasing trade between developing and developed countries; and (5) the problem of tariff escalation. It does not appear that a meeting at the ministerial level was necessary to establish such a work programme, nor is it clear that the meeting improved the chances for future negotiations on the various issues covered.

Another quite different initiative that might have been proposed relates to the growing recognition among governments of the inter-relations between their international and domestic economic policies. In particular, other governments have increasingly come to appreciate the extent to which US monetary and fiscal policies affect their own and world economic conditions through trade, capital and exchange-rate movements. They feel frustrated in their efforts to cope with these repercussions, since little serious effort is made to coordinate policies or even inform them of contemplated US actions. Protectionist policies, export subsidies and capital controls are in part manifestations of this frustration.

The United States could have exercised its economic leadership role by exploring more fully the possibility of greater coordination among the industrial nations on domestic and international economic policies. A possible institutional structure to utilize is the annual summit meetings of leaders of the major industrial nations, but representation from the smaller industrial countries and the developing nations would also be required. The finance ministers already meet concurrently with the top political leaders. These sessions, along with separate and joint meetings among trade and monetary officials, could be increased in frequency and a secretariat established to facilitate studies of issues that arise. The initial purpose would be to exchange ideas and explore possibilities of improved economic coordination. As the largest trading nation and dominant financial power, it is in the political and economic interests of the United States, as well as of developed and developing countries as a whole, for this country to assume the leadership role in the endeavour.


## NOTES

1. I am grateful for comments on an outline of this paper presented at a pre-conference working meeting held in Washington on 29 April 1983. In addition, I thank the many individuals in the government and various private

organizations who provided information and perspective for the paper. Three government publications that were especially helpful are: Executive Office of the President (1982), *Twenty-Sixth Annual Report of the President of the United States on the Trade Agreements Program, 1981–2*; United States International Trade Commission (1982), *Operation of the Trade Agreements Program*, 33rd Report, 1981, USITC Publication 1308; and United States International Trade Commission (1983), *Operation of the Trade Agreements Program*, 34th Report, 1982, USITC Publication 1414.

2. The June 1983 Supreme Court decision that congressional veto provisions of executive branch actions are unconstitutional may reverse somewhat the recent shift in governmental power to Congress but is not likely to change the basic relationship of shared authority in the trade field.

3. The average level of industrial tariffs in Japan is only about 3 per cent, lower than that of the United States or the EC.

# REFERENCES

Brock, William E. (1981), *Opening Statement before a Joint Oversight Hearing of the Senate Committee on Finance and the Senate Committee on Banking, Housing, and Urban Affairs on US Trade Policy*, Washington: Office of the United States Trade Representative.

Cohen, Stephen D. and Ronald I. Meltzer (1982), *United States International Economic Policy in Action*, New York: Praeger.

Council of Economic Advisers (1983), *The Annual Report of the Council of Economic Advisers*, Washington: US Government Printing Office.

Executive Office of the President (1982), *Twenty-Sixth Annual Report of the President of the United States on the Trade Agreements Program, 1981–2*, Washington: US Government Printing Office.

*General Agreement on Tariffs and Trade* (1982), Ministerial declaration adopted on 29 November 1982, Geneva: GATT, L/5424.

Saxonhouse, Gary R. (1982), *The Micro and Macroeconomics of Foreign Sales to Japan*, Ann Arbor: Department of Economics, University of Michigan.

United States International Trade Commission (1982), *Operation of the Trade Agreements Program, 33rd report, 1981*. Washington: United States International Trade Commission.

# PART III
## Trade Policy Theory

# 5 The Political Economy of Protectionism*

Although economic historians have traditionally studied international trade policies in both economic and political terms, it has only been within the last decade that trade economists have manifested much more than casual interest in this approach.[1] Over a dozen articles or papers have been written since 1974 in which trade economists have analysed in quantitative terms the relationship between the level of protection (or a change in the level) afforded different industries or income classes and various political and economic characteristics of these sectors or groups that appear to influence the level of protection.[2] This greater attention to the political economy of protectionism is only one indication of the growing interest of economists in public choice—a subject that Mueller (1976) defines as the application of economics to political science. According to Mueller, public choice developed as a separate field in response to the issues raised by Bergson (1938), Samuelson (1947), and Arrow (1951) in their pioneering work on social welfare, and also in response to the explorations in the 1940s and 1950s of the conditions in which the free-market mechanism fails to achieve a Pareto-optimum allocation of resources.

## 1 WELFARE ECONOMICS: BERGSON, SAMUELSON, ARROW, et al.

A discussion of the political economy of trade policy can usefully begin by placing the subject in the framework established by Bergson and Samuelson for analysing social welfare. The Bergson–Samuelson formulation of the social welfare function makes a clear-cut distinction between individual tastes or preferences for goods and services and individual values relating to general standards of equity or to other

---

* From Jagdish N. Bhagwati (ed.) (1982), *Import Competition and Response*, Chicago: University of Chicago Press, pp. 263–86. © 1982 by The National Bureau of Economic Research. All rights reserved.

ethical judgements. These authors also assume that an individual's preferences for economic goods and services depend only upon his own consumption of these items and not upon what other individuals consume. Thus, social welfare $(W)$ is written as:

$$W = W[U^1(X_1^1, \ldots , X_n^1; V_1^1, \ldots , V_m^1), \ldots$$
$$U^s(X_1^s, \ldots , X_n^s; V_1^s, \ldots V_m^2)]$$

where the $U$ terms represent ordinal utility measures for the $s$ individuals, the $X$ terms stand for the $n$ commodities and the $V$ terms stand for the $m$ productive services.

As Samuelson points out, the social welfare function characterizes some set of ethical beliefs that permits an unequivocal answer as to whether one configuration of the economic system is 'better' than, 'worse' than or 'indifferent' to any other.[3] Bergson also stresses that the social welfare function rests on ethical criteria.[4] Neither author analyses in any detail the nature of the value judgements, nor how the community selects a particular social welfare function. Bergson utilizes an egalitarian welfare function to indicate how a maximum welfare position would be determined, but he points out that any set value of propositions sufficient to evaluate all alternatives could be used. He states that the determination of prevailing values for a given community is a proper and necessary task for economists but does not pursue this topic at all himself.[5] With regard to the manner of selection of the welfare function, Bergson simply assumes—as Arrow notes—that there is a universally accepted ordering of different possible welfare distributions in any situation.[6]

The manner in which the social welfare function is used to determine a maximum social welfare point under a given set of economic circumstances is illustrated in Figure 5.1.[7] Letting $U^1$ and $U^2$ be ordinal utility indices for individuals 1 and 2 (assumed for simplicity to be the entire community), suppose that the curve $AA'$ represents the free-trade utility-possibility function for the community with its given set of individual preferences, factor supplies and technical production constraints. The necessary (but not sufficient) conditions for maximizing social welfare are the familiar Pareto-optimum conditions of production and exchange, and these enable one to reduce the level of indeterminacy in the system to points along the utility-possibility frontier. Next, the social welfare function is depicted in the figure by means of a set of social indifference contours, along any one of which (e.g., $ii'$) social welfare is constant. Since individuals are assumed to 'count', the indifference contours cannot intersect and must slope downward, although their absolute slopes at any point are arbitrary. Obviously social welfare is

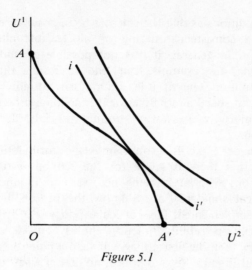

*Figure 5.1*

maximized at the point of tangency between a social welfare contour and the utility-possibility curve. At the tangency point it is ethically judged that the marginal social utility of income (or of any commodity) is the same for the two individuals.

Arrow defines the social welfare function somewhat differently from Bergson and Samuelson. He first points out that the distinction between tastes and ethical values is by no means clear cut.[8] To use his examples, there is little difference between the pleasure derived from one's own lawn and from one's neighbour's lawn or between an individual's dislike of having his grounds ruined by factory smoke and his distaste for the existence of heathenism in some distant area. Consequently, Arrow views each individual as ordering not only the various amounts of each type of commodity he may consume and the labour he may supply but the amounts of both private and collectively consumed goods in every one else's hands. Each of these distributions of goods and services (i.e., each social state) is also ordered as directly represented rather than by using the notion of a utility function. He then defines a social welfare function as a process or rule which, for each individual ordering of alternative social states, gives a corresponding social ordering of these social states.[9] As Arrow points out, whereas Bergson seeks to locate social values in welfare judgements by individuals, he locates them in the actions taken through the rules society uses for making social decisions.[10]

The problem posed by Arrow on the basis of this definition of a social welfare function is whether a rule exists for passing from individual orderings of social states to a social ordering without violating such reasonable conditions as that the rule not be imposed or dictatorial and that it give a consistent ordering of all feasible alternatives. He discovered that, in general, it was not possible to find such a rule. Majority voting, for example, can lead to results that violate the transitivity condition. Only if at least a majority of individuals have the same ordering of social alternatives or if individual orderings are single peaked will majority voting always produce a social ordering that meets these conditions.

An advantage of the Bergson–Samuelson formulation of welfare economics is that there is scope for the economist to make policy recommendations without it being necessary to inquire into a community's ethical standards or to know the process by which these standards are implemented. If a particular policy (e.g., free trade) gives a situation utility-possibility function entirely outside another policy (e.g., no trade), then the first policy will yield a point on a higher social welfare contour than the second policy, no matter what the shape of the social welfare contours. But since the implementation of a particular policy places the economy at some specific point on a situation utility-possibility function, redistributions of welfare along such a function must be permitted for this statement to have validity.

## 2  THE POSITIVE THEORY OF TRADE POLICY DETERMINATION

The contributions of Bergson, Samuelson and Arrow prompted the developments that led, in particular, to the consideration of the related but distinct theory of public choice. In particular, the question was raised whether Pareto-efficient resource-allocational policies, delineated as such by economic analysis, would in fact be adopted under the political processes characterizing modern industrial democracies.

Writers pursuing the latter line of thought, such as Downs (1957) and Buchanan and Tullock (1962), postulate that voters and their elected representatives pursue their own self-interest in the political market place just as they do in the economic market place. The difference is that preferences are expressed by ballot-box voting rather than dollar voting.

Applying this approach to trade policy, economists generally hypothesize producers and particular income groups to be the demanders of protectionism, who seek to maximize the present value of the additional income they can obtain by reducing imports. Elected representatives (or the citizens themselves, if there is direct voting) are regarded as the suppliers of protection, who also seek to maximize their own welfare. Under conditions of perfect competition in political markets, this implies that they maximize their chances of election.

## 2.1 Perfect Markets

An important conclusion from this economic approach to political decision making is that Pareto-efficient policies will be implemented under majority rule, provided that such conditions prevail as perfect information, no voting costs and the absence of any costs of redistributing income.[11] Suppose, for example, that the foreign-offer curve facing a country shifts outward and thereby enables the country to expand its consumption possibilities. In a vote between a tariff policy that restricts the consumption possibilities to its initial set and a free-trade policy that enlarges this set, the latter policy will be selected, since it is possible to make a majority of voters (or even all voters) better off under the free-trade policy than they are initially. In selecting a particular point, however, among the many on the free-trade utility-possibility frontier on the basis of majority rule, the cycling problem noted by Arrow can arise for the community. Each individual will order the alternative social states along this frontier on the basis of the utility he obtains from each. But while individual preferences are transitive, majority voting will not generally yield transitive social preferences. If all points on the utility-possibility functions are to be considered, the only way out of the difficulty without abandoning majority rule is, as Arrow has shown, either to assume a universally agreed-on ordering of all welfare distributions (the Bergson approach) or at least to assume that a majority of voters possess identical orderings of these distributions. The latter approach means that the social welfare function is dictatorial; on the other hand, in accepting majority voting as the selection rule, the condition of non-dictatorship loses its intrinsic desirability.[12]

## 2.2 Redistribution Limitations

Those who apply public choice theory to trade policy generally rule out the possibility of redistribution along a utility-possibility frontier. They assume in their analyses that the selection of a particular point on the frontier results from the operation of market forces as modified by trade taxes and as influenced by individual tastes and the prevailing distribution of productive factors.[13] This, for example, is the framework in which the Stolper–Samuelson (1941) theorem is sometimes utilized to account for protectionism in a capital-abundant economy. Since in the standard Heckscher–Ohlin–Samuelson trade model with two factors (capital and labour), two goods and fixed trading terms a tariff will raise the real return to labour, protectionism will emerge if workers have more voting power than capitalists.[14]

But labour could always improve any position it attains under protectionism by permitting free trade and then redistributing income in its favour through lump-sum taxes that it could impose by majority voting. This possibility usually is not mentioned in discussing this application of economics to the politics of protection. Likewise, writers who analyse protection to particular industries and who assume that factors are industry-specific in the short run generally do not introduce the possibility of free trade coupled with lump-sum redistribution to the factors in the industry as an option to be explained.

While most countries have some forms of automatic compensation to factors adversely affected by imports, such as extended unemployment compensation, retraining payments, migration allowances, technical assistance and governmental purchasing and scrapping of excess capital equipment, they usually do not compensate fully for the economic loss to these factors. Moreover, the measures are used to supplement protection from imports that takes the form of higher duties or quotas rather than to substitute for protection. Just why this is so is itself an important topic for investigation within a political economy framework. Some comments are made about this matter in the next section in the discussion of possible extensions of the usual analysis. The point here is simply that, although the assumption made by previous writers in this field concerning limited redistribution possibilities may be consistent with the actual policies of most governments, it is a severe restriction on first-best welfare analysis.

## 2.3　Information and Voting Costs

Besides generally ruling out the possibility of income redistribution within the context of free trade or protectionism, writers in the field focus on the existence of various other imperfections in political markets that prevent a complete expression of the preferences of the population through the voting process. Information costs and costs of registering one's preferences through the voting process are two sources of such imperfections.

For example, in an environment of imperfect information, some consumers may be unaware that the prices of an imported product and its domestic substitute have risen in response to a higher import duty. Moreover, if the increase in prices is modest compared with their budget outlays on the items, it may not be rational for these consumers to invest the time and funds to find out about the cause of the price rises in order to try to reverse these increases through the political process. Even if a consumer is aware of the reason for the price increases, he may find that the costs of registering his opposition through the political process are greater than his resultant loss in consumer welfare.

The existence of these types of costs and the point that the welfare losses from protecting a particular industry are so widely dispersed that the loss to any one consumer is small were first emphasized by Downs

(1957) as an explanation of why producers succeeded in obtaining protection from imports.

## 2.4 Elected Representatives and Political Parties

Another type of imperfection in political markets introduced in the literature on the subject concerns the fact that representative democracy with political parties prevails rather than direct democracy. If political markets operate perfectly, the actions of elected officials will merely reflect the wishes of the voters. Otherwise, new candidates will enter the market and unseat existing representatives of the voters. The existence of imperfections that provide incumbents with special election advantages and make it very costly for new candidates to make their views widely known modifies this conclusion and increases the possibility that the wishes of a majority of the voters will not be carried out.

Brock and Magee (1974, 1980) have utilized game theory to analyse the manner in which one political party selects a particular trade policy and how a second party reacts to this choice. For example, they pose the problem of choosing preelection tariff positions by a pro-tariff and a free-trade party in the following way. The pro-tariff party maximizes its probability of election by increasing the level of protection it supports until the positive marginal effect on the party's election probability from the increased resources given by the protectionist lobby is just offset by the negative effect of lost voters and resource flow from free traders to the free-trade party. The free-trade party, on the other hand, chooses a position that minimizes the election chances of the protectionist party. Thus, it will lower its tariff below the other party's tariff until the marginal positive effect on its election probability from resources and votes provided by free traders is just offset by the negative impact of increased funds flowing from the protectionist lobby to the pro-tariff party. Assuming equilibrium is of the simple Cournot–Nash variety, they are able to derive such results as: (1) in the neighbourhood of equilibrium, one party will become more protectionist when the second does, but the second party will adopt a more liberal position when the first party becomes more protectionist: (2) if the protectionist lobby becomes more powerful, it is not inevitable that both parties will become more protectionist; one of the parties may favour a lower tariff.

## 2.5 The Free-Rider and Externality Problems

Another type of imperfection in the operation of political-economic markets emphasized by writers in this field (e.g., Olson (1965) and Pincus (1972, 1975)) is the free-rider problem that is associated with the provision of a public good. A tariff (or the absence of one) has the characteristic of a public good in that a beneficiary from a tariff cannot be excluded from the benefits, even though he does not contribute to the costs of providing the tariff. For example, a firm in a protected industry benefits even if it does not contribute to the lobbying efforts required to secure the protection. Thus, there is an incentive for each firm not to reveal its true preferences regarding its benefits in the hope that others will pay the lobbying costs. Olson argues that the voluntary formation of an effective lobbying group is more likely if the group is small and if the benefits are unevenly distributed, since under these circumstances the benefits to each individual member, or at least one member, increase. [15] Pincus adds that the costs of coordinating and monitoring a pressure group tend to reduce lobbying activity if an industry is widely dispersed geographically.

This framework has been applied to explain both why protectionism exists despite the fact that consumers represent a majority of voters as well as why some industries are more highly protected than others. Consumers are too numerous and widely dispersed for effective liberal-trade pressure groups representing their interests to be formed. While these factors generally do not prevent producers from organizing into pressure groups, one does expect that pressure groups will be more effective if the industries they represent are characterized by high levels of firm and geographic concentration. However, Olson notes a possible exception. Some groups provide both private and public goods and collect funds for organizing and lobbying from the sale of the private good. For example, a group may sell a magazine or journal that provides helpful technical information to its members. Consequently, even though the structure of an industry appears unfavourable for organizing into an effective pressure group, it may in fact be well organized for this reason. [16]

While a tariff has the public-good characteristic that all producers in a protected industry benefit from the higher price no matter whether they contribute to the costs of obtaining protection, it lacks the characteristic of a pure public good, namely, that increases in benefits to one producer do not reduce the benefits to other producers. The producer-benefits from protection mainly take the form of temporary rents, although expansion in the protected sector may also increase long-run returns to some factors. The distribution of these benefits among existing producers depends on how rapidly and to what extent they respond on the supply side as well as on how fast new domestic competitors take advantage of the enhanced profit opportunities. In deciding how much to invest in lobbying activities, an individual producer must estimate the supply response of others as well as his own to be sure he earns at least the market rate on his rent-seeking investment. Even if there is only one producer, he must be concerned with the possibility that his lobbying investment will create profit opportunities so attractive that other firms will enter the market and prevent him from earning an acceptable return on his lobbying activities. In other words, just as a protective duty is no guarantee that individual entrepreneurs in an infant industry will make greater investments in acquiring technological knowledge, so too is the existence of net benefits from lobbying no guarantee that the rent seeking will be undertaken.

This externality problem may in part explain why protectionist efforts over the last fifty years have focused on depressed industries. It is not rational for capitalists outside such an industry or even within the industry to invest in new productive capacity, nor for outside workers to seek employment in the sector, if a tariff increase occurs that still leaves the rate of return on investment and the wage rate below what they are generally. Those involved in the industry know that the distribution of rents on existing physical and human capital in the industry is likely to be closely related to existing factor supplies and can be more certain of their return from such a tariff.

## 3   MODIFYING THE POSITIVE THEORY OF TRADE POLICY DETERMINATION: SOCIAL VALUES AND INTERPERSONAL EFFECTS

The public-choice theory of trade policy determination reviewed above is based on the assumptions that all individuals in the economy seek to maximize their welfare and that individual welfare depends only on the goods and services a person consumes directly.

It is evident that considerations of equity and social justice may well affect policy choices. The fact that low-income workers, including women and migrants, are substantially employed in textiles may account partly for the protection granted to this industry in some of the developed countries. The desire to protect the incomes of the under-privileged groups, whether defined by sex or citizenship or by regional location (e.g., depressed regions), can thus well provide an input into the tariff-making process, though, it must be stressed, this does not in itself explain the choice of tariff protection rather than other policy instruments in granting this element of redistribution to the concerned group.

Among the many studies of tariff making or tariff reduction that have stressed this issue, one may include Cheh (1974), Caves (1976), Helleiner (1977) and Anderson (1978). Corden (1974, p. 107) has suggested that societies may have a 'conservative welfare function' requiring that trade policy should be implemented so as to avoid 'any significant reductions in real incomes of any significant section of the community'.[17]

If altruistic notions do contribute to protection, one may well ask what prompts such altruism. Arrow (1975) gives three reasons why an individual undertakes actions that are, or seem to be, expressions of altruism. First, the welfare of the individual may depend not only on the goods he consumes but also on the economic welfare of others. An altruistic relationship exists if the individual's welfare decreases when the welfare of others decreases.[18] As will be recalled, interpersonal relationships of this type are excluded from the Bergson–Samuelson formulation of the social welfare function, though not from Arrow's. Second, not only may the individual derive satisfaction from seeing someone else's satisfaction increased, but he may gain satisfaction from the fact that he himself has contributed to that satisfaction. Third, an individual may be motivated entirely by his own egoistic satisfaction, but 'there is an implicit social contract that each performs duties for others in a way calculated to enhance the satisfaction of all'—an argument that implies enlightened self-interest.[19]

Of these reasons for altruistic behaviour, the last may have particular relevance to protectionist policies. It may be that an individual supports a tariff increase outside his own industry because he thinks this action will enhance his own chances of receiving tariff protection should his industry come under severe import competition in the future. It is this idea that serves as the basis for regarding tariffs as a type of insurance policy (see Corden 1974, pp. 320–1; Cassing 1980, pp. 396–7). Workers and capital owners who are risk-averse wish to avoid human and physical capital losses due to sudden and significant increases in imports that compete with the domestic products they produce. However, private markets to insure against this risk do not exist, apparently for reasons of inadequate data or 'moral hazard'. The import-relief legislation involving recommendations from the ITC can, for example, be viewed as a means of providing the desired insurance. But if this view is adopted, one is left guessing why the implicit contractual behaviour agreed on by different industry groups chooses tariffs as the method of providing relief against import competition, since this policy leaves consumers worse off and thereby reduces the scope of the implicit contractual arrangements embracing other groups with a political role.

Moreover, protection may well reflect broader goals, such as those discussed by Johnson (1960) in his seminal analysis of the 'scientific tariff' in which he analysed the optimal tariff structure to promote collective goals such as industrialization, self-sufficiency, 'a way of life,' and military preparedness.[20] While Johnson considers the question of optimal tariff structures to reflect these goals at minimal cost, the question as to whether protection or alternative policy interventions will

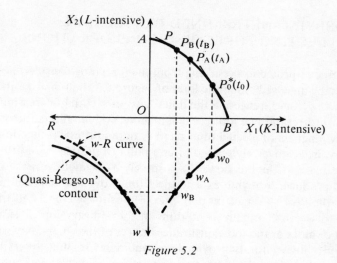

*Figure 5.2*

be the least-cost policies to adopt in pursuit of such goals is explored in other papers by Johnson (1965) and Bhagwati and Srinivasan (1969).

That altruism, a Bergsonian approach, and the pure public-choice theoretic solution can result in different tariff outcomes may now be simply illustrated. Thus, in Figure 5.2, $AB$ is the production-possibility curve for goods $X_1$ and $X_2$. A shift in the terms of trade of this small, open $2 \times 2$ economy will shift production from $P$ to $P_0^*$. The optimal solution, in Paretian economic terms, is then at $P_0^*$ with zero tariff. It is also the pure public-choice theoretic majority-rule solution under the ideal restrictions set out in section 2. But suppose now that there is an 'altruistic', 'empathetic' feeling toward labour in this model, and depict the real wages of labour in the lower RHS quadrant. There, as the production of $X_1$ (the $K$-intensive good) falls with the imposition of successively higher tariffs that raise the relative price of good $X_2$, the real wages of labour rise *à la* the Stolper–Samuelson theorem. Therefore, an 'altruistic' tariff ($t_A$) may be depicted as that which brings production to $P_A$ and real wages up from $W_0$ to $W_A$. On the other hand, one may envisage a government that instead maximizes a quasi-Bergson social welfare function, such as that represented in the lower LHS quadrant. This social welfare function is defined directly on wage and rental incomes (R) in the $2 \times 2$ model, rather than on the utilities of the wage and rental earners as in the classic Bergsonian social welfare function. The tangency of the social indifference contour with the wage-rental locus in the lower LHS quadrant then determines the corresponding production at $P_B$ and the associated 'Bergsonian' tariff rate $t_B$.[21]

## 4   LOBBYING-DETERMINED PROTECTION REFLECTING FOREGOING CONSIDERATIONS

The degree of protection resulting from the foregoing considerations can be formally analysed along the lines of Figure 5.3. Let $Ot_0V$ be the 'cost of lobbying' curve, reflecting the dollar cost of securing increasing levels of tariff protection by a lobby. Such a curve, which reflects factors such as the willingness of elected officials to grant additional protection to an industry, is; (1) inversely related after a point to the degree of protection already given to the industry; (2) positively associated with the magnitude of producer lobbying expenditures (both of these relationships are part of the Brock–Magee model); and (3) positively correlated with the degree to which economic conditions in the industry match either the altruistic values or the social insurance desires of the voters. Not only are industry lobbying funds provided to candidates so that voters can be informed about how they have been, or will be, helped by the candidates, but they are also spent by an industry to convince voters that the industry's condition or cause of injury merits assistance on such grounds as fairness and equity. In other words, lobbying funds deployed by an industry will tend to reflect, in varying degrees, the diverse factors that have been discussed earlier in this paper. Reflecting the fact, therefore, that altruism may result in some protection at zero or negligible cost, the $Ot_0V$ curve has the stretch $Ot_0$ along the horizontal axis.

The curve $OQS$ in Figure 5.3, on the other hand, reflects the benefits from tariff protection. These are assumed to increase until they level out at $Q$ with maximal protection implied by the prohibitive tariff.

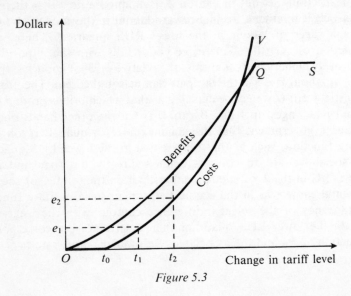

*Figure 5.3*

The equilibrium, endogenous tariff then emerges in the usual profit-maximizing fashion. That is, the industry in question will select the particular lobbying-expenditure level at which the additional cost of an increment in the tariff (i.e., the marginal cost of a tariff increase) is just equal to the marginal revenue from the tariff increase. The expenditure level that maximizes the industry's net benefits is $Oe_2$ in Figure 5.3, and the associated tariff increase is $Ot_2$.[22]

Other industries that may or may not be faced with a recent decline in the foreign-import supply curve will have similarly shaped gross benefit curves indicating the increase in producer surplus associated with further increases in any existing tariffs and also similarly shaped voter-support curves indicating the highest duty increases obtainable by the industry at various expenditure levels. For many industries, the voter-support curve may lie entirely above the benefits curve so that no duty change will be supported. Another possibility is that the voter curve, though intersecting the tariff-increase axis at a positive level, rises more rapidly than the benefit curve. In this case the best policy for the industry to follow is not to lobby at all.[23] It may also be the case that the voter-support curves for different industries are not independent of each voter. For example, if voters have recently supported tariff increases in other industries, the voter-support curve for the industry depicted in Figure 5.3 may lie farther to the left than if there had not been these increases.

The voter-support curve of an industry receiving protection may also rise over time (and thus lead to a lower optimal tariff increase for the industry) as voters learn from their experiences with a higher tariff. The industry may not live up to its promise to become internationally competitive again or the workers may not appear to be so deserving of assistance as voters learn more about them after the initial duty rise. It is for such reasons that import protection for a particular industry is often only temporary. But the model can also account for indefinite increases in protection. The information disbursed by an industry concerning why it deserves assistance may remain valid indefinitely in the minds of voters or else never be disproved by information from other sources.[24]

Many variations and extensions on the analysis presented thus far suggest themselves.[25] One would be to introduce various degrees of imperfection in political markets. For example, on the basis of his control of a party's political mechanisms or his greater previous political exposure, the incumbent may be able to obtain a higher duty for an industry than any other candidate who is given the same amount of campaign funds. In this case, the official will share in the producer-surplus generated by the tariff increase by becoming the recipient, say, of campaign contributions that reduce the need to campaign as hard as would otherwise be necessary. Another modification would be to introduce interindustry differences in the ability to raise lobbying funds from firms and workers. Because of the free-rider problem many industries, for example, may not be able to make the expenditures needed to maximize net benefits.

More broadly, investigations are needed concerning the different forms of assistance received by industries. Why is one industry helped by the imposition of quotas, while another only receives tariff protection or perhaps extended unemployment insurance? Or why is one industry aided directly by subsidies in various forms and another indirectly by import protection? The reasons the political process does not yield the free-trade solution, coupled with income transfers to compensate individuals who lose under this policy, must also be studied and empirically tested.

Although this last question is worthy in itself of a separate paper, a few economic and political reasons come immediately to mind. First, under the free-trade–income-subsidy approach, it would be necessary to set up a costly administrative mechanism both for determining which firms and workers are injured by cheaper imports and the extent of their income loss and for channelling the appropriate compensation to them. On the other hand, a tariff increase that in part offsets a decrease in import prices partially compensates injured individuals through the operation of the price system. The drawbacks of a tariff increase as a means of compensation are that it provides extra income for those who may not be very seriously injured by the fall in import prices and does not help those who are too inefficient to remain in the industry with only a partial reversal of the price decline.

The unfavourable experience with actual income-compensating schemes (in contrast to the ideal lump-sum redistribution arrangements assumed in welfare economics) may help account for the failure of the free-trade–income subsidy approach to be extensively implemented. For example, there is evidence suggesting that the special unemployment benefits extended to trade-displaced workers in the United States may make employers more willing to lay off workers and may encourage those who do lose their jobs to remain unemployed for longer periods than otherwise.[26] Such behaviour tends to turn both government officials and the general public against this approach. The tariff-raising method also has the deficiency that firms may lay off workers and reduce their efficiency-increasing efforts in the expectation of receiving import protection, but such abuses are probably politically less transparent than those associated with direct income payments.

Gainers from free trade also may be reluctant to support income-compensating measures because they are unsure of the tax burden they will bear under these schemes. If, in response to a decrease in the price of an import good, a tariff is introduced that completely restores the initial price, a voter whose money income is unaffected by the change knows that he will be no worse off than before the price decline, even if he does not receive any of the tariff proceeds. Voters who are risk-averse may prefer this situation to free trade coupled with an uncertain redistribution scheme that could reduce their real income. Moreover, since it is extremely expensive to levy an income tax that captures part of the consumer surplus gains of just those who benefit from lower import prices, some voters might expect any income-subsidy programme to be financed through the progressive income tax system used to support most redistributive programmes. Those who think they will lose on balance under this arrangement will tend to oppose the free-trade–income-subsidy approach. A politically appealing feature of increasing the tariff to restore in part the initial domestic price of the imported good is that those who gain from cheaper imports pay the costs of partially compensating those who are injured.

Finally, losers from trade liberalization are likely to oppose exclusive reliance on direct income redistribution. Direct income transfers clearly separate the subsidized and productive parts of one's income-receiving activities and tend to demean the recipients. Price-increasing schemes do not seem to be as objectionable to beneficiaries on this ground, since the subsidy element is less transparent. The greater transparency of tax-financed subsidies to voters is another likely reason for opposition to the free-trade–income-subsidy approach by those who are injured by free trade. Experience suggests that the duration of voter support for this compensation method is likely to be less than under the tariff-raising approach.

A political–economic analysis of import policy or any other public issue in which various second-best constraints are imposed, it should be stressed, does not mean that discussions of welfare-increasing policies are no longer relevant. Rent-seeking activities are themselves often regarded as a completely wasteful use of economic resources. In the political-economy model outlined here where the absence of perfect information is a key assumption and where rent-seeking activities mainly take the form of informational expenditures (rather than, say, of income-redistributing bribes), the matter is not as clear-cut as this. Some of the information provided may be socially valuable from a benefit–cost viewpoint, even though the self-interest goal of an industry leads it to present the type of information that maximizes its likelihood of receiving protection.[27] Nevertheless, the general public is unlikely to obtain the particular set of information it would prefer to receive from any given level of informational outlays. Levying a tax on the industry's information expenditures and spending the proceeds on the type of information about the industry preferred by the general public would be an example of the kind of policy that could bring about a potential increase in welfare for the majority of voters, who are outside the industry.[28] Moreover, some industries that the community would want to assist if their economic conditions were better known may be unable to organize their members for the purpose of providing such information. As a result, the particular set of industries actually assisted may not be the ones that maximize the welfare of the voting majority for any given magnitude of information expenditures, even if the expenditures made in each industry are of the type desired by the public. Other areas of policy interest involve devising fiscal and institutional mechanisms for selecting and financing the volume of information expenditures that maximizes the community's welfare within the given set of constraints.

## 5   EMPIRICAL RESULTS: A REVIEW

The industry characteristics that have been used in empirical efforts to account for industry differences in tariff rates (or changes in these rates) can be divided into three groups: (1) those that indicate the ability and willingness of the productive factors employed in an industry to provide funds and other resources for lobbying efforts; (2) factors that reflect the willingness of the majority of voters and their elected representatives to grant protection; and (3) features that relate to the magnitude of the benefits obtained from different levels of (or increases in) protection. [29]

The first set of factors relates to the voter-support curve $Ot_0V$ in Figure 5.3, which indicates the tariff increases voters would support at various levels of lobbying expenditures. Because of the free-rider problem associated with voluntary lobbying contributions, the feasible range of this curve for the particular industry may be such that the optimum tariff increase cannot be attained. As mentioned earlier, the ability to overcome the free-rider problem and form a common interest group (thus extending the range of the voter-support curve beyond only minimum expenditure levels) is supposedly positively correlated with the degree of industry concentration and negatively related both to the size of the industry in terms of number of firms and to the degree of geographic dispersion. In addition, as Olson (1979) points out, usually a lobbying organization is not formed immediately—or, if the organization already exists, resources are not forthcoming in significant amounts from the membership—upon the emergence of a new common interest for a group. A crisis or repeated series of crises may be necessary to shock the individuals in the group into establishing the organization or increasing their contributions to it. To capture this effect, such variables as growth conditions and the level of (or, preferably, the change in) the import-penetration ratio have been employed in various regression analyses. In general, the concentration ratio has not been significant in most studies. The number of firms, the import-penetration ratio, and (especially) measures of growth perform better in the expected manner.

When an industry is subject to greater import competition, the relative change in producer income caused by a given decline as well as the ability of capitalists and workers to move into alternative productive lines may also affect the willingness of those in the industry to contribute to lobbying efforts. The first effect is usually measured by the share of value added in total output and the second by such variables as the average age of the workers, their average wages, an industry's specialization ratio and the share of capital income in value added. The value-added ratio has turned out as expected in some studies, while among the measures of resource flexibility the average wage is almost always highly significant, and the average age is significant in most instances. The other measures of resource flexibility do not perform as well. Still another variable influencing the absolute size of lobbying expenditures by an established pressure group is simply its size in terms of the total income of its members. This variable does not turn out to be significant in most regression analyses.

It should be noted that several of the variables affecting lobbying pressures by domestic producers also influence counter-lobbying pressures by both foreign producers and domestic consumers. The assumption is usually made that the impact of domestic producers dominates that of the other two groups.

Aside from the ability of an industry to undertake lobbying efforts, the shape of the voter-support curve depends on the willingness of voters and their elected officials to grant import protection. For example, if voters are particularly sympathetic toward low-income workers who suffer income losses and to those who have difficulty in adjusting to income losses, one would expect that tariff rates would be higher (or GATT-related tariff cuts less) in industries with relatively low wages, high proportions of unskilled workers, high average age of workers, etc. But the higher the growth rate in these industries, the less favourable is the voter likely to be toward a given tariff increase. Because of attitudes of 'fairness' on the part of voters, variables such as the level of import penetration and the particular reason for a sudden increase in imports (e.g., dumping) may also influence the shape of the voter-support curve. Voter views on whether an industry's decline jeopardizes some desirable national goal (e.g., national defence or relations with an important foreign country) may also play a significant role in determining the nature of a voter-support curve.

A selfish reason why voters may resist tariff increases is the fear that foreign-tariff retaliation will decrease output in the industries where they are employed. Thus one expects increased protection for a particular industry to be easier to obtain if only a few other industries are also pressing for import relief. Similarly, general tariff-cutting efforts by a government are likely to be easier to undertake if other governments are also cutting their import duties. If the majority of voters favour protection primarily for selfish, long-run insurance purposes, one would expect this policy to operate mainly in industries in which average wages are near those of the voters as a whole, on the grounds that these are more similar to the industry for which the average voter wants insurance, his own industry.

The size of the industry in sales or employment terms is likely to affect the voter-support curve for several reasons. Each individual voter realizes, for example, that when the foreign import-supply curve is completely elastic in an industry, the producer-surplus benefits obtained from a given import price rise are greater, the greater is the domestic industry's supply. A voter may also be more willing to grant this price increase, the larger is the number of workers per dollar of increase in net benefits. On the other hand, the more significance the protected item has in his budget, the less ready is he likely to be to support increased duties. In addition, industry size influences the curve because of the voting strength of those employed in an industry itself, the magnitude of general tax revenues lost from the declining industry, and how much voters know about the sector. The relation of other industries, as import suppliers or output users, to the particular industry under consideration should also be considered in the context of the preceding factors.

Among the variables included in the second group of factors influencing the shape of the voter-support curve, measures of human capital, such as average wages and the proportion of unskilled workers, perform the best and, indeed, seem to be the most significant variables in the various studies, taken as a whole. Tests of different international policy variables are not numerous enough to generalize, but Caves (1976) did find some support for Canada's tariffs' being related to their economic development goals. Fieleke (1976), on the other hand, found that a national defence variable was not significant in accounting for the United States' tariff structure. Industry size as measured by number of employees is significant in the expected manner in some of the studies.

Though not included thus far in any of the regression analyses, various factors relating the ability of elected officials to deviate from the preferences of the voters (and still get re-elected) could also be included as influences on the shape of the curve indicating the support of decision makers for tariff increases.

The magnitude of industry benefits from different levels of protection or increases in protective levels (i.e., the position of the producer-benefits curve *OQS* in Figure 5.3) depends on the elasticity of the industry's short-run supply curve, the level of output from which tariff increases are being considered, and any other supply-curve shifts due to factors other than the initial downward pressure on price. If, for example, productive factors are completely immobile in the short run, the short-run supply curve will be vertical and the benefits curve will therefore be steeper up to the tariff increase that restores the initial price. This will raise the equilibrium tariff level *ceteris paribus*.[30] As already noted, the degree of factor mobility can be measured by such variables as the average wages in an industry, the average age of its employees or, if one considers capital to be more immobile than labour, capital's income share, and the elasticity of substitution of labour for capital in other sectors. Furthermore, the higher the degree of product specialization in the industry, the more likely it is that a higher proportion of the factors in the industry will be immobile in the short run.

Since a given percentage increase in domestic supply in response to a 1 per cent increase in price will increase producer surplus by a large sum if the initial output level is large, the slope of the benefits curve is also related to the industry's output level. While short-run shifts in the domestic-demand curve will not affect the short-run benefits of a given tariff increase in cases where the foreign-supply curve is perfectly elastic, these shifts will have an independent price effect when this curve is less than perfectly elastic. An increasing demand curve will add to the short-run benefits of a given tariff increase. Still another factor of this type is the extent to which producers in an industry own comparable facilities abroad that export either back to the home country or to third countries. In the latter case, the producers do not wish to set off tariff increases in their export markets.

As the preceding discussion indicates, it is difficult to find variables that enable one to discriminate among different hypotheses concerning the reason for interindustry differences in protection. For example, should the fact that protection is comparatively high in industries with comparatively low per-worker levels of human capital be interpreted as support for the hypothesis that voters behave in an altruistic manner or for the hypothesis that, because of their poorer adjustment ability, low-income groups are more likely to overcome the free-rider problem that tends to limit lobbying efforts? Moreover, quite aside from interindustry differences in voter attitudes or in the free-rider problem, the equilibrium tariff increase after a given decline in the foreign-supply curve will be greater if low levels of human capital are associated with inelastic short-run industry supply curves. One way in which the first two hypotheses might be disentangled would be to determine whether per-capita lobbying resources, in terms of money, letter-writing efforts, and other measures of political pressure, on the part of low-wage workers are in fact greater than for high-wage workers in response to a given decline in income. Furthermore, it might be possible to separate the last hypothesis from the others by introducing measures of short-run supply elasticity as well as average wages into the regressions.

Most of the other variables mentioned also can be interpreted as affecting both curves in Figure 5.3. The direction of their impact on tariff levels is generally the same, but again existing analyses do not enable one to discriminate among the underlying forces for which these variables serve as proxies. Yet, if one of the objectives of such investigations is to suggest policies or institutional changes that will increase welfare in the second-best world of trade policy formation, the ability to make such distinctions is essential. The possibility of succeeding in this regard would seem to require greater efforts to determine the various separate relationships that make up a total model of the political economy of protectionism.

## ACKNOWLEDGEMENT

The author is grateful for the valuable comments of the discussants and other conference participants and especially for Jagdish Bhagwati's help in tightening up the paper. Thanks are due to the Office on Foreign Economic Research, United States Department of Labor and the World Bank for financial support in undertaking the research underlying this paper.

## NOTES

1. The most famous United States historical study along these lines is that of Taussig (1931). *See* also Schattschneider (1935).
2. Several of the articles will be discussed in the text, while all are listed in the references at the end of the paper.
3. Samuelson (1947, p. 221).
4. Bergson (1968 reprint, p. 413).
5. Bergson (1968 reprint, p. 413).
6. Arrow (1963, p. 71).
7. Samuelson (1956, p. 15).
8. Arrow (1963, p. 18).
9. Arrow (1963, p. 23).
10. Arrow (1963, p. 106).

11. It has also been pointed out by Coase (1960) that, with these conditions, some market failures, e.g., certain externalities, will be corrected through private contracts without requiring any government intervention.

12. Arrow (1963, p. 74).

13. The only redistribution generally mentioned relates to the tariff proceeds, and this is not brought into a discussion of attracting additional votes.

14. If workers pursue their self-interest, they will raise tariffs to the levels that eliminate trade. In fact, they could even lobby for export subsidies.

15. *See* Brock and Magee (1974) for a modelling of some of Olson's concepts in terms of a non-cooperative game.

16. One could say that, in these cases, the cost of lobbying is low because it is marginal to a public-good activity already in place.

17. The question of what is a 'significant section' of the community can depend, in a pluralistic democracy, on lobbying by the section itself, so that it is not clear that the explanation of protection provided by resort to such a notion as Corden's is truly independent of the kind of explanation resulting from public-choice theory based wholly on self-interest.

18. If the individual's welfare increases, the relationship is one of envy rather than altruism.

19. Arrow (1975, p. 17). Arrow is discussing the reasons why people give blood to individuals they do not personally know.

20. One of the hypotheses tested by Caves on Canadian data is that there is a 'collective national preference for industrialization while also promoting prairie settlement and a national transportation system' Caves (1976, p. 279).

21. The diagram assumes the necessary convexities for an interior maximum, of course.

22. If the industry is initially in a tariff-equilibrium position but the voters change their views and agree upon a general tariff-cutting rule under a GATT-sponsored trade negotiation, the point $Ot_2$ can be interpreted as the tariff increment above the formula cut that minimizes the industry's losses relative to its initial income level.

23. If the absolute slope of the voter support curve is less at all points than the absolute slope of the non-horizontal portion of the benefits curve, a prohibitive duty will be imposed.

24. In the narrow self-interest model where voters are in effect tricked into permitting increased protection, it is much more likely that the protection to an industry will decline as voters gain experience from repeated 'plays' of this political 'game'.

25. Lobbying-determined tariffs are analysed, in explicit models, by Findlay and Wellisz (1982) and Feenstra and Bhagwati (1982). In fact, Feenstra and Bhagwati develop benefits and costs curves much like those in Figure 5.3.

26. *See* Richardson (1982) and Neumann (1979).

27. The appropriability problem may prevent this information being provided through the private market mechanism.

28. Since these voters would have the option to ask for the same type of information the industry would have furnished with the taxed funds, the ability to select a different information set provides the opportunity for a potential welfare increase.

29. Since the 1930s the average tariff level for dutiable manufactures has decreased very significantly in the industrial countries. For example, in the

United States the ratio of duties collected to the value of dutiable imports declined from 59 per cent in 1932 to 10 per cent in 1970. Consequently, existing interindustry differences in tariff rates are closely related to the ability of industries to resist the general downward pressure on tariffs.
30. Presumably in the initial position the marginal benefits of a tariff increase are less than the lobbying expenditures needed to achieve the tariff increase.

# REFERENCES

Anderson, Kym (1978), Politico-economic factors affecting structural change and adjustment, In *The Economics of Structural Change and Adjustment*, eds, C. Aislabie and C. Tisdell, University of Newcastle: Institute of Industrial Economics, Conference Series no. 5.
——. (1979), Toward an explanation of recent changes in Australian protectionism. Mimeographed.
Arrow, Kenneth J. (1951), *Social Choice and Individual Values*, New York: Wiley.
——. (1963), *Social Choice and Individual Values*. 2nd edn., New York: Wiley.
——. (1975), Gifts and exchange, In *Altruism, Morality, and Economic Theory*, ed. E. S. Phelps, New York: Russell Sage Foundation.
Baldwin, Robert E. (1976), The political economy of postwar US trade policy, *Bulletin*, 1976–9, New York University Graduate School of Business Administration, Center for the Study of Financial Institutions.
Bale, M. D. (1977), United States concessions in the Kennedy Round and short-run labor adjustment costs: further evidence, *Journal of International Economics* 7, no. 2 (May): 145–8.
Bergson, Abram (1938), A reformulation of certain aspects of welfare economics, *Quarterly Journal of Economics* 52 (February): 310–34. Reprinted in Alfred N. Page (ed.) (1968), *Utility Theory: A Book of Readings*, New York: Wiley, pp. 402–22.
Bhagwati, J. N. and T. N. Srinivasan (1969), Optimal intervention to achieve non-economic objectives, *Review of Economic Studies* 36 (January).
Brock, William A. and Stephen P. Magee (1974), An economic theory of politics: the case of tariffs. Mimeographed.
——. (1978), The economics of special interest politics: the case of tariffs, *American Economic Review* 68, no. 2 (May): 246–50.
——. (1980), Tariff formation in a democracy, In *Current Issues in Commercial Policy and Diplomacy*, eds, J. Black and B. Hindley, London: Macmillan.
Buchanan, James M. and Gordon Tullock (1962), *The Calculus of Consent*, Ann Arbor: University of Michigan Press.
Cassing, James H. (1980), Alternatives to protectionism, In *Western Economies in Transition*, eds, J. Leveson and J. W. Wheeler, Boulder: Westview Press, pp. 391–424.
Caves, Richard E. (1976), Economic models of political choice: Canada's tariff structure, *Canadian Journal of Economics* 9, no. 2 (May): 278–300.
Cheh, J. H. (1974), United States concessions in the Kennedy Round and short-run labor adjustment costs, *Journal of International Economics*. 4: 323–40.

——. (1976), A note on tariffs, nontariff barriers, and labour protection in United States manufacturing industries, *Journal of Political Economy* 84: 388–94.

Coase, Ronald (1960), The problem of social costs, *Journal of Law and Economy* 3: 1–44.

Constantopoulos, M. (1974), Labour protection in Western Europe, *European Economic Review* 5: 313–18.

Corden, W. Max (1974), *Trade Policy and Economic Welfare*, Oxford: Clarendon Press.

Downs, Anthony (1957), *An Economic Theory of Democracy*, New York: Harper & Row.

Feenstra, Robert C. and Jagdish N. Bhagwati (1982), Tariff-seeking and the efficient tariff, In *Import Competition and Response*, ed. J. N. Bhagwati, Chicago: University of Chicago Press, ch. 9.

Fieleke, N. (1976), The tariff structure for manufacturing industries in the United States: a test of some traditional explanations, *Columbia Journal of World Business* 11, no. 4 (Winter): 98–104.

Findlay, Ronald C. and Stanislaw Wellisz (1982), Endogenous tariffs, the political economy of trade restrictions and welfare, In *Import Competition and Response*, ed. J. N. Bhagwati, Chicago: University of Chicago Press, ch. 8.

Helleiner, G. K. (1977), The political economy of Canada's tariff structure: an alternative model, *Canadian Journal of Economics* 4, no. 2 (May): 318–26.

Johnson, H. G. (1960), The cost of protection and the scientific tariff, *Journal of Political Economy* 68, no. 4 (August): 327–45.

——. (1965), Optimal trade intervention in the presence of domestic distortions, In *Trade, Growth, and the Balance of Payments*, eds, R. E. Caves, H. G. Johnson and P. B. Kenen, Amsterdam: North-Holland.

Magee, Stephen (1976), Three simple tests of the Stolper-Samuelson theorem. December, xeroxed.

Mayer, Wolfgang (1974), Short-run and long-run equilibrium for a small open economy, *Journal of Political Economy* 82, no. 5 (September/October): 955–67.

Mueller, Dennis C. (1976), Public choice: a survey, *Journal of Economic Literature* 14, no. 2 (June): 395–433.

Mussa, Michael (1974), Tariffs and the distribution of income: the importance of factor specificity, substitutability, and intensity in the short and long run, *Journal of Political Economy* 82, no. 6 (December): 1191–1203.

Neumann, George R. (1979), Adjustment assistance for trade-displaced workers. In *The New International Economic Order: A US Response*, ed. D. B. H. Denoon, New York: New York University Press.

Olson, Mancur (1965), *The Logic of Collective Action: Public Goods and the Theory of Groups*. Cambridge, Mass.: Harvard University Press.

——. (1979), The political economy of comparative growth rates. Mimeographed.

Pincus, Jonathan (1972), A positive theory of tariff formation applied to nineteenth century United States. Ph.D. thesis, Stanford University.

——. (1975), Pressure groups and the pattern of tariffs, *Journal of Political Economy* 83, no. 4 (August): 757–78.

Rawls, J. (1971), *A Theory of Social Justice*, Cambridge, Mass.: Harvard University Press.

Ray, Edward J. (1979), Tariff and nontariff barriers to trade in the US and abroad. October, Xeroxed.

Richardson, J. David (1982), Trade adjustment assistance under the United States Trade Act of 1974: An analytical examination and worker survey, In *Import Competition and Response*, ed. J. N. Bhagwati, Chicago: University of Chicago Press, ch. 12.

Riedel, James (1977), Tariff concessions in the Kennedy Round and the structure of tariff protection in West Germany: An econometric assessment, *Journal of International Economics* 7, no. 2 (May): 133–43.

Samuelson, Paul A. (1947), *Foundations of Economic Analysis*, Cambridge, Mass.: Harvard University Press, Ch. 8.

——. (1956), Social indifference curves, *Quarterly Journal of Economics* 70, no. 1 (February): 1–22.

Schattschneider, E. E. (1935), *Politics, Pressures, and the Tariff: A Study in Free Private Enterprise in Pressure Politics, as Shown in the 1929–1930 Revision of the Tariff*, New York: Prentice-Hall.

Stolper, Wolfgang and Paul A. Samuelson (1941), Protection and real wages, *Review of Economic Structure* 9, no. 1 (November): 58–73.

Taussig, Frank W. (1931), *The Tariff History of the United States*, Cambridge Mass.: Harvard University Press.

# 6 Rent Seeking and Trade Policy: An Industry Approach*

## 1 INTRODUCTION

In recent years economists have modelled the process by which particular industries and income groups seek protection against import competition through lobbying and bloc voting.[1] The earliest theoretical work on the subject is the classic paper by Stolper and Samuelson (1941) in which the authors demonstrate that in a standard two-good, two-factor Heckscher–Ohlin model, the factor used intensively in the import-competing sector will gain in real income terms from protection whereas the other factor will lose. Unfortunately, the Stolper–Samuelson theorem does not seem to be very useful for understanding the nature of present-day protectionist pressures. As Magee (1980) found in analysing testimony given during the congressional hearings on the 1974 US Trade Act, representatives of labour and capital from the same industry almost always take the same position concerning the desirability of granting the president the authority to undertake another trade-liberalizing multilateral negotiation. The divergence in views on the issue of further trade liberalization is along industry lines rather than between capital and labour.

For earlier years, when arguments such as the need for tariffs to maintain labour's standard of living were widely accepted (more, it seems, on grounds of political ideology than of economic analysis), the Stolper–Samuelson relationship may be useful in interpreting tariff history. However, modern economists appear to have been reasonably successful in convincing most political leaders of the fallacy of the pauper-labour argument and of similar arguments for protection. To obtain import protection today, it seems to be necessary (but not sufficient) for an income group or industrial sector to demonstrate to the satisfaction of government officials and the general public that the industry is being injured due to increased imports or to unfair trade

* From *Weltwirtschaftliches Archiv*, Band 120, Heft 4 (1984), pp. 662–76.

practices by foreign suppliers, in the sense these concepts are defined in the GATT and national legislation. Import injury (or the threat of injury) is defined in these documents as a short-run phenomenon resulting from such conditions as the significant idling of productive facilities, significant unemployment or underemployment, and rising inventories, Furthermore, any relief provided in the form of higher tariffs, quotas, adjustment assistance and so forth is generally specified as being only temporary. Consequently, a short-run economic model such as the one formulated by Mayer (1974) and Mussa (1974) seems more appropriate than the long-run Heckscher–Ohlin model for analysing the particular protectionism that characterizes recent trade policy history.[2]

In the Mayer–Mussa specific-factor model, it is assumed that the stock of capital is fixed in each of the economy's two production sectors while the third factor, labour, is mobile between the two sectors.[3] As Mussa (1974) demonstrates, under these conditions an increase in the relative domestic price of one of the two goods (due, for example, to an increase in the duty levied on imports) increases the real income of the specific factor employed in this import-competing sector and reduces the real income received by the owners of capital in the export sector. The real rewards to the labour employed in both sectors may increase or decrease. Since per-worker relative wages increase less than the relative prices of the protected product, the real income level of labour in both sectors declines when measured in terms of the protected commodity but increases when measured in terms of the other commodity. Whether the net result is an increase or decrease in labour's real income depends upon the proportions in which the two goods are consumed.

This impact of protection on labour is also not consistent with Magee's findings concerning the positions of labour and capital in each sector on the liberalization-versus-protection issue. For example, if labour gains, both labour and capital in the protected import-competing sector will favour protection, but labour and capital in the export sector will disagree on the desirability of protection.

One model that does yield results consistent with Magee's findings is, as Magee (1980, p. 138–9) points out, Cairnes's (1874) non-competing-groups model in which all productive factors are industry-specific. However, this framework is inconsistent with what several studies of workers displaced by import competition indicate, that a high proportion of permanently displaced workers do move to other industries to obtain employment (see, e.g., Richardson, 1982, p. 334).

What these studies also show, however, is that workers permanently displaced from an industry due to import competition generally suffer a significant loss in earnings, both because of the search time involved in obtaining another job and because of the lower level of earnings in their new jobs.[4] An important reason for this decline in earnings is that industry-specific skills acquired by workers through learning-by-doing are worthless when the workers transfer to another industry. Consequently, because of the threatened loss in the rents earned on sector-specific human capital, workers in an industry facing increased import competition join capitalists in the same industry, who also are threatened with a loss in rents from their sector-specific physical capital, in seeking protection against the increased import competition.

## 2   A MODEL OF RENT SEEKING THROUGH PROTECTION

This rent-seeking behaviour of workers and capitalists can be analysed with the following two-commodity, specific-factors, small-country model. Assume there are fixed stocks of sector-specific physical capital, capital in sector X and capital in sector Z. There is also a given supply of labour, part of which has acquired unique skills for producing commodity X and the rest of which has acquired unique skills for producing commodity Z. Initially it will be assumed that these two types of labour are fully employed in the sectors for which they have special skills and that wages are equal for the two types of labour. Unlike physical capital, labour is assumed to be mobile between the two sectors in the short run. However, when skilled workers from either sector move to the other sector, their productivity level is only a certain fraction of that achieved by skilled labour.

This situation is depicted in Figure 6.1, which is a modified version of Mussa's (1974, p. 1194) diagrammatic representation of the specific-factors model. The horizontal axis indicates the total fixed labour supply for the economy, with the quantity of labour employed in sector X being measured to the right from $O_x$ and the quantity employed in Z being measured to the left from $O_z$. The vertical axis measures the value of the marginal productivity of labour in sectors X and Z (measured from $O_x$ and $O_z$, respectively) in terms of units of Z per unit of labour. At the given initial price of X in terms of Z, the curves $VMPL_{xs}$ ($P_x^0$) and $VMPL_{zs}$ show the value of the marginal productivity of skilled labour in sectors X and Z, as successive units of only this type of labour are employed in each sector. The intersection of the two curves at $A$ indicates the assumed initial long-run equilibrium point where $O_xL^0$ of labour has been employed in sector $X$ for sufficient time to acquire the unique skills used in producing this commodity, and the $O_zL^0$ of labour employed in producing Z has also been similarly trained. Since perfect

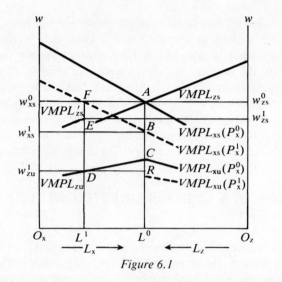

*Figure 6.1*

competition is assumed, the wage in each sector is equal to the value of the marginal productivity of the skilled labour employed in each sector. The wages of skilled labour in sector X, $O_x w_{xs}^0$, and in sector Z, $O_z w_{zs}^0$, are equal because the long-run equilibrium is one in which sufficient time has elapsed for labour to shift from one sector to the other and acquire the latter sector's specialized skills.[5]

The curve labeled $VMPL_{zu}$ that begins at the point $C$ on the vertical line $AL^0$ indicates what the value of the marginal productivity of skilled labour displaced from sector X would be when this labour is employed as unskilled labour in sector Z in addition to the $O_z L^0$ of skilled labour already employed in the Z sector. Similarly, the curve $VMPL_{xu}(P_x^0)$ depicts the schedule of the value of the marginal productivity of labour displaced from sector Z and employed in sector X in addition to $O_x L^0$ of skilled labour employed there. Both of these curves are assumed to be some (not necessarily equal) fraction (less than one) below the marginal productivity schedules of skilled labour in these two sectors.[6]

Now suppose the initial long-run equilibrium situation is disturbed by a fall in the price of commodity X because of increased import competition. The curves $VMPL_{xs}(P_x^1)$ and $VMPL_{xu}(P_x^1)$ are determined by multiplying the physical marginal productivity schedules of skilled and unskilled labour employed in sector X (in the previously described manner) by this lower price of X in terms of Z. Since the curve $VMPL_{xs}(P_x^1)$ intersects the vertical line $AL^0$ between the points $A$ and $C$, there will not be any reallocation of labour between the two sectors; $O_z L^0$ of skilled labour will remain employed in sector Z and $O_x L^0$ of skilled labour in sector X. However, the wage of the skilled labour in X will decline to $O_x w_{xs}^1$ as part of its rents are transferred to consumers. Similarly, the rents collected by capitalists in sector X will decrease from the area of the triangle above the line $w_{xs}^0 A$ and under the $VMPL_{xs}(P_x^0)$ line to the area of the triangle above the line $w_{xs}^1 B$ and below the $VMPL_{xs}(P_x^1)$ line. The skilled labour employed in sector Z continues to receive a wage of $O_z w_{zs}^0$, while capitalists also continue to receive a rent on their capital equal to the area above the line $A w_{zs}^0$ and under the $VMPL_{zs}$ line.[7]

The real income of workers and capitalists in sector X measured in terms of commodity X remains unchanged, since their income measured in terms of good Z decreases by the same proportion as the price of X in terms of Z decreases. However, since the price of Z in terms of itself is unchanged, labour and capital in sector X incur a reduction in their real income measured in terms of good Z. Thus, as long as both groups consume some of commodity Z, both groups suffer an unambiguous reduction in their real income level. Since the returns to labour and capital in sector Z remain unchanged when measured in terms of Z, these groups enjoy an unambiguous increase in their economic welfare, since the price of X falls. If we think of sector X representing a particular industry and sector Z representing a composite of many industries, one can appreciate why labour and capital in sector X are likely to lobby the government vigorously for import protection that will raise the price of X back toward its initial level. With a price rise they will benefit significantly from the increase in rents that will accrue to them. On the other hand, the decrease in real income for the typical worker or capitalist employed in the rest of the economy is likely to be too small to warrant counter-lobbying efforts by these individuals.

An alternative to assuming that wages are flexible in sector X is to assume they are fixed in the short run at $O_x w_{xs}^0$, owing, perhaps, to a collective bargaining contract on wages that holds throughout the time period. Consequently, in response to the price decline in sector X, firms will lay off $L^0 L^1$ $(=AF)$ skilled workers in this sector. These workers will be forced to shift to sector Z and take jobs as unskilled workers. Their marginal productivity schedule as they supplement the skilled workforce already employed in the Z sector is indicated by the $VMPL_{zu}$ curve originating at the point $C$. Their wage will be $O_x w_{zu}^1$. Furthermore, the possibility of firms substituting unskilled workers for skilled workers will drive the wage of skilled workers in this sector down to $O_z w_{zs}^1$.[8]

The skilled workers still employed in sector X gain in real income terms since their wage in terms of Z remains unchanged when the price of commodity X declines. The workers displaced from sector X who end up as unskilled employees in sector Z suffer an income loss in terms of Z equal to the area $FARD$. They also lose in terms of commodity X since the proportion by which their wages decrease, that is, $FD/FI^1$, is greater than the proportion by which the price of X declines, that is, $AB/AL^0$. As long as these workers continue to belong to the labour union in sector X and there is a threat of continued price decreases in this sector due to import competition, the workers employed in X are likely to be willing to use part of their earnings to lobby for import protection for this sector. They will be joined by the owners of capital in sector X since their rent declines to the area above the line $w^0_{xs}F$ and below the $VMPL_{xs}(P^1_x)$ curve. This decline is relatively greater than the decrease in the price of X and thus represents an unambiguous drop in real income.

The rental return accruing to capitalists in sector Z increases to the area under the $VMPL_{zs}$ curve but above the $Ew^1_{zs}$ line and to the right of the line from $A$ to $B$ plus the area $CRD$. Since the price of X has declined, this increase represents a real income increase measured in terms of either commodity. Skilled workers in sector Z lose in terms of commodity Z since their wage in terms of Z declines to $O_zw^1_{zs}$ and could either gain or lose in terms of commodity X.[9]

Figure 6.2, which is a redrawing of the essential parts of Figure 6.1, shows the effect of a greater decline in the price of commodity X. Now the new marginal productivity curve for skilled workers in sector X, $VMPL_{xs}(P^2_x)$, intersects the marginal productivity curve for unskilled workers in sector Z at $G$ rather than intersecting the vertical line $AL^0$ between points $A$ and $C$. This means that $GH$ of skilled workers initially employed in sector X are displaced and forced to obtain jobs as unskilled workers in sector Z at a wage equal to $O_zw^2_{zu}$. Moreover, the wage of the remaining skilled workers in sector X is also driven down to $O_xw^2_{xs}$ and

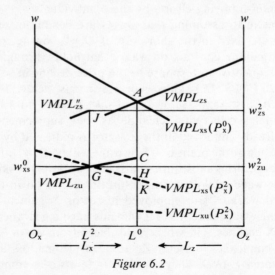

*Figure 6.2*

they lose all the rent derived from their specialized skills for this sector. The wage of skilled workers employed in sector Z is also driven down to $O_z w_{zs}^2$.

Since the relative decline in the price of X, $AK/AL^0$, is greater than the relative decline in wages in sector X as well as in the wages of workers formerly employed in sector X, $AH/AL^0$, the real income of those still employed in X as well as of the newly employed Z workers increases in terms of commodity X but declines in terms of commodity Z. Skilled workers in sector Z also gain in terms of X and lose in terms of Z. In contrast, capitalists in sector X lose in terms of both commodities whereas capitalists in Z gain in terms of both commodities.

## 3 PROTECTION SEEKING

If capitalists and workers in industry X lose in real income terms (or fear they will lose in the future) and are able to overcome the free-rider problem associated with the collective-good nature of import protection, they will organize into a common interest group, raise funds through 'voluntary' contributions, and seek protection or some other form of assistance from the government. In doing so, they will maximize their gains from these efforts by collecting and spending funds up to the point where the additional cost of their protection-seeking activities equals the additional income benefits from further protection.

Since the tariff-seeking process involves the expenditure of real resources, the effect of this lobbying activity on economic welfare is of interest. Suppose that skilled labour and physical capital in sector X (the import-competing sector) can be used for lobbying purposes. In terms of Figure 6.1, the employment of physical capital for this purpose lowers the marginal productivity curve for labour in sector X, while the utilization of this sector's skilled labour for lobbying shifts the origin, $O_x$, to the right and causes the marginal productivity of labour curve to shift to the right in a parallel fashion. As long as the equilibrium labour distribution point remains between points $A$ and $C$ so that the output of Z is unchanged while the output of X declines, the lobbying will reduce the economy's output of X and Z valued at free-trade prices. In other words, the lobbying activity will always be welfare-reducing.

If, however, sector X's marginal productivity curve for skilled labour intersects sector Z's labour productivity curve for unskilled labour in the downward-sloping part of this curve (as in Figure 6.2), so that the output of Z increases as the output of X declines, then, as Findlay and Wellisz (1982) point out, the outcome first noted by Bhagwati and Srinivasan (1980) is possible. The output of X and Z valued at international prices can be greater under import protection that is gained through resource-using lobbying activities than under the same level of protection but in a situation where no resources are expended in obtaining this protection.

## 4   THE SIZE OF THE STAKES IN PROTECTION SEEKING

In Figures 6.1 and 6.2 the area under labour's marginal productivity curve for sector X indicates, of course, the value added by labour and capital in this sector at a particular price of X and employment level in the sector. The magnitude of the value added by these two productive factors in some of the industries that have sought protection can be obtained from national input/output tables. For example, the 1972 US input/output table prepared by the US Department of Commerce (1979) shows the value added by labour and property in the motor vehicles and equipment sector to be $20.7 billion, in the apparel sector $10.1 billion, and in footwear and other leather products $1.9 billion. This means that if the prices of the goods produced in these sectors fall by 1 per cent because of greater import competition, the short-run income of these factors will, as previously explained, fall by 1 per cent. This amounts to $207 million in motor vehicles, $101 million in apparel and $19 million in footwear. Value-added data for some of the smaller industries that have petitioned for protection can sometimes be estimated from information published in reports of the US ITC on import-injury cases. For example, 1 per cent of the 1982 value added by labour and capital employed in the stainless steel and alloy tool steel industry was approximately $9 million, in contrast to only $145 thousand in the industry producing tubeless tyre valves.

If these are the rents that can be obtained by labour and capital with a protection action that raises the prices of the products supplied by these sectors by 1 per cent, what are the costs of seeking protection? Jackson (1984) estimates that the US system for the regulation of imports through the dozen or so different formal types of procedure cost the private sector about $40 million in 1982 and the government $200 million. The number of such cases in which government determinations were made or were pending in 1982 were: escape-clause cases, 4; preliminary and final antidumping decisions, 61 and 10 respectively; preliminary and final countervailing duty decisions, 111 and 13 respectively; unfair trade cases 15; and cases alleging unfair or unreasonable trade practices by foreign governments, 19.

What the comparison of these value-added and cost figures seems to indicate is that, even without expressing all the value-added figures in 1982 prices or capitalizing the gains over the period for which the protection is designed to increase value added, the possible benefits are very large compared with the costs. As Adams and Dirlam (1984) emphasize, the cost side is favourable to protection petitioners who utilize the established administrative channels because the government pays most of the costs involved. Furthermore, as ITC cases indicate, downward price pressures of 5–10 per cent or more due to increased import competition are not at all unusual.


## 5   ALTERNATIVE MEASURES FOR CAPTURING RENTS

Thus far it has been assumed that the industries being considered lobby for protection against imports. However, this leaves open the particular form of import protection and ignores the fact that some industries seek various forms of government subsidization as an aid to competing in international markets. Obviously, a general determinant of the type of assistance sought by an industry is the nature of its balance of trade. An import-competing industry will seek protection against imports in such forms as tariffs, while an export-oriented sector will press for export subsidization through such means as subsidized export financing and special export-related tax benefits. Both types of industries will lobby the government for domestic subsidies such as access to capital funds at below-market interest rates or an outright grant.

Import-competing industries generally prefer quotas over tariffs on the grounds that their effects are more predictable. A tariff increase may be offset by lower foreign prices as foreign suppliers accept lower profits or continue to lower their unit costs. Some government officials also prefer quotas since, with orderly marketing agreements and 'voluntary' export restraints, the government can apply protection selectively and thus avoid complaints or possible retaliation by countries whose exports to the protecting country have not increased. Well-established foreign firms also often favour quotas over tariffs since they usually reap most of the windfall gains and need not be as concerned with their new or rapidly expanding domestic competitors. However, the protected domestic industry often finds that the quotas do not have the expected restrictive effect due to quality upgrading and increased imports from third countries. As a result of these responses, industries often follow a pattern of protection seeking that involves progressively more restrictive means, for example, more and more bilateral quota agreements, as in the case of textiles and apparel, or domestic content requirements, as in the case of the US automobile industry.

Within recent years more and more US import-competing industries have sought protection under the laws dealing with such 'unfair' trade practices as foreign dumping, foreign subsidization and market disruption. The antidumping, countervailing duty and market-disruption laws have a much weaker injury requirement than the traditional 'escape-clause' route for securing protection. Furthermore, it is easier to rally public support for protection on grounds of unfair actions by foreign suppliers than on the basis of injury that might be caused by inefficient management of the domestic industry. The country-specific nature of the protective response also appeals to some government officials.

Government subsidies directed only at an industry's exports are more difficult to obtain for an industry than import protection, due to the explicit GATT ban on export subsidies. However, subsidized export credits are permitted provided the government is a signatory to an international undertaking on official export credits, such as the one operated under the Organization for Economic Cooperation and Development (OECD) auspices. Special tax breaks for exporting firms are also allowed under certain conditions, although the DISC legislation of the US was declared to be in violation of the GATT export-subsidy rule. Consequently, lobbying by export-oriented firms in the developed countries usually is aimed at both of these forms of export subsidization.

Assistance that does not distinguish between exports and output destined for domestic consumption is sought by both export-oriented and import-competing industries. The variety of domestic aids is also wider than the assistance to export-oriented industries because GATT rules in this area are much less well defined than in the export field. This type of aid includes general loans at below-market interest rates, the provision of equity capital, accelerated depreciation allowances, tax holidays, government financing of needed infrastructure investment, wage subsidies, etc. While I do not know of any empirical work on the subject, one would expect that workers prefer import protection, export subsidization and wage subsidies over capital subsidies. The modernization of capital facilities generally associated with such subsidies is more likely to be labour displacing than labour using.

An alleged drawback of most forms of subsidization is that they appear as a cost item in the budget, whereas tariff protection, for example, is actually a revenue-producing activity. But this drawback does not appear to have been very effective in restraining the extensive subsidization that some countries undertake. When an export-oriented industry suffers injury due to loss of foreign markets, it is just as difficult to refuse adjustment assistance in the form of subsidies as to deny tariff assistance to an injured import-competing industry. Moreover, it is apparent to all what the adverse effects will be from cutting off a subsidy, whereas because of its uncertain effects, it can be argued that eliminating a tariff may not hurt an industry at all.

## 6   RENT SEEKING DUE TO PROTECTION

The analysis thus far has focused on the process by which increased import competition in an industry may lead to lobbying by the industry for import protection. Some economists, for example Krueger (1974) and Bhagwati and Srinivasan (1980), have also modeled the manner in which import protection leads to lobbying for the windfall gains or tariff revenue associated with the protection. As Krueger (1974) pointed out in her pioneering article on rent seeking, when there is a system of binding quantitative restrictions in which the right to import depends on the possession of an import license, resource-using competition is likely to arise among importers for the windfall gains associated with the ownership of import licenses. This can range from investment in excess capacity in order to obtain a large share of import licenses to lobbying or actually bribing government officials who make the allocative decisions.

In most instances when developed countries enter into agreements with other countries that quantitatively limit imports from these countries, the governments of the exporting countries are given the right to allocate the quotas among their domestic producers. [10] In these cases foreign producers lobby their governments for the rents attached to the right to export. For example, under the Japanese voluntary export restraints on auto exports to the United States, the smaller auto producers in Japan have lobbied their government for a larger share of the export quotas.

Bhagwati and Srinivasan (1980) introduce the term 'revenue-seeking' to describe the situation in which economic agents lobby for a slice of the tariff revenue resulting from the adoption of protective tariffs. This case is somewhat different from the rent seeking analysed by Krueger (1974). When quantitative restrictions (QRs) are applied to all imports or just to imports of a single sector, the government must devise a system to allocate the rights to import (or export) among traders and producers. Since holders of rights to import specified amounts of a commodity subject to QRs can earn a premium by purchasing the commodity at a lower price than they sell it for, competition will arise among importers for these rights to import.

Under a tariff arrangement, the allocation of imports is carried out via the price system, with the tariff revenue usually going automatically into the public treasury in the same way as any tax revenue. Generally, neither customs officials nor any other government officials associated with the importation process have the authority to allocate the tariff proceeds among particular economic agents. The distribution of government revenues customarily involves a decision process by the legislature and chief executive that is only loosely related to their revenue-raising decisions. Consequently, the many different groups lobbying for government allocative decisions favourable to their interests usually do so without regard to any particular tax source.

One revenue situation that is likely to intensify competitive lobbying activity is a substantial rise in tax revenues that is unrelated to increased government-spending plans. This could come about, for example, because of an appreciable rise in protective tariffs on most imports. As Bhagwati and Srinivasan (1980) point out, various interest groups will then lobby government officials for a share of these extra revenues. However, when the protective tariff for only a particular industry is increased, the increment in tax revenue is likely to be too small to trigger increased lobbying activity aimed at obtaining a part of this extra revenue. The extra tariff proceeds tend to become part of the country's general tax revenues, and they are spent for purposes that do not require separate spending decisions by the legislature or chief executive.

Sometimes particular tax revenues are earmarked for specific distribution purposes. For example, state gasoline taxes are often regarded as user fees and only utilized for the maintenance and expansion of the highway system. Presumably, this arrangement is the consequence, at least in part, of lobbying by groups representing truckers and private automobile users.

Recently, Hufbauer and Rosen (1983) have proposed earmarking tariff revenues generated by escape clause tariffs to help the impacted domestic industry adjust to the changed comparative-cost conditions. Feenstra and Bhagwati (1981) have also analysed the effects of using tariff proceeds to increase the incomes of workers in protected industries and thereby influence the amount of tariff-seeking lobbying by these groups. However, as yet there does not seem to be much evidence that workers and capitalists in such industries have lobbied for these revenues or for the release of other existing revenues on the grounds that there has been a net increase in government revenues. They do, of course, often lobby for government assistance beyond the increase in their incomes due to increased tariffs, but this does not appear to be related to the increase in the government's tax revenues.

## 7   CONTROLLING RENT-SEEKING BEHAVIOUR

As the cost and benefit figures cited earlier indicate, the incentives for workers and capitalists in industries faced with injurious foreign competition in domestic or foreign markets to seek import protection or subsidization are extremely strong. Since the US government bears most of the investigatory costs, even relatively small industries find it worthwhile to petition for import relief through the various administrative channels where such agencies as the ITC and the Commerce Department determine the outcome of petitions for protection on the basis of criteria established by law or administrative regulation. Where small industries are at a distinct disadvantage, however, is in seeking protection via the political route. This involves bringing direct political pressure on the president and members of Congress so that the president will take the lead in negotiating with foreign countries such arrangements as voluntary export restraints and orderly marketing agreements. As Hufbauer and Rosen (1983) point out, only five US industries have been successful at this level: textiles and apparel, steel, automobiles, meat, and sugar. Collectively, these industries account for over 25 per cent of US imports.

In considering the decisions reached in the fifty-three import-relief cases on which the ITC has made findings since 1975, one can only conclude, I think, that protection via this route has been kept reasonably under control. Of these 53 cases the ITC determined that serious injury had occurred as the result of increased imports in 28 instances or 57 per cent of the total number. In addition, in 3 cases the vote of the commission was evenly split. Of these 31 cases sent to the president for final determination, import relief was granted in only 13 of the cases. In 6 other cases the president provided adjustment assistance to the workers, while for the remaining 12 he turned down assistance in any form. Thus, in only 13 of 53 cases, or 25 per cent of the total, did the industries alleging serious injury receive assistance in the form of higher tariffs or quotas.

The major part of the increase in protection in the United States has occurred not via administrative channels but as a consequence of industries exerting political pressure on elected officials, often, as in the auto case, after their petitions have been rejected by government agencies such as the ITC. Of course, no one would want to block the use of the political route, since the availability of this avenue of expression is essential for a democracy. Consequently, relying on such a solution as making lobbying too expensive for any industry to undertake is not appropriate. It is also important for a democracy that the full implications of protection on the economy as a whole be made known to political leaders and the general public. At the present time the ITC considers the effects of increased imports and of temporary import relief only on the workers and capitalists in the petitioning industries. The real income implications of increased protection on consumers or employment and trade in other sectors is ignored. When a case goes to the president, an interagency committee considers these effects, but this is not made available to the general public. Thus, when industries seek protection via the political route after they fail to obtain import relief through the ITC route, political officials and the general public tend to know about only one side of the case.

One suggestion for providing a more balanced economic evaluation of the ITC's recommendations to the president for increased tariffs or quotas is to require the commission also to include an evaluation of the probable economic effects of these protectionist recommendations. [11] This evaluation would include such economic effects as the likely magnitude of the price increases to final consumers on the products covered, the increased costs to other producers using the products as inputs, the expected employment changes in the protected industry as well as in sectors using the products as inputs, and the likelihood that the injured industry can become competitive again.

Just as the findings of the ITC with regard to injury are widely disseminated to political officials and the public through various media channels, their assessment of the probable economic effects would also become widely known. This would make it easier for public officials to render political decisions that take into account not only the welfare of workers and capitalists in the injured industry but the welfare of others affected by import protection.

## NOTES

1. *See*, for example, Baldwin (1976, 1982), Bhagwati (1980), Brock and Magee (1980), Findlay and Wellisz (1982) and Mayer (1983).
2. Jones (1971) also developed a two-product model with two sector-specific factors and one mobile factor but used it to analyse long-run trade issues. Earlier, Haberler (1936, ch. 12) outlined the effects of the existence of specific factors on a country's production possibilities curve.
3. Other properties of the model are that the production function for each of the two commodities is linear–homogeneous with declining marginal physical products for each factor, that the aggregate supply of labour is fixed and that perfect competition prevails.
4. The study in which Richardson (1982) participated found that three years after being permanently displaced by import competition, the average weekly wage of workers was only 92 per cent of their preseparation wage. Another study (Jacobson, 1978) indicated that between the third and sixth year after displacement, workers in such sectors as automobiles, steel, meat packing, aerospace and women's clothing earned about 15 per cent less than prior to displacement. Still another study (Neumann, 1979) places the wage reduction at about 20 per cent.
5. A skilled worker who shifts from one sector to the other is assumed to lose the first sector's skills by the time he acquires the other sector's unique skills.

6. For simplicity it is assumed that skilled and unskilled labour are perfect substitutes for each other in production in the same fixed proportion in each sector; for example, 1.5 unskilled workers equal 1 skilled worker. In the long run, the unskilled-labour productivity curves will shift up to the skilled-labour curves for the two sectors as the unskilled labour acquires the unique skills through learning by doing.

7. In the long run, as skilled workers in both sectors retire and are replaced by young unskilled workers, enough new workers will go into sector Z that the new long-run equilibrium will be where the $VMPL_{zs}$ curve intersects the new schedule of the value of the marginal productivity of labour in sector X, namely, the $VMPL_{xs}(P_x^1)$ curve.

8. Employing $L^0 L^1$ unskilled workers in the Z sector in addition to the $O_z L^0$ skilled workers drives down the marginal productivity of skilled workers to the point where it equals the marginal productivity of the unskilled workers, namely, $L^1 D$, multiplied by the assumed ratio for the productivity of a skilled worker compared with that of an unskilled worker, for example, $1.5 \times L^1 D$. The curve $VMPL'_{zs}$ indicates the marginal productivity of skilled labour in sector Z, given the employment of $O_z L^0$ of skilled labour and $L^0 L^1$ of unskilled labour in the sector.

9. On Figure 6.1 they gain in terms of X, since the proportion by which their wage in Z declines is less than the proportionate decline in the price of X. The reverse relationship is also possible.

10. Transferring the rents connected with the quotas to foreign governments serves as a form of compensation that makes it easier for these governments to accept quantitative limits on their exports.

11. The ITC is already required to carry out such an assessment when the president decides to undertake a tariff-modifying negotiation with other countries.

# REFERENCES

Adams, Walter and Joel Dirlam (1984), The trade laws and their enforcement by the International Trade Commission, In *Recent Issues and Initiatives in US Trade Policy*, ed. Robert E. Baldwin, NBER, Chicago: Conference Report, pp. 128–53.

Baldwin, Robert E. (1976), The political economy of postwar US trade policy, *The Bulletin* no. 4, New York: New York University, Graduate School of Business Administration.

———. (1982). The political economy of protectionism, In *Import Competition and Response*, ed. Jagdish Bhagwati, Chicago: University of Chicago Press, pp. 263–86.

Bhagwati, Jagdish (1980), Lobbying and welfare, *Journal of Public Economics*, 14: 355–63.

———. and T. N. Srinivasan (1980), Revenue-seeking: a generalization of the theory of tariffs, *Journal of Political Economy*, 88: 1069–87.

Brock, William A., and Stephen P. Magee (1980), Tariff formation in a democracy, In *Current Issues in Commercial Policy and Diplomacy*, ed. John Black and Brian Hindley, Papers of the 3rd Annual Conference of the International Economics Study Group, London: Macmillan, pp. 1–9.

Cairnes, John Elliot (1874), *Some Leading Principles of Political Economy—Newly Expounded.* London: Macmillan.

Feenstra, Robert C. and Jagdish N. Bhagwati (1982), Tariff-seeking and the efficient tariff, In *Import Competition and Response*, ed. Jadgish N. Bhagwati, Chicago: University of Chicago Press, pp. 245–58.

Findlay, Ronald E. and Stanislaw Wellisz (1982), Endogenous tariffs, the political economy of trade restrictions, and welfare, In *Import Competition and Response*, ed. Jagdish N. Bhagwati, Chicago: University of Chicago Press, pp. 223–34.

Haberler, Gottfried (1936), *The Theory of International Trade*, London: Hodge.

Hufbauer, Gary C. and Howard Rosen (1983), Managing comparative advantage, unpubl. paper.

Jackson, John H. (1984), Perspectives on the jurisprudence of international trade, *American Economic Review* 74: 277–81.

Jacobson, Louis S. (1978), Earnings losses of workers displaced from manufacturing industries, In *The Impact of International Trade and Investment on Employment*, ed. William G. Dewald, A Conference on the US Department of Labour Research Results. Washington pp. 87–98.

Jones, Ronald W. (1971) A three-factor model in theory, trade and history, In *Trade, Balance of Payments and Growth*, eds, J. N. Bhagwati, R. W. Jones, R. A. Mundell and J. Vanek, pp. 3–21.

Krueger, Anne O. (1974), The political economy of the rent-seeking society, *The American Economic Review* 64: 291–303.

Magee, Stephen P. (1980), Three simple tests of the Stolper–Samuelson Theorem, In *Issues in International Economics*, ed. Peter Oppenheimer, London: Oriel Press, pp. 138–55.

Mayer, Wolfgang (1974), Short-run and long-run equilibrium for a small open economy, *Journal of Political Economy* 82: 955–67.

——. (1983). *Endogenous Tariff Formation*, University of Cincinnati, mimeo.

Mussa, Michael (1974), Tariffs and the distribution of income: the importance of factor specificity, substitutability, and intensity in the short and long run, *Journal of Political Economy* 82: 1191–2043.

Neumann, George R. (1979), Adjustment assistance for trade-displaced workers, In *The New International Economic Order*, ed. David B. H. Denoon: A US Response, New York: New York University Press, pp. 109–40.

Richardson, J. David (1982), Trade adjustment assistance under the United States Trade Act of 1974—an analytical examination and worker survey, In *Import Competition and Response*, ed. Jagdish N. Bhagwati, Chicago: University of Chicago Press.

Stolper, Wolfgang F. and Paul A. Samuelson (1941), Protection and real wages, *Review of Economic Studies* 9: 58–73.

US Department of Commerce (1979), *Survey of Current Business* 59, No. 4: 51–72.

# 7 The Economics of the GATT*

As international trade in goods and services continues to expand at a considerably more rapid rate than the growth of world output, the institutional arrangements for maintaining order in international trading relations take on added significance. The main international organization established for this purpose, the GATT, was highly successful in the early post-World War II years not only in resolving international disputes but in facilitating significant tariff reductions by the industrial nations. However, since the mid 1950s and especially since the conclusion in 1967 of the Kennedy Round of trade negotiations, the influence of the GATT has declined. So-called 'voluntary' export constraints and 'orderly marketing agreements' covering trade in such items as footwear, steel and TV sets have been introduced entirely outside of the GATT framework. Such trade-distorting measures as domestic-production subsidies, government purchasing policies that favour domestic producers, and state trading on a non-commercial basis have also been used more extensively in recent years. Furthermore, the consultative and reporting roles of the GATT have diminished in importance.

Many had hoped that the decline in GATT's role would be reversed as a result of the Tokyo Round of trade negotiations. But it is now evident that, although some important improvements in behaviour codes have been made, these negotiations have not completely removed the danger of a breakdown in the international trading order through the continued introduction of trade-distorting measures. Given this possibility, it is important for economists and others to examine closely the economic and political basis of the various rules of GATT with a view towards again attempting to re-establish the basis of an open and stable international trading order.

* From Peter Oppenheimer (ed.) (1980), *Issues in International Economics*, Oxford International Symposia, Vol. V, London: Oriel Press, pp. 82–93.

# THE POLITICAL BASIS OF THE GATT

Economists tend to judge the rules of organizations like the GATT on the basis of whether they promote economic efficiency, growth and stability. Trade economists are somewhat ambivalent, however, as to whether it is world efficiency, growth and stability they wish to promote or only the economic welfare of their own country. Analysts of domestic issues by and large act as if income redistribution will be undertaken to offset any losses to particular income groups when there is a net gain to the community as a whole. Trade economists, on the other hand, cannot even pretend that redistribution among countries is likely to occur, and this may be the reason why they often adopt a nationalistic viewpoint.

Maximizing the collective economic welfare of individuals making up either a country or the world is, however, not the main policy objective of the GATT. The GATT is an international legal document whose primary purpose is to promote or protect certain political goals of nation-states. Economic factors influence these political goals, but to the extent that economic interests are promoted in GATT rules and procedures, it is mainly the interests of the more politically effective producers rather than of consumers. In the GATT, as in such other postwar economic organizations as the International Monetary Fund (IMF) and the World Bank, the broad objective is to help to maintain international political stability by establishing rules of 'good behaviour' as well as mechanisms for settling disputes.

Those who played the major role in shaping these agreements, especially the Americans, placed great importance on economic factors as the cause of World War II. These factors include the 1930s depression itself, the uncertainty about the international financial system, the burden of reparations payments and—what is of concern here—the many restrictions introduced on international trade. In the trade field, it was a policy act by the United States, namely the passage of the Smoot–Hawley Tariff Act of 1930, that initiated trade relations in the 1930s and worsened the trade contraction associated with the depression. To try to prevent this from again happening, Cordell Hull and his colleagues at the State Department pressed for an international trade organization that would facilitate the type of liberalizing negotiations held successfully under the US Trade Agreement Act and that would provide a set of rules minimizing the use of discriminatory measures, quantitative controls and other government trade-distorting policies. A broad agreement (the Havana Charter for an International Trade Organization) was proposed covering, in addition to traditional trade issues, commodity agreements, restrictive business practices and international investment, but the ITO was not approved by key governments and a more limited organization covering only trade matters (the GATT) emerged from the discussions.


# THE ECONOMIC AND POLITICAL RATIONALE FOR REDUCING TRADE DISTORTIONS

The tariff-cutting mechanism and safeguards rule of GATT illustrate the relationships between political and economic objectives in this agreement. On the basis of the type of first-best economics usually taught introductory students, a country should unilaterally reduce its import duties, since this will increase its economic welfare. The possibility that the country's terms of trade might deteriorate so much as a result of the cuts that the nation's net welfare in fact declines is mentioned but this is usually not dwelt upon very long, since it raises the question as to why tariff increases are not being recommended. However, if pressed on this latter point, economists generally argue that any potential terms-of-trade gains are likely to be lost through retaliation, though Harry Johnson (1953–4) pointed out long ago that this is not necessarily true and economists are vague on the politics of retaliation. Reciprocal tariff cutting is thus presented as a process by which all the participants can obtain the kind of gains possible to any one country facing fixed terms of trade, and the troublesome issue of choosing between a nation's welfare and world welfare is avoided. Still another economic argument used to support reciprocal duty reductions is that, compared with unilateral reductions, these cuts have less unfavourable effects on such macro-economic variables as aggregate employment and the balance-of-payments or exchange rates.

Even if the above reasoning of trade economists is valid in most cases, it seems to be more the result of a happy coincidence of economic and political objectives than of foresight and deliberate choice by the founders of GATT. They viewed tariffs, especially the high ones existing at the end of World War II, as trade barriers that antagonize foreign producers and lead to big-power economic domination of small countries for marketing purposes as well as to coalitions of the larger powers. Such developments, in turn, increase the possibilities of international political instability and its ultimate manifestation, military conflict. The framers of the GATT believed that cutting duties multilaterally would reduce these international political tensions without significantly disturbing existing power relationships. However, where these power relationships were very unequal, as was the case between the developed and developing countries or between the United States and the other industrial countries at the end of World War II, they were prepared to not insist upon reciprocity.

Since the reduction of international political tension is a public good, its provision in society involves the free-rider problem. All wish to enjoy greater international political stability but hope to get others to pay the costs involved in obtaining it. Moreover, except when relations among nations are strained, the benefits of an alleged marginal improvement in political stability are generally perceived to be very small by any one individual, as are the economic benefits from reciprocal tariff reductions. Because of this and the fact that political action involves costs, active domestic support for reciprocal tariff cutting by the gainers from this policy tends to be weak, whereas opposition can be very strong from import-competing industries that fear significant producer surplus losses as duties are cut. Thus, while there may be unambiguous political and economic gains for individual nations as a whole, the losers may be able to block the achievement of these gains through active political opposition. The framers of GATT attempted to prevent this by permitting exceptions in any tariff-cutting negotiations and by allowing the withdrawal under Article XIX of tariff concessions previously granted. They recognized, in other words, the pressure-group nature of international economic policymaking and established a safeguards rule to moderate the major source of opposition to trade liberalization.

On the basis of economic efficiency criteria, taxes and subsidies on imports and exports all have the same type of distorting effect. The rate of transformation between exports and imports is equal in production and consumption but differs from the transformation rate in international exchange. Consequently, in terms of the objective of an efficient allocation of world resources, one would expect the GATT to have one statement recommending the elimination of all direct trade taxes and subsidies, but this is not the case. Export subsidies are banned outright as of a particular date (Article XVI), while import and export taxes are to be reduced only gradually. No mention at all of import subsidies is made in either the GATT or the ITO.

The rationale for these differences rests on the political nature of the GATT and the economic forces that shape political objectives. The 1930s experience with export subsidies as well as with competitive devaluation, which has the effect of a general export subsidy and import surcharge, apparently convinced the GATT founders that export subsidies exacerbate international tensions and should be eliminated. Though consumers in the importing country gain from export subsidization by other nations, domestic-producer groups in the importing countries are forced to curtail output and incur a producer surplus loss. The greater ability of the latter groups to make their views the determining ones in national policy is what increases the likelihood of increased international tensions as various counter-restrictions or subsidies are urged on the government of the country receiving the subsidized goods. While eliminating export subsidies may improve international relations, their removal can also cause serious injury in the subsidized industries, much as tariff reductions can. However, the political power of domestic producers to insulate themselves from possible injury-causing actions by their government is much less when the government's actions affect the income they earn in foreign markets in contrast to their earnings based on domestic sales. The view that domestic producers are somehow more entitled to domestic than foreign markets is still widely held by the general public. Thus, the founders of GATT did not implement their political objective with regard to export subsidies gradually (as with tariffs); they were banned outright.

Export taxes, like tariffs, are permitted under the GATT, although the preamble of the agreement implies that they are to be reduced along with tariffs through trade negotiations. The GATT founders were less concerned over the political dangers associated with controls over exports than over imports. In part this was probably due to a recognition that the political power of domestic producers, who tend to be hurt by export taxes, acts as a strong restraining force on the imposition of such taxes. The political danger from these taxes arises mainly because of the antagonism of foreign producers who use taxed products as intermediate production inputs and therefore are hurt by their increased cost. At the time GATT was established, however, the great dependence of many raw material suppliers on the developed industrial nations made the likelihood of significant price-increasing export taxes much less than at the present time.

Interestingly, the general prohibition of quantitative restrictions under GATT rules is lifted for exports when critical domestic shortages arise. The quantitative controls over exports are to be administered in a non-discriminatory manner, however. This GATT rule recognizes that the sharp price increases often associated with domestic shortages can cause consumers to modify their usually passive role on trade matters and exercise their basically greater political strength over both local producers of the products in short supply and those concerned with the foreign-policy implications of supply restrictions.

While export subsidies are prohibited and warnings raised about possible adverse effects of domestic subsidies, no mention of import subsidies is made in the GATT. These do occasionally occur, however, not directly but in the form of government purchases of essential commodities that are then resold to domestic consumers at lower prices than paid by the government. Again, the political power of domestic producers of substitute goods holds such subsidies to a minimum. Because of this and the fact that the income benefits to foreign producers from the subsidies minimize any international tension-creating aspects of this trade distortion, the framers of the rules of GATT apparently believed any political problems arising from the use of import subsidies would be *de minimus*.

## SELECTIVE DOMESTIC TAXES AND SUBSIDIES

How selective indirect taxes versus selective subsidies are handled in the GATT further illustrates the asymmetrical economic features of the existing code of 'good' international behaviour. For indirect taxes, such as an excise tax on a particular commodity, the destination principle of taxation is followed; the product bears the tax in the country where it is destined for use. Therefore, the excise tax is levied on imports and rebated on exports. For selective subsidies, such as a production subsidy on a particular product, the origin principle of taxation is adopted. Since this means that the subsidy applies only to goods produced in the subsidizing country, imports do not receive the subsidy, but exports do.

Under the simplifying assumption of fixed terms of trade, adopting the destination principle for indirect taxes has the effect of leaving domestic production unchanged but decreasing foreign purchases when the product is imported and increasing foreign sales when it is exported. The price domestic consumers pay for the product rises by the amount of the tax. On the other hand, following the origin principle when a production subsidy is introduced has the effect of increasing the production of the subsidized good and either increasing exports or reducing imports. The domestic price of the subsidized product remains unchanged from its free-trade level. If the origin rather than destination principle is followed in the tax case, the domestic price of the good remains unchanged, while domestic production declines. Similarly, in the subsidy case using the destination rather than origin principle results in a lower price for consumers but no change in the output of the subsidized product.

These various relationships are shown in Figure 7.1. Let the fixed terms of trade be indicated by the slope of the line $d_s D_t$, production by the point $P$ (fixed factor supplies and competitive conditions are assumed), and free-trade consumption by the points $F$ and $f$ depending upon whether the Y good is exported or imported, respectively. If a production tax is imposed on the Y good and the destination principle is followed, passing the tax on to consumers will reduce the domestic consumption of Y but this decline will be matched by either an equal increase in exports or decrease in imports. The points $D_t$ and $d_t$ indicate

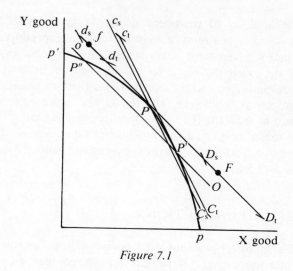

*Figure 7.1*

the consumption bundles in the export and import cases and the reciprocal of the slope of the line through these points the price of Y in terms of X. Under the origin principle where only domestically produced Y is taxed, production shifts to $P'$ and consumption to either $O$ or $o$, depending upon whether Y is exported or imported. The price of Y remains unchanged.

The same figure can be used to depict the case where the domestic production of Y is subsidized and either the origin or destination principle is followed. If Y is subsidized without any rebate on exports or subsidy of imports (the origin principle), the domestic production of Y will shift to $P''$ and consumption change to $O$ in the export case or $o$ in the import case. On the other hand, if the subsidy is rebated at the border for exports and given to imports of the item (the destination principle), the production point would remain at $P$ and the consumption points be $D_s$ or $d_s$, respectively.

It should be noted that the increase in exports (or reduction in imports) can be just as large when Y is taxed and the destination principle is followed as when Y is subsidized and the origin principle used. It should also be pointed out that, from the viewpoint of the nation's total welfare, nothing can be said about the superiority of the origin versus destination principle without detailed knowledge about the country's tastes and cost conditions. Adjustments at the border in both the selective indirect tax and subsidy cases merely convert a production inefficiency into a consumption inefficiency. In second-best terms, such an international adjustment does not get at the basic domestic reason for the initial inefficiency.

The differential GATT treatment at the border of goods affected by taxes and subsidies is simply a by-product of the producer bias that affects so many government interventions into domestic markets. The purpose of the excise tax is not to tax domestic production but to tax domestic consumption, and the use of the destination principle makes it a consumption tax. Collecting the tax at the manufacturing stage is merely aimed at reducing the costs of collection. Similarly, the purpose of selective subsidies is usually to subsidize the domestic production of a product and not the domestic consumption of the good. Thus, the origin principle is adopted.

## COUNTERVAILING ACTIONS

As noted above, under present GATT border adjustment rules, domestic subsidies increase exports or reduce imports compared to what they would be under free-trade conditions. Should the increase in exports cause or threaten material injury to an established industry in the importing country, this country can impose a countervailing duty under Article VI of the GATT equal to the subsidy granted. Under conditions of an infinitely elastic foreign demand for the product, the foreign duty will fall entirely upon the subsidizing country and the price its producers receive will fall by the duty. The situation is depicted in Figure 7.1 with the line $c_s C_s$. The cost of producing Y exclusive of the subsidy falls from the reciprocal of the slope of the production possibilities curve at $P''$ to the reciprocal of its slope at $P$, with production shifting to the latter point and consumption to $C_s$. The price received by the country for Y (and paid by its consumers) will equal the reciprocal of the slope of the line $c_s C_s$. As is evident from the figure, the countervailing duty restores exports to their free-trade level only by chance; exports after the duty can be greater or less than their free-trade level. If the subsidizing country's demand for the import good is inelastic (i.e., the supply curve of the export good is backward bending), the countervailing duty will have the effect of increasing the country's exports above their subsidized level.

There is no GATT provision for countervailing against domestic subsidies on imported products, but injury to foreign exporters could be just as substantial in this situation as in the export-subsidy case. The counterpart of permitting a levy in the export case would be to allow the exporting country to introduce a countervailing subsidy on exports equal to the subsidy granted domestic producers abroad. The effect in Figure 7.1 would be to shift output in the country subsidizing production from $P''$ to $P$ and consumption from $o$ to $c_s$. The apparent rationale for not permitting this type of countervailing action is, as mentioned earlier, that the producer bias of GATT extends only to domestic markets. Actions are permitted to counter foreign measures that cause injury to domestic producers as a result of increased imports but are not allowed when the injury is the consequence of a loss of export markets.

For consistency, similar countervailing actions to those in the subsidy case might also be permitted for indirect taxes. Since the use of the destination principle increases exports above (or imports below) their free-trade level, countervailing action by foreigners might be allowed. Specifically, in the export case a duty equal to the rebated tax, or, in the import situation, an export subsidy equal to the border tax might be permitted. In Figure 7.1 the line $c_t C_t$ would depict this case, with $P'$ being the production point and $C_t$ and $c_t$ the final consumption points in the export and import cases respectively.

As in the case of the border adjustments analysed earlier, none of the countervailing actions discussed above entirely offset the initial Pareto inefficiency. Again, this inefficiency is caused by a domestic policy and cannot be completely eliminated by an international measure.


## CONCLUSIONS

It is hoped that the preceding discussion is sufficient to indicate the rather unsatisfactory nature of the GATT in terms of the behaviour standards generally applied by economists. The objectives of those who established the organization were mainly political, and they were quite willing to slant the rules in favour of a particular domestic pressure group, producers, to help gain acceptance of their broad trade-liberalizing recommendations.

The view that trade-distorting measures can be an important source of increased international tension still seems to be valid today. However, levels of tariffs, the main distortion that the founders of the GATT focused on, are currently low enough in the industrial nations on most imported items to no longer be a significant source of irritation to exporting countries. Instead of tariffs, quantitative import controls now stand as the major type of import barrier, especially against the exports of developing countries. Many of these countries are rapidly increasing their industrial potential, and they are increasingly frustrated by the unwillingness of the established industrial nations to open up certain markets for simply produced manufactures. This leads to the very form of international tension that the founders of GATT wished to prevent. Similarly, the growing shortage of certain key raw materials, coupled with the greater ability and willingness of developing countries to restrict exports of these items, is increasing the dissatisfaction of the older industrial economies towards the developing nations. Disputes among industrial countries, especially with regard to the trade implications of various domestic aids, will occasionally be important, but the main area of concern in the foreseeable future for trade policy and international political relations is North–South trade.

The implications of this are that the GATT should focus both on gradually dismantling existing quantitative restrictions in the industrial countries on products of potential export interest to the developing nations and on establishing mechanisms to assure the developed nations that their industrial activity cannot suddenly be disrupted seriously by export-restriction actions by raw material suppliers. Unfortunately, the recent Tokyo Round of trade negotiations made very little progress in either of these crucial areas.

Since producers (including workers) are more likely to incur significant reductions in real income as a result of changes in trade than are consumers, there is some justification for the producer bias of the GATT on income distribution grounds. However, assistance to producers should only be temporary and occur only when they are significantly injured. Moreover, ideally, aid should be provided in a manner that does not distort optimum production and exchange relationships. Given the apparent inability of most countries to provide aid of this sort promptly, temporary trade-distorting measures may be justifiable as a second-best way of furnishing producer assistance. The existing safeguard provisions of the GATT (Article XIX), which permit a temporary increase in duties to help counter serious injury due to increased imports arising from free-market forces, illustrate the use of this principle. Such duty increases should, however, be tied to substantive domestic adjustment measures, should be carefully monitored by the GATT, and should not be allowed when import increases are related to macroeconomic factors and thus better handled by using macroeconomic tools. Carrying this principle over to a country's export-competing industries would imply that, if serious injury occurred in one of these sectors as a result of sudden export losses related to free-market, microeconomic factors abroad, temporary export subsidies might also be permitted. Efforts would continue to eliminate all the various types of direct trade distortions, but temporary assistance in the form of counter-trade-distorting measures would be allowed until more satisfactory domestic adjustment policies are generally accepted.

Temporary assistance to producers also seems to be the proper way to deal with domestic actions by governments that have unfavourable trade effects. Progress in directly negotiating reductions in the distorting effects of the measures is sometimes possible, but for the foreseeable future, governments are likely to continue to insist they be given a free hand to deal with matters they consider to be mainly internal in nature. Selective indirect taxes and production subsidies fit into this category of policies. Under the approach just outlined and where existing border adjustment rules are being followed, an import-competing industry seriously injured by increased imports, either diverted from the internal market of another country that increases its indirect taxes on the industry's product or resulting from the subsidization of domestic production by the foreign country, would be permitted to impose a temporary tax on the imported goods. Similarly, an export industry injured as a consequence of an increase abroad in indirect taxes on its product or in production subsidies might be allowed to introduce temporary countervailing export subsidies.

The principle could be applied in other international trading relationships as well as, for example, in dealings with state-owned or-controlled enterprises or with private industries engaged in dumping. It is based on the notion that changes in a country's imports or exports of selective products (whether these are due to private microeconomic market forces or selective government policies that distort these forces) that are so rapid and extensive as to cause significant injury to foreign industries do not represent 'good' international behaviour in terms of promoting harmonious international relations. Under careful international supervision, a country with an injured industry would be permitted to introduce on a selective basis temporary trade measures to help offset the injury and permit smoother adjustments in their economic structures. A by-product of this approach is that GATT rules would be more balanced in their treatment of producers and consumers. For example, in cases in which foreign countries are prepared to subsidize more or less indefinitely domestic production that is exported, consumers in other countries would not be prevented by permanent countervailing duties from benefiting from the lower price of the commodity. On the other hand, export industries that are injured through trade changes just as seriously as import-competing industries would qualify for possible assistance in the way import-competing sectors now do.

# REFERENCES

Johnson, Harry G. (1953–4), Optimum tariffs and retaliation, *Review of Economic Studies* XXI (2): 142–53.

# 8 The Case against Infant-Industry Tariff Protection*

## 1

The classical infant-industry argument for protection has long been regarded by economists as the major 'theoretically valid' exception to the case for worldwide free trade.[1] What controversy there is over the concept tends to centre not on analytical issues but rather on empirical matters. Some writers—for example, Myrdal (1957, pp. 96–7) and Rosenstein-Rodan (1963)—maintain that the economic conditions on which the case is based apply to most manufacturing industries in LDCs, and they believe, therefore, that general protective measures are justified in these economies. Others—for example, Haberler (1936, pp. 281–5) and Meier (1964, pp. 302–3)—are more sceptical about the pervasiveness of these conditions and stress the high costs of making incorrect decisions. Unfortunately, the views of both groups are based largely on casual empiricism. Careful, detailed investigations of the empirical issues involved in the infant-industry case have been rare.[2]

The purpose of this note is not to discuss these empirical matters but rather to suggest that economists have too readily accepted the theoretical arguments set forth for infant-industry protection. I will not deny that there are unique factors affecting new industries that may require market intervention by public authorities if a socially efficient allocation of resources is to be achieved. What I will question is the effectiveness of tariffs in accomplishing this result. In particular, I will argue that for some of the main conditions cited as warranting temporary tariffs, protection may well either decrease social welfare or at least fail to achieve the socially optimal allocation of resources in new industries that is the purpose of the duty.

Other writers have also recently argued that the infant-industry dogma has less generality than commonly claimed. Kemp (1960) and Grubel (1966) have pointed out, for example, that where acquired skills and

---

* From *Journal of Political Economy* Vol 77, no. 3 (May/June 1969): 295–305.

knowledge are 'specific' to a firm, there is no need for tariff protection as a means of encouraging socially justifiable investment in human resources. Johnson (1965) has emphasized that infant-industry protection, like other protective measures designed to correct domestic distortions, causes a relative welfare loss to consumers by raising the domestic price of the imported good above its world level.[3] The point stressed here relates to the production side. Not only is a consumption loss associated with protection but, as a general principle, one cannot be sure that a temporary tariff will result in the optimum increase in production, or, indeed, in any increase at all in the production-possibility curve.

Four principal infant-industry cases will be considered in the following sections. Part 2 examines the case for protection based upon the point that the acquisition of knowledge involves costs, yet that knowledge is not appropriable by the individual firm. The familiar argument that infant-industry protection is needed because costs associated with on-the-job training cannot be recouped by the training firm is evaluated in part 3. The existence of static and reversible externalities as a justification for temporary protection is discussed in part 4. This part also considers the argument for protection that imperfect information leads to systematic overestimates of investment risks or of the unpleasantness of working in particular industries. In all four cases I conclude that temporary protection by means of an import duty on the product of the industry is not likely to achieve the goal of a more efficient allocation of resources in production.

2

The essential point stressed by infant-industry proponents since Hamilton (1971) and List (1856) first wrote on the subject is that production costs for newly established industries within a country are likely to be initially higher than for well-established foreign producers of the same line, who have greater experience and higher skill levels. Over time, new producers become 'educated to the level of those with whom the processes are traditional' (Mill, 1909, p. 92) and their cost curves decline. The infant-industry argument states that during the temporary period when domestic costs in an industry are above the product's import price, a tariff is a socially desirable method of financing the investment in human resources needed to compete with foreign producers.

The first point to note about this statement is that, as Meade (1955, p. 256) has noted, the existence during early stages of production experience of higher costs than those of foreign competitors is, by itself, insufficient justification for tariff protection on grounds of economic efficiency. If, after the learning period, unit costs in an industry are enough lower than those during its early production stages to yield a discounted surplus of revenues over costs (and therefore indicate a comparative advantage for the country in the particular line), it would be possible for firms in the industry to raise sufficient funds in the capital market to cover their initial excess of outlays over receipts.[4] These circumstances are no different from those in which firms go to the capital market for funds to cover the excess of expenditures over revenues incurred during their early stages because of the need to purchase indivisible units of physical capital.

As Meade (1955, p. 256) also pointed out, the key argument on which the infant-industry case must rest relates to the technological externalities frequently associated with the learning process. Consider the matter of acquiring the technological knowledge needed to compete effectively with foreign producers.[5] An entrepreneur who incurs costs in order to discover the best way to produce a particular product may face the problem that this information becomes freely available to potential competitors who can utilize it at the same time that the initial firm does. Competition then either pushes up factor prices or drives the product's price down to a point where the initial firm is unable to recover its total costs, including the sum spent on obtaining the knowledge—assuming its other costs are the same as those for competing firms entering the field. Because of this type of response, individual entrepreneurs will be reluctant to invest in knowledge acquisition unless they are sure they can easily prevent others from obtaining the knowledge or can reap a high enough reward during the time it takes others to copy them. Investments in knowledge that are profitable from a social point of view may, therefore, not be undertaken in the economy.

For many types of knowledge acquisition no externality problem exists, since entrepreneurs are able to keep their knowledge about production or markets from their competitors. Thus they are able to reap exclusively the profit benefits of their investments in securing knowledge. Similarly, in industries in which there are significant economies of scale in relation to the size of the market and therefore a small number of firms, interfirm negotiations are likely to result in arrangements that offset the externality problem (see Coase, 1960; Buchanan and Stubblebine, 1962). Nevertheless, cases in which there are many firms and knowledge acquired by one entrepreneur becomes freely available—or available at a nominal cost—to other entrepreneurs cannot be ruled out as unlikely to be numerous or significant. The instances where these conditions hold could result in a significant divergence between private and social benefits.

A protective duty is, however, no guarantee that individual entrepreneurs will undertake greater investments in acquiring technological knowledge. A duty raises the domestic price of a product and, from the viewpoint of the domestic industry as a whole, makes some investments in knowledge more profitable. But the individual entrepreneur still faces the same externality problem as before, namely, the risk that other firms in the same industry will copy, without cost to themselves, any new technology discovered by the firm and will then drive the product's price or factor prices to levels at which the initial firm will be unable to recover the costs of acquiring the knowledge. If there were always some technologically fixed time lag between the introduction of a new, cheaper production technique and the changes in product or factor prices caused by the entry of the firms who freely copied the new production method, a duty would operate to make investment in knowledge acquisition more profitable for an individual firm in an industry. But, to make a point too often ignored in such discussions, the speed with which firms respond to market opportunities is a function of the level of profit prospects. A duty will make it worthwhile for firms to incur the costs of acquiring the knowledge discovered by other firms (if it is not completely free) faster and also to move into production more rapidly and with greater output rates (see Alchian, 1959). Setting the duty so high that both initial current production costs and the direct costs of acquiring technological knowledge can be covered from current receipts also will be ineffective. Since production under existing socially inefficient technology will be made profitable, firms that make no attempt to discover better productive techniques will enter the industry and drive out of business any firms that spend extra sums on knowledge acquisition. Thus, unless the rate of entry of new firms is relatively unresponsive to the level of profit rates of existing producers, there is no reason to assume as a general rule that any single firm will be more successful in recouping its investment in knowledge with a high duty than with none at all. A duty tends merely to encourage socially inefficient production as long as the state is willing to provide protection. A production subsidy on an industry-wide basis will have the same effect. What is needed, of course, is a subsidy to the initial entrants into the industry for discovering better productive techniques.

Only if during the period of knowledge acquisition there are no costs beyond those needed for efficient production under existing techniques would a tariff clearly accomplish its purpose—improving the long-run allocation of resources.[6] Then any firm considering the possibility of initiating domestic production in the industry need not be concerned with competition from subsequent entrants into the field who do not have to incur learning costs. But learning through experience does involve direct costs for any firm. Unless a firm experiments on a random basis—a procedure that will not bring about the consistent decline in costs postulated under the infant-industry argument—it will be necessary for management to devote resources to analysing previous performance before evaluating new productive practices. These are resources that could have been used to increase output and thus lower unit costs under existing production techniques. Consequently, as long as these learning-by-experience costs are greater than what other firms must pay to acquire the knowledge, it cannot be assumed as a general rule that firms will be prepared to incur the initial direct-learning costs even if the government imposes a tariff on the product. On the other hand, if the costs of learning by experience are actually less than the costs of acquiring known technology in the industry, all firms will follow the learn-by-experience route. A duty is still not needed in this case, since firms can borrow funds to tide them over the period during which their costs are not competitive with those of well-established foreign firms.

In many instances, the relationship among the costs of learning, the ease with which potential competitors can take advantage of newly discovered knowledge, and the benefits from this knowledge may be such that individual firms need not be concerned with recovering their learning costs. The point is that when the technological spillover flows from one firm to other firms in the same industry, protection of the entire industry—including new entrants— cannot be counted upon to induce firms to incur the volume of learning costs needed either to achieve a social optimum or to gain the knowledge possessed by foreign competitors.[7]

Recent writers on externalities have emphasized the same point in more general terms. They have shown that in order to achieve optimality when technological externalities exist, it is not enough merely to place taxes or subsidies on an industry's output. First, as Plott (1966) illustrates with the standard smoke-diseconomy case, this type of corrective effort may actually reduce welfare. What is needed is a tax on smoke output or on the resource input from which smoke is generated. This example corresponds to the case discussed above in which an infant-industry tariff reduces welfare by being ineffective in shifting a country's production-possibility curve outward, yet causing a consumption loss due to the rise in the price of the imported good above its world level.[8] Moreover, as Turvey (1963), Buchanan (1966) and Plott (1966) have noted, even if a tax is effective in raising welfare, it may not lead to the optimum set of production techniques. Specific taxes or subsidies directed toward particular types of inputs—for example, in the infant-industry case, toward research activities—may be necessary to achieve this goal. In the infant-industry context, this means that a tariff is a second-best solution not only because of its consumption effects but also, even under the best of conditions, because of its effects on production.

3

Another frequently cited example of technological spillover that creates a divergence between the private and social rates of return on investment concerns on-the-job training. If—so the argument goes—a firm could count on its workers to remain with it after they have been provided with on-the-job training, the firm could incur the costs of training and recoup them later by paying the workers wages just enough below their subsequently higher marginal productivity to cover these costs.[9] But workers in a free-market economy are not slaves, and they will be bid away by new firms after their training period if they receive less than their marginal productivity. Because of this ownership 'externality' (that is, a divorce of scarcity from effective ownership), it is argued that temporary protection is justified.

Kemp (1960) has already noted an important qualification of this argument. If the learning process is internal or 'specific' to the firm in the sense that the skills and experience acquired are not useful to other firms, then there are no economic-efficiency grounds for government intervention. Each firm can borrow funds to finance the costs of training and recoup these outlays by paying slightly less than the subsequent marginal productivity of the workers. The workers are still being paid at least as much as they can earn in alternative employments, and they will not leave.

But what if the skills are not restricted to the particular firm providing the training but can be used by potential competitors in the industry? Without government intervention, firms will still furnish on-the-job training, and thus a socially optimal resource allocation will be achieved. Although no firm will finance on-the-job training, the workers will. It is the workers who will benefit over their working lives from this on-the-job training, and it will be in their interest to pay for its cost. They can, for example, work during the training period at a wage rate low enough that the firm's labour costs are not initially higher than foreign competitors' (see Grubel, 1966; Becker, 1964). Alternatively, they can borrow on the capital market to tide them over this low-income period or even pay the firm with these borrowed funds to provide on-the-job training. This will be the rational course for workers to follow (and optimal for the economy) as long as the present value of their net income stream over their working life is greater with the training than under any other income alternatives.

If, for some reason, such as a lack of knowledge of earning opportunities, workers do not bear the costs of their own training, a protective tariff still cannot be counted on to induce firms to pay for these training costs.[10] Competition from existing firms in the industry as well as from potential entrants will force firms to pay workers their marginal productivity both during and after their training period. Consequently, no firm undertaking the costs of training will be able to recoup them. All that a tariff can do is raise the price of the product high enough that production is profitable without training the workers. This merely creates an inefficient industry in the country.

4

Static externalities can also result in divergences between private and social returns. A traditional example of such spillover effects is the increase in honey production resulting from an increase in the production of apples (and apple blossoms) near the location of beehives. How significant these sorts of spillovers are in practice is not clear. Most writers (for example, Scitovsky, 1954) do not regard them as very important. In any event, they do not constitute grounds for infant-industry protection. The infant-industry argument is a case for temporary protection, whereas duties justified because of reversible static economies will be needed on a continuing basis.

Although static externalities are now generally treated as quite separate grounds for protection from those included under the infant-industry case, the same is not true for market imperfections. Popular usage suggests that the infant-industry case covers any grounds for *temporary* protection and not just those that are unique to infant industries. Thus, for example, monopolistic factor prices could make the establishment of a new industry privately unprofitable, although it would be socially beneficial. A temporary tariff can, under these conditions, move resources into the infant industry and thereby improve welfare levels in the country. Monopolistic factor markets can, of course, block socially desirable factor movements not only in new industries but also in well-established productive lines as an economy grows and taste patterns shift. Because this type of market distortion is by no means unique to new industries, it would seem more logical to consider the existence of monopolistic practices apart from the infant-industry argument for justifying tariff protection. If it is not treated separately, authors should at least note that the argument covers both new and old industries.

As Kafka (1962) pointed out, however, there is one type of market imperfection that tends to be particularly applicable to infant industries. In this situation a lack of knowledge about an industry causes investors to overestimate the risks of investing in the industry and causes workers to overrate the unpleasantness of moving into this line of production.[11] Whether a tariff will be effective in compensating for these imperfections depends on whether there are costs involved in knowledge acquisition other than those associated with current production, and whether the knowledge that is acquired becomes freely available to others.

Suppose, for example, that a potential entrant into a new industry, if it could provide potential investors with a detailed market analysis of the industry, could borrow funds from investors at a rate that would make the project socially profitable. Should this information become freely available to other investors and potential competitors, however, the initial firm might not be able to recoup the cost of making the market study. As in the earlier cases dealing with acquiring technological knowledge or training labour, under these circumstances the firm will not finance the cost of the study and a socially beneficial industry will not be established. Suppose also that, in the absence of this market information, investors will insist on such high interest charges that the investment will not be privately profitable. A tariff on the industry's product can overcome this unprofitability and enable firms to pay the high interest rates demanded by investors.

If this high return over a period of time is all that is needed for investors to acquire sufficient knowledge about the industry for the lending rate to be bid down to a rate reflecting actual risk levels in the industry, a temporary tariff may be socially desirable. But, while some information about earning prospects is likely to be conveyed to investors by their payments experience, it is doubtful if the full information that is socially profitable in terms of investment in knowledge acquisition will ever be conveyed to them simply by this sort of costless experience. The mere fact of tariff protection will make it difficult for investors to infer from their payments experience that they are overestimating investment risks in the industry. If this is so and the spillover problem also exists when outlays to obtain information are made, a temporary tariff cannot be relied on to move production in the infant industry to a socially optimal level. [12] Direct subsidies to pay for the costs of knowledge acquisition will be needed. The same general point holds for providing information about working conditions to employees in a new industry. It is a gross oversimplification of the nature of the learning process to assume that all the information that is socially justifiable in terms of the return on knowledge-producing investment will eventually be provided simply by experience. Consequently, it cannot be assumed as a general rule that a tariff will be an effective device in enabling investors or workers to obtain the information needed for a socially efficient use of their factor services.

5

If the infant-industry argument for tariff protection is worthy of its reputation as the major exception to the free-trade case, it should be possible to present a clear analytical case, based on well-known and generally accepted empirical relationships unique to infant industries, for the general desirability and effectiveness of protective duties in these industries. The contention of this paper is that such a case cannot be made.

The infant-industry case rests on the notion that a freely functioning price system will—in the absence of temporary duties—fail to bring about socially optimal levels of training, knowledge and factor endowment in new industries. The main difficulty usually cited is the technological-spillover effects associated with the learning process. Learning involves costs; yet the knowledge acquired frequently becomes freely available to those who are potential competitors. The importance of these spillovers is not denied here: what is argued is that a duty cannot be relied on to correct for these externalities and to achieve an optimal learning level. When learning involves costs other than those needed for efficient production with existing techniques and skills, as in the case of acquiring technological knowledge or training labour, a tariff may not compensate for the spillover problem at all. More generally, even though some knowledge can be obtained by production experience alone, it is highly unlikely that the socially optimal knowledge and training levels are acquired without some direct outlays for knowledge acquisition. When the technological-spillover problem is present, imposing tariffs is no guarantee that these socially desirable kinds of expenditures will be made. What is needed is a direct subsidy devoted to knowledge acquisition.

Technological externalities, however, may not be the source of the difficulty in obtaining an optimal allocation of resources (including resources devoted to knowledge acquisition); a lack of knowledge or monopolistic prices for inputs may be the cause of the economic inefficiency. Undoubtedly, a tariff-induced move of productive factors into new industries is sometimes sufficient for these factors to acquire the knowledge that will make the duty unnecessary at a later date. But there would also seem to be many cases in which the knowledge that must be acquired to make the tariff subsequently unnecessary involves outlays in addition to current production costs and also becomes freely available to others. Under these circumstances, protective duties are likely either to fail completely in achieving their purpose or else to fail in directing sufficient resources into infant industries to achieve a social optimum. As far as monopolistic factor markets are concerned, it appears that these are as important impediments to efficient resource allocation in established industries as in infant industries. It would seem more logical, therefore, from a pedagogical point of view, to consider this as a protectionist argument separate from the infant-industry case. In short, not only do infant-industry duties distort consumption—as do all duties—but they may fail to achieve a socially efficient allocation of productive resources in new industries and may even result in a decrease in social welfare. What is required to handle the special problems of infant industries is a much more direct and selective policy measure than non-discriminatory import duties.

## ACKNOWLEDGEMENTS

I am especially grateful to W.M. Corden, Gottfried Haberler, Harry Johnson, Robert Mundell, Theodore Morgan, and Burton Weisbrod for valuable comments.

## NOTES

1. This paper deals with the traditional 'infant-industry' dogma associated with such writers as List, Hamilton, Bastable and Mill in contrast to modern arguments for 'infant-economy' protection based on the work of such writers as Rosenstein-Rodan, Scitovsky and Dobb. *See* Grubel (1966) for a comprehensive analysis of the differences between the modern and traditional infant-industry arguments.
2. Taussig's (1915) work still stands as the classic but inconclusive empirical study of the subject.
3. The consumption loss referred to by Johnson (1965) can be prevented by subsidizing domestic production rather than taxing imports.
4. The case in which the existence of imperfect capital markets prevents this type of response is considered in part 4.
5. Although it may be possible to acquire the basic technology for a new industry from foreign producers at little cost, it usually is necessary to modify this technology somewhat before production under domestic conditions has a chance of competing successfully with foreign production.
6. In supporting the use of tariffs in the learning-by-experience case, Meade (1955, pp. 270–1) and Kemp (1960) both seem to be making this assumption. At one point in his analysis Meade (1955, pp. 256–7) does present an example in which knowledge acquisition involves costs beyond those needed for efficient current production, and at that point he states that a temporary subsidy to the *firm* may be socially desirable. But he does not distinguish between these cases in his summary of the arguments for temporary state intervention.
7. If, however, the technological spillover affected only firms in entirely different industries, then a tariff would be effective in inducing firms within the protected industry to incur learning costs.
8. Terms-of-trade effects are being ignored in this statement.
9. Training costs are the excess of current wage and other costs associated with the new workers over their current marginal productivity. As Haberler

(1936, p. 284) has pointed out, in order for the establishment of the new industry to represent a socially desirable shift in resources, the discounted marginal productivity stream of the workers who transfer into the new industry must be higher than in the industries from which they are drawn.

10. If a monopoly price on capital funds prevented workers from borrowing to finance their training, a tariff would enable the industry to pay higher wages and thus could make it profitable for workers to pay the socially excessive interest charges. In this case a temporary duty would be socially beneficial.

11. Lack of perfect knowledge is also one of the major grounds used to support the modern 'infant-economy' argument. For a critical view of this argument, *see* Haberler (1964), Baldwin (1965) and Grubel (1966).

12. It will be necessary to maintain the duty on a permanent basis if investors do not revise their risk evaluation as they accumulate payments experience. The tariff improves the efficiency of resource allocation, but this case for protection is quite different from the argument for temporary protection of infant industries.

# REFERENCES

Alchian, Armen (1959), Costs and outputs, In *The Allocation of Economic Resources*, ed. M. Abramovitz, Stanford, Calif.: Stanford University Press.

Baldwin, Robert E. (1965), Investment policy in underdeveloped countries, In *Economic Development in Africa*, ed. E. F. Jackson, Oxford: Blackwell.

Becker, Gary S. (1964), *Human Capital*, New York: National Bureau of Economic Research.

Buchanan, James M. (1966), Joint supply, externality, and optimality, *Economica* XXXIII (November): 404–15.

——. and Stubblebine, W. Craig (1962), Externality, *Economica* XXIX (November): 371–84.

Coase, Ronald H. (1960), The problem of social cost, *Journal of Law and Economics* III (October): 1–44.

Grubel, Herbert G. (1966), The anatomy of classical and modern infant-industry arguments, *Weltwirtschaftliches Archiv* XCVII (December): 325–42.

Haberler, Gottfried (1936), *The Theory of International Trade*, London: Hodge.

——. (1947), An assessment of the current relevance of the theory of comparative advantage to agricultural production and trade, *International Journal of Agrarian Affairs* IV (May).

Hamilton, Alexander (1913), *Report on Manufactures* (1791), Reprinted in US Senate Documents XXII, no. 172, Washington: US Congress.

Johnson, Harry G. (1965), Optimal trade intervention in the presence of domestic distortions, In *Trade, Growth, and the Balance of Payments: Essays in Honor of Gottfried Haberler*, Chicago: Rand McNally.

Kafka, Alexandre (1962), A new argument for protection?, *Quarterly Journal of Economics* LXXVI (February): 163–6.

Kemp, Murray C. (1960), The Mill-Bastable infant-industry dogma, *Journal of Political Economics* LXVIII (February): 65–7.

List, F. (1856), *National System of Political Economy*, Translated by G. A. Matile, Philadelphia: Lippincott.

Meade, James E. (1955), *Trade and Welfare*, New York: Oxford University Press.

Meier, Gerald M. (1964), *Leading Issues in Development Economics*, New York: Oxford University Press.

Mill, John Stuart (1909), *The Principles of Political Economy*, London: Longmans, Green.

Myrdal, Gunnar (1957), *Rich Lands and Poor*, New York: Harper.

Plott, Charles R. (1966), Externalities and corrective taxes, *Economica* XXXIII (February): 84–7.

Rosenstein-Rodan, P. N. (1963), Notes on the theory of the 'big push', In *Readings in Economic Development*, eds T. Morgan, G. W. Betz and N. K. Choudry, San Francisco: Wadsworth.

Scitovsky, Tibor (1954), Two concepts of external economies, *Journal of Political Economy* LXII (April): 145.

Taussig, Frank W. (1915), *Some Aspects of the Tariff Question*, Cambridge, Mass.: Harvard University Press.

Turvey, R. (1963), On divergences between social cost and private cost, *Economica* XXX (August): 309–13.

# 9   The Inefficacy of Trade Policy*

## 1   INTRODUCTION

Economists typically evaluate alternative trade or domestic policies on the basis of their effects on social welfare. For example, in their pioneering analysis of government intervention to achieve non-economic objectives, Bhagwati and Srinivasan (1969) rank different policies that can be used to attain a particular non-economic objective in terms of their welfare costs.[1] The optimal policy is the one that achieves the desired objective, say, a minimum output level in an industry, in the least-cost manner.

It is invariably assumed in such analyses (as well as in those dealing with the optimal manner of offsetting market distortions) that trade policy is an effective means of achieving the desired objective. On this assumption, the criticism of trade policy in situations in which the objective relates to a domestic rather than a trade matter is not that it will not work but that it will create a new welfare-reducing distortion in the process of achieving the desired objective.

There is, however, a considerable body of analysis scattered throughout the trade literature demonstrating that trade policy often does not achieve the objective for which it is introduced. For example, the well-known Metzler paradox points out that, under some conditions, the imposition of a tariff on an imported good may lower rather than raise the domestic price of that good and thus decrease rather than increase domestic production of the protected item. Similarly, the analysis of smuggling by Bhagwati and Hansen (1973) shows that smuggling in response to a tariff may increase a country's welfare compared with the tariff situation by itself and can prevent the attainment of the desired minimum level of domestic production for the

---

* *The Inefficiency of Trade Policy*. Frank D. Graham Memorial Lecture, Essays in International Finance No. 150, December 1982. Copyright © 1982. Reprinted by permission of the International Finance Section of Princeton.

import-competing good. Frank Graham also appreciated the limitations of commercial policy, as is indicated by the statement in his excellent little volume, *Protective Tariffs*, that 'The importance of a sound foreign commercial policy, though by no means insignificant, has been greatly exaggerated by partisans of both the *laissez-faire* and the restrictionist schools' (1934, p. 6). In evaluating protection as a means of improving a country's terms of trade, he specifically notes (p. 83) that retaliation by foreign partners can negate a country's monopolistic objectives.

It makes sense for writers on the subject of distortions to assume that trade policy is effective in achieving its stated objective because they are concerned with the costs of an effective policy, but a more complete welfare analysis of policy alternatives would involve an integration of the literature on distortions with the literature on the effectiveness of both trade policies and various domestic policies.

Pulling together and elaborating on the reasons why trade policy may not operate as intended is also a desirable objective in itself. An increasing variety of non-tariff trade measures are being utilized to favour particular industries and income groups. Although the specific measures selected are the result of complex political compromises involving various domestic and foreign pressures, each is invariably presented as being adequate to achieve its stated purpose. Yet experience shows that frequently the measures do not accomplish their objectives, and the aided sectors press for more help. However, standard economic analysis suggests that such outcomes should not be at all unexpected. As a contribution to more rational policymaking and a fuller analysis of the welfare implications of various trade policies, this paper surveys the conditions under which those policies may be ineffective in carrying out their purpose. Most have already been noted by various authors, but they have not been pulled together within a common framework.

Trade policies operate directly on the relative prices and quantities of imported or exported goods and, by affecting the domestic prices of traded goods, indirectly influence levels of production, employment, factor rewards and consumption in domestic industries producing similar goods. Sometimes the primary reason for utilizing trade policies is to affect the volume or prices of traded goods, but more frequently the objective is to influence one of the variables that is only indirectly affected by trade measures, such as production or income. In its effort to influence the magnitude of these latter variables, the government may be pursuing either an economic objective (raising national economic welfare) or some non-economic goal (raising non-economic welfare at the expense of economic welfare).

There are three general ways in which a trade policy can be ineffective in attaining its stated purpose: (1) domestic prices of imports or exports move in the opposite direction to that intended; (2) domestic prices tend to change in the predicted direction but not by as much as policymakers expect; and (3) domestic prices move in the direction and to the extent desired, but the new prices fail to produce the indirect effects expected. If the objective of trade policy is to improve the country's terms of trade, there is still another kind of ineffectiveness: the terms of trade may worsen. But, as Kemp (1969, pp. 64–7 and 95) indicates, this result cannot occur if—as is usually assumed—trade taxes are redistributed to the private sector, there is a unique non-intersecting set of social indifference curves, and multiple equilibria are ruled out.

Underlying these ways in which trade policies can be ineffective are three economic principles that influence their effectiveness. The first and third principles have their counterparts in the literature on the welfare effects of economic distortions, while the second proposition is familiar from standard trade theory.

First, if an international economic distortion exists, it is possible for a trade measure introduced to increase the domestic production of a good by raising its domestic price to have the opposite effect. This principle is briefly discussed in section 2.

Second, the less comprehensive a trade policy measure is in its commodity and country coverage, the less effective is it likely to be. Section 3 describes various responses—both legal and illegal—to trade measures that limit their effectiveness.

Third, the less directly the change in the price of imports or exports affects the economic variable that is the object of trade policy, the less effective the policy is likely to be. Section 4 describes some unexpected indirect results of trade policies.

## 2    INTERNATIONAL DISTORTIONS

If a country has unexploited monopoly power over the international terms of trade, that is, $FRT \neq DRT = DRS$, where $FRT$ is the marginal foreign rate of transformation through trade, $DRT$ is the marginal domestic rate of transformation in production and $DRS$ is the marginal domestic rate of substitution in consumption, a trade measure may have the opposite effect to that intended. This principle was discovered by Metzler (1949), although he did not state it in this manner. Metzler demonstrated that when a country introduces a tariff or export tax, the price of its importables will decline if the elasticity (in absolute terms) of the foreign demand for the exports of the tariff-imposing country plus the tariff-imposing country's own marginal propensity to spend on imports is less than unity. The necessary but not sufficient conditions for this outcome are, as he stated, that the foreign elasticity of demand is less than unity or that imports are an inferior good in the taxing country. It can easily be shown that if a country already has introduced an optimum tariff, so that $FRT = DRT = DRS$, any further tariff increase will raise the domestic price of the import good and thus tend to raise domestic production. Thus, the Metzler paradox depends upon the existence of an international distortion.

# 3   OFFSETTING SUPPLY AND DEMAND RESPONSES

As noted above, a second condition determining the effectiveness of trade policies is their comprehensiveness and thus the extent to which they can prevent trade from being shifted to new supply or demand sources.

There is a variety of both legal and illegal ways in which trade can be shifted, and policymakers often do not take account of them sufficiently (or at all) in introducing a particular trade policy.[2] Legal responses include importing or exporting the product in either more or less processed forms that are not covered by the trade measure, changing the quality mix of a traded product, shifting to a substitute product, varying the country or domestic-customer distribution of imports or exports, shifting the country distribution of production, and retaliating with another trade policy measure. Furthermore, trade policies can have offsetting macro effects. Illegal ways of avoiding the restraining or promoting effects of a trade measure include smuggling, transshipping through third countries, incorrect invoicing and bribing customs officials. As the following discussion shows, the extent to which these responses offset the intended price and quantity effects of a particular trade policy depends upon the nature and comprehensiveness of the trade policy being used. One important point emerging from the analysis is that quantitative restrictions are likely to be less effective in limiting offsetting supply or demand shifts than *ad valorem* duties.

## Shifts in the Degree of Processing of Traded Goods
When a trade-distorting measure is introduced at a particular production stage of a product, the product is often imported or exported in a more or less processed form. The resulting shift in composition of traded goods is familiar from the literature on effective protection. Nevertheless, policymakers often fail to take it into account when they establish levels of protection (or export subsidies), either from lack of

knowledge or because of constraints imposed by the provisions of existing trade policy legislation.

Avoiding an import restriction by exporting the product in less processed form is illustrated by the recent experience with Japanese shipment to the United States of small trucks. The US tariff rate on assembled trucks had been raised earlier to 25 per cent, but the rate on unassembled trucks was left at 4 per cent. The difference between the duty-inclusive prices of assembled and unassembled small Japanese trucks exceeded the cost of assembling 'knocked-down' trucks in the United States. Therefore, those trucks were shipped unassembled, and integrated domestic producers of trucks did not receive the degree of protection intended from the tariff on fully assembled trucks. In general, the imposition of an import tax on a processed item will produce a smaller-than-expected domestic price increase because the item will be imported in less processed form. Furthermore, a quota on the processed good that is set to produce the same expected increase in the domestic price will result in an even smaller actual price increase.

These points can be shown by Corden's (1971, p. 30) well-known diagrammatic representation of effective protection. In Figure 9.1, quantities of assembled and unassembled trucks are shown along the horizontal axis, where units are chosen so that one unit of unassembled trucks is needed to make one assembled truck. The foreign supply curves for unassembled and assembled trucks are $GG'$ and $SS'$, respectively. The domestic supply curve for the components needed to assemble trucks is $EE'$. The domestic supply curve for fully assembled trucks is $HJ'H'$ under free-trade conditions. This curve indicates that, beyond $OK$ units

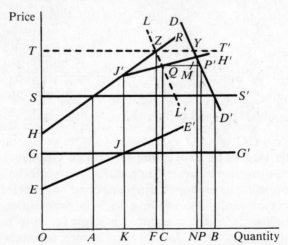

*Figure 9.1: Shifting from assembled to unassembled trucks*

of finished trucks, it is cheaper to import unassembled trucks and assemble them domestically than to produce a finished truck within the integrated domestic truck industry. The domestic demand for assembled trucks is $DD'$.

In the absence of any duties, $OA$ of assembled trucks are produced domestically, $AB$ are imported, and the equilibrium price is $OS$. Since the unassembled trucks ($OA$) needed to produce $OA$ of assembled trucks domestically are cheaper at home than abroad, there are no imports of unassembled trucks under completely free trade.[3]

Suppose that policymakers wish to protect the domestic truck-manufacturing industry and, not observing any imports of unassembled trucks, mistakenly believe that the domestic supply curve of assembled trucks will continue beyond $J'$ along the curve $HJ'R$ rather than along $HJ'H'$. They introduce a tariff of $TS/OS$ with the expectation that imports of assembled trucks will decline to $ZY$, the difference between $DD'$ and $HJ'R$ at the price OT. In fact, imports of unassembled trucks begin when the price of finished trucks rises above $J'K$, and the actual equilibrium is reached when the domestic price of trucks reaches $MN$. The tariff has eliminated imports of assembled trucks, but $KN$ of unassembled trucks are now imported and assembled domestically. The integrated domestic truck industry expands from $OA$ to $OK$ rather than, as expected, to $OF$. (The volume of assembly activity is greater than expected, but the individuals involved in assembling foreign-made trucks may not be those the government wants to help.)

The effect of imposing a quota rather than a tariff to reduce imports of finished trucks to the expected level, $ZY$, can be indicated by shifting the demand curve to the left by the maximum amount of permitted imports, that is, to $LL'$. The new equilibrium level for the domestic price of trucks will be $QC = P'P$ (rather than $MN$), and $KC$ of unassembled trucks will be purchased abroad and assembled domestically, whereas $KN$ were imported with the tariff. $CP$ units of assembled trucks will also be imported. Thus, fewer foreign-made trucks will be assembled domestically with the quota and, although the volume of production in the integrated domestic truck industry is $OK$, the same as it was with the tariff, producer surplus in the integrated industry is less (because the domestic price is $QC$ rather than $MN$). The tariff is more comprehensive in protecting total domestic assembling activity by keeping finished foreign trucks out of the domestic market. But the price of a licence for importing finished trucks represents a windfall gain and can range from zero to the amount by which the tariff would increase the price of assembled trucks.

Imports of a product in a more fully processed form can undercut government's efforts to protect an intermediate-goods industry. This

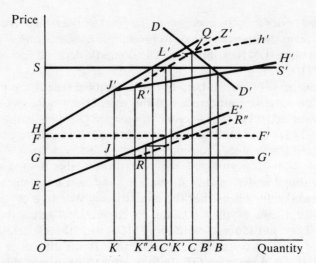

*Figure 9.2: Shifting from tool-making steel to cutting tools*

point can be illustrated by the same diagram. In Figure 9.2, let quantities of tool-making steel and of cutting tools be represented along the horizontal axis. As before, a fixed coefficient is assumed for the use of tool-making steel in making cutting tools, and units are chosen so that one unit of steel is needed to make one unit of cutting tools. The curves *GG '* and *SS '* are the foreign supply curves for steel and cutting tools, respectively, while *EE '* and *HJ 'H '* are the domestic supply curves for these goods.

In the absence of any protection, *OK* units of steel are produced domestically and *KB* units imported. There are no imports of cutting tools; all are produced domestically from either domestically produced or imported steel. Now suppose that the government imposes a duty at the rate *FG/OG* on steel with the expectation that the resulting shift in the domestic supply curve of cutting tools to *HL 'h '* will increase the domestic output of steel from *OK* units to *OK '* units, raise the domestic price of cutting tools to *QC*, and reduce imports of steel to *K 'C*.[4] In fact, imports of cutting tools begin when their price reaches *OS*, so that the domestic output of steel expands only to *OA*, imports of cutting tools become *AB '*, and imports of steel disappear.

A quota on steel set equal to the amount expected to be imported under the tariff, *K 'C*, will be less effective than the tariff in protecting the steel industry. As Corden (1971, pp. 216–17) explains, a quota on the intermediate good shifts the supply curve of steel from *EJG '* to *EJRR "*, where *JR = K 'C* is the maximum of steel imports permitted. This causes the domestic supply curve of cutting tools to shift from *HJ 'H '* to

$HJ'R'Z'$. In the new equilibrium, $C'B'$ of cutting tools are imported and $OC'$ produced domestically from domestically produced and imported steel. The domestic production of steel is $OK''$ (rather than $OA$, as with the tariff), and steel imports are $K''C' = K'C$.

Grossman (1981) analyses two other situations involving protection of intermediate goods in which there may be a perverse outcome. Protection based on domestic-content requirements, he points out, can decrease value added in the targeted industry rather than achieve its purpose of increasing value added. The reason is that the value-added effect of increasing the output of domestic components may be more than offset by the decrease in final-good production. The typical tariff-preference arrangement involving a content requirement imposed on the exporting countries also may decrease the volume of exports from the countries receiving preferential treatment.

## Changes in the Quality Composition of Traded Products

Another likely market reaction to the introduction of an import or export restriction is a change in the quality composition of the affected goods. The introduction of quantitative restrictions on imports of textiles, shoes and automobiles into the United States, for example, has led to the importation of higher-unit-value goods in these three product sectors. Suppose that $D_hD_h'$ and $D_lD_l'$ in Figure 9.3 are a trade-restricting country's import-demand curves for high- and low-quality shoes, respectively, and $S_h$ and $S_l$ the import-supply curves for the two types of shoes. Assume that the qualities are fixed but the import mix can be changed.

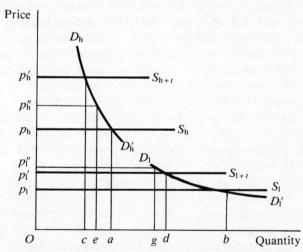

*Figure 9.3: Shifting from low-quality to high-quality shoes*

(For an analysis of the change in the quality of goods produced, as distinct from the mix of goods, as a result of import restrictions, see Rodriguez (1979) and Santoni and Van Cott (1980)). Furthermore, assume initially that the cross-price demand elasticities for the two types of shoes are zero. The equilibrium prices and quantities under free trade and competitive conditions are $Op_l$ and $Ob$ for the low-quality shoes and $op_h$ and $oa$ for the high-quality shoes.

Now assume that a 50 per cent duty is imposed on shoes, so that the import-supply curves and domestic prices of both grades of shoes rise by 50 per cent, that is, prices rise to $Op'_h$ and $Op'_l$. Suppose that the elasticities of import demand for the two types of shoes are the same, say, unity. The quantities imported of both types of shoes fall by the same percentage, $db/Ob = ca/Oa$. The quality mix remains unchanged. Obviously, if the import-demand elasticity (treated as a positive number) is greater for low-quality than for high-quality shoes, there will be a relative shift in imports toward high-quality shoes, and vice versa.

Instead of using a tariff to reduce total imports of shoes from $Oa + Ob$ to $Oc + Od$, suppose the government utilizes an import quota. Competitive conditions in the quota market ensure that all quota licences are used and that the price paid for a licence will be the same whether it is used to import high-quality or low-quality shoes. The absolute difference between the prices of shoes under the quota arrangement and free-trade conditions will be the same for both high-quality and low-quality shoes. With the *ad valorem* duty, by contrast, the absolute price increase was greater for high-quality shoes. Therefore, the shift from an *ad valorem* tariff to a quota will lead to an expansion of imports of high-quality shoes and a contraction of imports of low-quality shoes. Given the assumption made about equal import-demand elasticities, this also means that a higher proportion of high-quality shoes is imported under the quota than under free trade.[5] Equilibrium prices and imports with quotas are $Op''_l$ and $Og$ for low-quality shoes and $op''_h$ and $oe$ for high-quality shoes. The total imports of shoes are the same under the tariff and quota, $Oc + Od = Oe + Og$, but both prices rise from their free-trade levels by the same absolute amount under the quota arrangement, $Op''_h - Op_h = Op''_l - Op_l$, so that the total value of shoe imports (net of the quota premium) is greater. This may reduce the total value of domestic production.

Next, suppose that the cross-price elasticities of import demands are not zero. If these (as well as the own-price elasticities) equal each other or, as Falvey (1979) assumes, the sum of the own-price and cross-price elasticities is the same for both goods, the quality mix will not change with the *ad valorem* tariff, since the two prices rise by the same percentage. As Falvey (1979) points out, it also follows under these assumptions that a quota will cause a shift toward high-quality shoes.[6]

Policy officials often assert that a quota is preferable to a tariff because, given completely elastic supply curves, it is necessary to know the shape of import-demand curves to determine what will happen to the value of imports when a tariff is introduced. In fact, as has been shown, in the typical quota case where (as usually happens) different qualities of a good are included in the quota category, it is necessary not only to have a knowledge of own-price import-demand elasticities but also cross-price import-demand elasticities to determine the change in the value of imports resulting from the introduction of a quota.

## Shifts to Substitute Products

Instances where product substitution has limited the price-increasing effects of restrictive trade policies are familiar to all, and thus there is no need to dwell on this offsetting response. One interesting recent illustration relates to the EC's Common Agricultural Policy. The Community has consistently increased the target price of feedgrains, yet the consumption of EC feedgrains has stagnated. The reason seems to be an import shift not only to oilseed meals but to such non-traditional nutrients as tapioca, beet pulp and citrus pulp. Duties on these products were bound at zero or near-zero levels in the Dillon Round of GATT negotiations.

## Shifts in the Country or Domestic-Customer Distribution of Traded Goods

One situation in which changes in the country distribution of traded goods can completely offset a trade-restricting measure is when a country restricts trade on a discriminatory basis. Suppose, for example, that the United States negotiates an orderly marketing agreement or voluntary export-restraint agreement that establishes a quantitative limit on imports of shoes from a particular foreign supplier, say, Brazil.

As long as the international supply at the free-trade price from all countries other than Brazil plus the quantity of imports permitted from Brazil equals or exceeds import demand by the United States at the free-trade price, the quantitative restriction will have no effect on the price of shoes. If US consumers initially are purchasing more shoes from Brazil than the amount allowed under the quota, they simply shift to other foreign sources, while foreign consumers shift to Brazilian suppliers.

These relations can be seen from Figure 9.4. Let the free-trade world price and traded quantity of shoes be $Op$ and $Oc$ respectively. The US import-demand curve is depicted as $D_{US}$, the import-demand curve by the rest of the world as $D_{RW}$, and the world import-demand curve as $D_W$, where $D_{US} + D_{RW} = D_W$. The export-supply curve of Brazil, the country against which the quota is imposed, is $S_B$, while the world supply curve is $S_W$. The export-supply curve of all countries other than Brazil is shown as $S_{RW}$. Even if the United States purchased all its imported shoes, that is, $Ob$, from Brazil under free trade, a quota would have no price effect, provided it was no smaller than $ab$ shoes.

Figure 9.4 can be used to indicate the conditions under which an export quota against a particular country will be ineffective. Suppose that Brazil will not supply more than $ab$ shoes to the United States. Since this quantity plus the free-trade supply of the rest of the world is as large as the free-trade import demand of the United States, the export quota does not raise the price of shoes for the United States. A redistribution of the world's traded supplies of shoes takes place among consuming countries to offset any price-increasing pressure.

As pointed out by Baldwin (1970, p. 73) and Baldwin and Richardson (1973), a preferential government purchasing policy is still another restrictive trade measure that can be completely offset by a shift in available supply among consumers. In this case, the condition for ineffectiveness is simply that the government's demand at the free-trade price be less than the supply available from domestic suppliers at that price. Suppose in Figure 9.4 that $D_{US}$ is the government's demand curve for shoes, $D_{RW}$ the demand curve on the part of private US consumers, and $D_W$ the demand curve of the government plus private domestic consumers. Furthermore, let $S_B$ be the supply curve of domestic producers and $S_{RW}$ the import-supply curve of foreign producers, where $S_W = S_B + S_{RW}$. If the government refuses to buy any shoes from

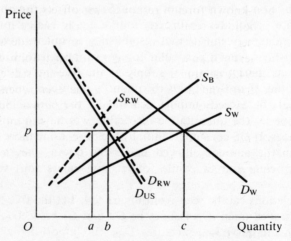

*Figure 9.4: Shifting the supply sources of shoes*

foreigners, the price will still remain at the free-trade level. Private US consumers will satisfy their demand at the free-trade price by purchasing the entire foreign supply at this price plus the excess domestic supply available after the government's purchases. If, instead, $S_{RW}$ is the domestic supply curve and $S_B$ the foreign supply curve, the price received by domestic producers will rise to the intersection point of $S_{RW}$ and $D_{US}$, and the price to domestic consumers will fall to the intersection point of $D_{RW}$ and $S_B$.

## Shifts in the Country Distribution of Production

The developing countries have long deliberately used protectionist trade policies to attract foreign investment. Government officials may fail to appreciate, however, that the increase in foreign investment within their own countries in response to a general protectionist policy (and the increase in the supply of imports from other countries if the protection is discriminatory) can lead to a smaller domestic price increase than expected from an import-restricting policy. The aim may be, for example, to stimulate shoe production in a relatively depressed area of the economy. The additional foreign investment (and thus the additional domestic output) resulting from the domestic price-increasing effects of a tariff will limit the price rise and consequently limit the benefits to firms in the depressed region. As Mundell (1957) demonstrated in his classic article on factor mobility, an inflow of capital in response to a tariff can even increase the domestic output of the protected good sufficiently to restore its free-trade price.

## Retaliation

Perhaps the best-known foreign response that offsets the objective of a country's trade policy is retaliation. Retaliation is usually brought up in discussing a country's effort to improve its terms of trade and raise its real income by means of an optimum tariff. Although Johnson (1953–4) and Scitovsky (1942) demonstrate that a country may still end up with better trading terms and a higher real income even when retaliation occurs, Johnson also shows how all trading partners could lose. One circumstance in which retaliation is mandated by law in most countries (and permitted under the GATT) is when a foreign country attempts to increase its exports by subsidies of one form or another. Article VI of the GATT states that a countervailing duty that does not exceed the amount of the subsidy may be levied to offset the export-increasing effects of the subsidy.

## Macroeconomic Effects

The macroeconomic effects of trade policies can also offset the intended

purpose of these policies. For example, switching from a system of direct
to indirect taxes in order to introduce equivalent rebates on exports and
taxes on imports and thereby improve the country's trade balance will
not be effective if exchange rates or factor prices are flexible. Selective
protection or subsidization, aimed at stimulating domestic production in
certain sectors, will be partly offset if it is extensive enough to change the
exchange rate or the level of factor prices.

## A Naive View of Supply and Demand Elasticities

The ineffectiveness of some trade policies stems not from unexpected
shifts in the import or export supply or demand curves but simply from
an oversimplified view of the elasticities of these curves.

The border adjustments permitted under GATT rules are a case in
point. By law, for example, the US government must impose a countervailing import duty if foreign governments subsidize exports or production in export industries and thereby cause material injury to the
import-competing domestic industry. The countervailing duty must be
equal to the net amount of the subsidy. The purpose of the countervailing duty is clearly to restore domestic prices and production to the levels
prevailing prior to the foreign subsidy. This will be the outcome,
however, only if the foreign offer curve is infinitely elastic (see Baldwin,
1980, p. 90, for an analysis of this case). Otherwise, countervailing
against an export or production subsidy can raise or lower the domestic
price, depending on the relative income elasticities of demand and price
elasticities of supply at home and abroad.

The rationale behind border-tax adjustments is also naive. For
example, governments that impose an indirect production tax on an
industry are permitted by the GATT to rebate this tax at the border. The
reasoning is that the adjustment will restore the country's exports to their
pretax level. However, as can be readily seen from either a partial-
equilibrium or simple general-equilibrium analysis (Baldwin, 1970,
Appendix B, and 1980, pp. 87–91), the net effect of the export rebate will
be to increase the country's export supply and thus decrease price and
output levels abroad. Thus, rather than achieve its apparently benign
purpose, this trade policy has the effect of an export subsidy.

The levying of antidumping duties equal to the difference between the
prices that foreign suppliers charge at home and abroad is also ineffective
in its intended purpose of eliminating dumping.

## Smuggling and Other Illegal Responses

Smuggling, bribing customs officials and deliberately invoicing incor-
rectly can all be analysed by the method used to analyse legal attempts to
avoid a trade restriction on a final good by importing or exporting the

good in an unprocessed form. These illegal acts occur only when there are government border charges, and the avoidance of these charges involves costs. Therefore, the supply curve of a good imported under these conditions is above that for the same good shipped under free trade. Smuggling, for example, will affect the domestic price that would otherwise prevail when a good is protected by a tariff if the tariff-inclusive domestic price is higher than the unit cost of importing illegally the quantity of goods that would be imported legally if there were no smuggling. If the tariff-inclusive price is higher, all imports will flow through illegal channels and the tariff will not be fully effective. Cigarettes were smuggled into the Philippines several years ago to avoid border taxes, and trade through legal channels all but disappeared.

In Figure 9.5, let $SS'$ and $FF'$ be the foreign import-supply curve with and without a tariff, respectively. Let $D_m D_m'$ be the domestic import-demand curve. The price and volume of imports will be $OS$ and $OD$, respectively, with free trade, and $OF$ and $OA$, respectively, with the tariff and no smuggling. Assume, however, that $HH'$ is the supply curve of the smuggled good, where the vertical difference between $HH'$ and $SS'$ is the cost of smuggling. If a tariff is imposed at the rate of $FS/OS$, all imports (equal to $OB$) will enter through illegal channels and the domestic price of the imported good will rise only to $EB$. The effect of a quota equal to $OA$ units, the amount that will be imported if the tariff is effective, can be shown by shifting the demand curve to the left by $OA$ units, to $FD_{mq}$. There will be $OA$ of legal imports plus $OC$ of smuggled imports, and the price will rise only to $GC$. Even if the tariff is effective,

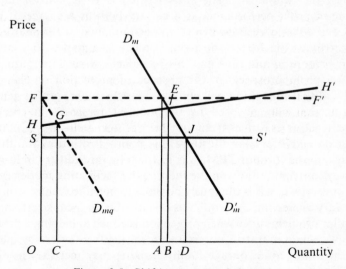

*Figure 9.5: Shifting to smuggled goods*

a quota will result in a lower price and larger volume of imports than the tariff.

Shipping goods via third countries to avoid import or export restrictions is relevant only in situations in which country discrimination is being practised. This method of avoiding country-specific controls places an effective limit, however, on the price-increasing effects of such controls.

## 4   UNCERTAIN INDIRECT EFFECTS

As noted at the outset, a trade policy may not accomplish the desired objective even when it produces the expected effects on domestic prices and trade. This is because trade policies are often used not simply to shift domestic production to particular levels, for reasons such as national defence, but to change economic variables that are only indirectly related to the prices and quantities of traded goods. For example, an industry faced with a surge of injurious imports frequently seeks temporary protection, arguing that protection will give the industry the time and resources needed to introduce new and more productive equipment and techniques. The modernization will supposedly eliminate the need for protection after a few years.

Standard price theory does not suggest this result. If an industry can be profitable with new equipment once protection is removed, why can't the industry enter the capital market to obtain the necessary funds to purchase the equipment? The answer often given is that an improved short-term profit performance is necessary both as a source of capital funds and as an encouragement to other investors. A rational investor may attribute the better short-run profit performance to the higher import protection and thus base his judgement about long-term investment on profit prospects in the absence of protection or else on the likelihood that protection will continue. Furthermore, profits generated by protection may be used by the industry to invest in completely different activities. Investment by the US steel industry in non-steel-producing activities may illustrate this point. Protection for the steel industry, in the form of TPM, was justified by the industry in large part as a way to maintain jobs in the industry by facilitating modernization. In any event, while it is obviously possible to imagine scenarios in which temporary protection pays off, this result is by no means certain.

Similar problems arise when protection is aimed at helping a particular group within an industry. For example, raising farm prices by means of trade measures to encourage family farming may increase the relative importance of corporate farms, since corporate farms may have easier access to capital markets and therefore be able to exploit new profit opportunities more rapidly. The short-run analysis of Mussa (1974) contrasted with the long-run analysis of Stolper and Samuelson (1941) also indicates how protection may at first raise a factor's real income but then decrease it as long-run adjustments take place.

Unexpected results can occur when there are domestic distortions. For example, temporary protection is often justified as a means of overcoming domestic externalities associated with the acquisition of knowledge and on-the-job training. But as has been pointed out in evaluating the case for infant-industry protection (Baldwin, 1969), the argument depends on a number of assumptions whose validity is not obvious. Protection may lead merely to expansion using existing productive techniques and skill mixes. Similarly, when domestic production is monopolized, raising a protective tariff beyond the point where all imports are eliminated will, as Corden (1971, p. 23) notes, cause the monopolist to reduce rather than to increase output. And Gene Grossman has pointed out to me that a monopolist will reduce output more when a quota is used to restrict imports to a particular level than when a tariff is used for the identical purpose. The existence of domestic factor-market distortions can also lead to 'abnormal' responses. Batra (1973, p. 249–50) demonstrates that, under these conditions, an increase in the domestic price of a product (brought about, for example, by a tariff) may lead to a decline in its output. Brecher (1974, p. 113) shows that import protection introduced to create employment may lead to the contrary outcome in an economy with a minimum wage and unemployed labour.

## 5 CONCLUSIONS

For an approach that is touted by many pressure groups and government officials as an effective remedy for a host of economic ills, the use of trade policy does not receive high marks for effectiveness. Occasionally, it may produce effects exactly opposite to those desired. In a not insignificant number of instances, it can be expected to have no effect at all in furthering the desired objective and may even promote some other undesirable outcome. More frequently, it probably operates in the direction intended, but policymakers either underestimate the extent of offsetting pressures or misunderstand the nature of its indirect consequences. Therefore, it does not fully accomplish its intended purpose. Furthermore, an important conclusion of the preceding analysis is that the ineffectiveness of trade policy tends to be greater when quantitative measures rather than tariffs are used to restrict imports.

Perhaps economists have understood this all along. Maybe we have not dwelt upon the inefficacy of trade policy because we know that usually the more effective trade policies are in achieving the purposes for which they are intended, the greater will be the resulting decline in national economic welfare.

It is also interesting to note that those trade policies that are growing in popularity, namely, discriminatory measures such as orderly marketing agreements, voluntary export restraints and selective embargoes, are the very ones likely to be least effective. Pressure groups seem to believe that they have a better chance of gaining public support if they focus on a particular country or set of countries and a product line in which a surge of imports or an apparently unfair practice can be observed fairly clearly. Government officials also like this approach, since it avoids political pressures from other countries supplying the same or similar products who cannot be accused of disruptive or unfair behaviour. Thus, protection may be easier to achieve when framed in this narrow manner. But it usually does not take long for recipients of this type of trade policy assistance to discover that their political achievement confers little economic benefit.

## NOTES

1. Bhagwati (1968) elaborated on this analysis in his 1967 Graham Memorial Lecture.
2. As will be pointed out in considering why particular trade policies are selected, the fact that these reactions are not taken into account when policymakers claim that a specific trade measure will achieve a particular goal does not necessarily mean that policymakers are unaware of them.
3. The existence of transportation costs or a foreign tariff on unassembled trucks is necessary to explain why unassembled trucks are not exported, since at $OA$ the foreign price, $OG$, is above domestic production costs. If they were exported, the domestic price of unassembled trucks would rise to $OG$ and eliminate the domestic production of finished trucks if $OG$ plus $EH$ (the domestic cost of assembling the first finished truck) exceeded $OS$ (the price of imported finished trucks).
4. If cutting tools were exported, a drawback equal to the duty could be claimed. Consequently, the domestic-supply curve for cutting tools would not shift.
5. With zero cross-price elasticities, the general condition determining whether the quality mix shifts toward or away from the high-quality good (compared with the free-trade composition of imports) is whether the ratio of the import-demand elasticities for the low- and high-quality goods, $\eta_l/\eta_h$, is greater or less than the ratio of the free-trade prices of those goods, $(\eta_l/\eta_h) \gtrless (p_l/p_h)$. Since $p_l/p_h < 1$, by assumption, a sufficient (but not

necessary) condition for a shift toward a higher-quality mix is $\eta_l > \eta_h$ (the elasticities being positive numbers).

6. The condition for there to be a shift in imports toward the high-quality product is $(p_h/p_l) > [(\eta_{hh} + \eta_{lh})/(\eta_{ll} + \eta_{hl})]$, where $\eta_{hh}$ and $\eta_{ll}$ are own-price elasticities and $\eta_{lh}$ and $\eta_{hl}$ are cross-price elasticities. (I am indebted to E. T. Chang for pointing out this relationship.)

# REFERENCES

Baldwin, Robert E. (1969), The case against infant-industry protection, *Journal of Political Economy* 68 (May/June): 295–305.

——. (1970), *Nontariff Distortions of International Trade*, Washington, DC: The Brookings Institution.

——. (1980), The economics of the GATT, In *Issues in International Economics*, ed. Peter Oppenheimer, London: Oriel, pp. 82–93.

——. and J. David Richardson (1973), Government purchasing policies, other NTBs, and the international monetary crisis, *Fourth Pacific Trade and Development Conference*, Ottawa.

Batra, R. N. (1973), *Studies in the Pure Theory of International Trade*, New York: St. Martin's.

Bhagwati, Jagdish (1968), *The Theory and Practice of Commercial Policy: Departures from Unified Exchange Rates*, Special Papers in International Economics no. 8, Princeton, NJ: Princeton University, International Finance Section.

——. and Bert Hansen (1973), A theoretical analysis of smuggling, *Quarterly Journal of Economics*, 87 (May): 172–87.

——. and T. N. Srinivasan (1969), Optimal intervention to achieve non-economic objectives, *Review of Economic Studies* 36 (January): 27–38.

Brecher, Richard A. (1974), Minimum wage rates and the pure theory of international trade, *Quarterly Journal of Economics* 88 (February): 98–116.

Corden, W. M. (1971), *The Theory of Protection*, Oxford: Clarendon.

Falvey, Rodney E. (1979), The composition of trade within import-restricted product categories, *Journal of Political Economy* 87 (October): 1105–14.

Graham, Frank D. (1934), *Protective Tariffs*, New York: Harper.

Grossman, Gene M. (1981), The theory of domestic content protection and content preference, *Quarterly Journal of Economics* 96 (November): 583–603.

Johnson, Harry G. (1953–4), Optimal tariffs and retaliation, *Review of Economic Studies* 21 (55): 142–53.

Kemp, Murray C. (1969), *The Pure Theory of International Trade and Investment*, Englewood Cliffs, NJ: Prentice-Hall.

Metzler, Lloyd A. (1949), Tariffs, the terms of trade, and the distribution of national income, *Journal of Political Economy* 57 (February): 1–29.

Mundell, Robert A. (1957), International trade and factor mobility, *American Economic Review* 47 (June): 321–35.

Mussa, Michael (1974), Tariffs and the distribution of income: the importance of factor specificity, substitutability, and intensity in the short and long run, *Journal of Political Economy* 82 (November): 1191–203.

Rodriguez, Carlos A. (1979), The quality of imports and the differential welfare effects of tariffs, quotas, and quality controls as protective devices, *Canadian Journal of Economics* 12 (August): 439–49.

Santoni, Gary J. and T. Norman Van Cott (1980), Import quotas: the quality adjustment problem, *Southern Economic Journal* 146 (April): 1206–11.

Scitovsky, Tibor (1942), A reconsideration of the theory of tariffs, *Review of Economic Studies* 9 (Summer): 89–110.

Stolper, Wolfgang F. and Paul A. Samuelson (1941), Protection and real wages, *Review of Economic Studies* 9 (November): 58–73.

# PART IV
Multilateral Trade Negotiations: Employment Effects and Negotiating Techniques

# 10 Trade and Employment Effects in the United States of Multilateral Tariff Reductions*

This paper summarizes certain aspects of my research into the trade and employment effects in the United States of a significant multilateral reduction in trade-distorting measures by the world's major trading nations. The study differs from earlier investigations into this question, such as those by Beatrice Vaccara and Walter Salant (1960), Robert Stern (1964), Giorgio Basevi (1968) and Stephen Magee (1973), in that the industry breakdown is much more detailed and the consequences of a multilateral tariff reduction on both US export and import-competing industries are taken into account. By estimating not only the net trade and employment effects of a significant tariff reduction in over 350 industries but also in the 50 states and on some 14 occupational groups, it is hoped that the results will be useful for those who are now embarked on the so-called Tokyo Round of trade negotiations within the framework of the GATT. Another novel feature of the study is the estimation of the net employment effects of multilateral tariff cuts under the assumption of flexible exchange rates.

## 1 ANALYTICAL FRAMEWORK

A key assumption of the analytical framework used in the study is that imports are imperfect substitutes for domestic production. The usual perfect-substitution model may be adequate for dealing with agricultural products and raw materials but it gives inconsistent results when empirical estimates of elasticities of import demand, domestic demand and domestic supply are compared with the theoretical relationships among these variables that must hold in a perfect-substitution model.[1] A more appropriate model for trade in manufactures is one in which imports and domestic production are imperfect substitutes and supply

* From *American Economic Review* 66, no. 2 (May 1976): 142–8. Research for the paper was financed by the US Department of Labor and the Ford Foundation.

curves for each of these types of goods are infinitely elastic. The assumption of an infinite-supply elasticity of imports is traditional in trade theory,[2] while the infinite-supply elasticity for domestic production of manufactured goods is widely supported by empirical estimation (e.g., Walters, 1963).[3]

Another simplifying assumption made in the analysis is that the compensated cross-price elasticity of demand is zero between any import good and all other goods except for the domestic substitute for this import good. Moreover, as is customary in tariff analysis, in order to eliminate any macro effects, it is assumed that total government expenditures and tax revenues remain unchanged. Consequently, if government expenditures are unchanged, as will be assumed here, and import duties are changed, it is assumed that income taxes are changed in such a way as to hold total tax revenue unchanged.

These points can be better understood with the aid of Figure 10.1 in which a simple exchange situation is depicted. Let $OA$ be the country's supply of the domestic good, the slopes of $AE$ and $AF$ reflect the domestic price and the fixed international price, respectively, of the import good, and $i_1$, $i_2$ and $i_3$ be three community-indifference curves. Postulating that consumers are identical in every respect, the point $N$ indicates the optimal combination of the domestic and import goods if a duty is imposed without any offsetting change in either taxes or government spending. If income taxes are reduced at the same time by a

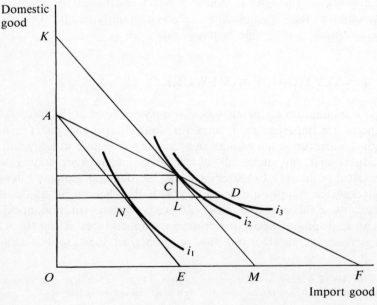

*Figure 10.1*

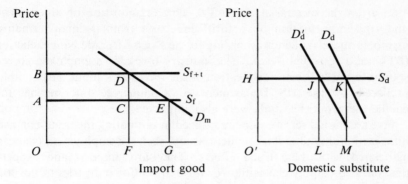

*Figure 10.2*

sum equal to the increased tariff revenues measured in terms of the domestic good (*AK* equals both the tariff proceeds and the additional disposal income due to the cut in the income tax), consumers divide the additional income between the two goods in such a way that the point *C* is reached. Consequently, to take the opposite case where the tariff on the import good is removed and the income tax is increased at the same time, consumers trade from the point *A* along the line *AF* until the point *D* is reached.

Since the line *AF* passes through *C*, consumers are able to purchase the same quantities of these two goods. In other words, apparent real income remains the same. Although consumers do not wish to substitute the import good for third goods, they do wish to purchase more of the import good and less of its domestic substitute. This substitution effect from *C* to *D* in Figure 10.1 indicates the increase in actual real income in the move to free-trade conditions.

A representation of these relationships using ordinary demand and supply curves is shown in Figure 10.2.[4] In the figure, $D_m$ and $D_d$ are income-compensated demand curves; $S_f$ and $S_{ft}$ are the foreign supply of imports without and with, respectively, the import tax; and $S_d$ is the domestic-supply curve of the import substitute. The area *ABDC* is equal to the tariff proceeds as well as the decrease in the income tax and corresponds to *AK* (or *EM*) in Figure 10.1. When the duty is eliminated and the sum paid to foreign producers increases by *FCEG* (equals *LC* in Figure 10.1), domestic expenditures on the local substitute decline by an equal sum, namely, *LJKM* in Figure 10.2 or *LC* in Figure 10.1.

## 2 DATA SOURCES

The trade and tariff data needed for the study are available for 1970 and

1971 from the secretariat of GATT. This organization obtained tariff and trade information on a tariff-line basis from its major trading members and classified it according to the Brussels Trade Nomenclature (BTN) at a four-digit level.[5] The industry breakdown employed corresponds to the 367-sector delineation of the 1967 sector input-output table prepared by the US Department of Commerce. Intermediate-use coefficients from this study were also employed.

Five additional sets of data are utilized in estimating the trade-balance impact of multilateral duty reductions and then the employment changes associated with these trade effects. They are: import- and export-demand and -supply elasticities for the 310 trading industries in the 367 input-output table; employment coefficients classified on the same industry basis; a breakdown of employment in each industry by skill groups; a breakdown of employment in each industry by state; and, finally, a set of price deflators to put the 1971 trade figures on a comparable basis with the 1967 input-output and labour-output coefficients used in the study.

Trade and employment effects were calculated using five alternative sets of import- and export-demand elasticities.[6] The preferred set (Set I) is based on the import- and export-demand elasticities calculated by Margaret Buckler and Clopper Almon (1972) for some seventy-five manufactured goods and import-demand elasticities calculated by Stephen Magee (1970) for crude foodstuffs, crude materials and manufactured food. Another set (Set II) consists of the Buckler–Almon elasticities modified by estimates for twenty industries calculated by the staff of the ITC. The remaining three elasticity sets consist of a fourfold grouping of one-digit Standard International Trade Classes and are based on a survey of the literature on trade elasticities by Robert Stern (1975). One set (Set III) is termed the 'best' by Stern; another set (Set IV) is made up of import-demand estimates of previous investigators that are on the low side and export-demand elasticities on the high side; and a final set (Set V) consists of high import and low export elasticities.

Labour coefficients for the 367 sectors of the 1967 input-output table were kindly supplied by Clark Bullard of the University of Illinois.[7] A breakdown of the labour coefficients into fourteen different skill groupings was supplied by the BLS and sector employment by state was obtained from the 1970 Sample Census of Population.[8] Finally, in order to express the 1971 trade figures in terms of the 1967 prices used for the input-output and labour coefficients, exports and imports classified into a four-digit level of the Standard Industrial Classification (SIC) were deflated by four-digit unit values obtained from the Bureau of Economic Analysis of the US Department of Commerce. After this deflation, the trade figures were classified on the basis of the 367 sectors of the 1967 input-output table.

# 3. ESTIMATES OF THE TRADE AND EMPLOYMENT EFFECTS OF TARIFF REDUCTIONS

The aggregate trade and employment effects in the United States of a 50 per cent multilateral tariff reduction are presented in Table 10.1. The Buckler–Almon–Magee elasticities are utilized in calculating these effects. In addition, certain products have been excluded from the tariff-cutting process: US exports to the EC of agricultural products subject to quantitative restrictions in this country, all US exports and imports of textiles covered by the international textile agreement and US imports of oil. All of these commodities are subject to non-tariff barriers that operate independently of tariffs. Cutting duties on these items will not increase trade.

While a 50 per cent duty reduction leads to changes in exports and imports that each exceed $1.5 billion, the net trade change is a negligible + $4 million for all industries and − $126 million for manufacturing alone. The net employment impact is also small: − 15,200 person-years for all industries and − 31,700 person-years for manufacturing.

As previously noted, estimates of trade and employment effects from a 50 per cent tariff cut were made with four other elasticity sets. Table 10.2 gives these results. Unless one combines import-demand elasticities taken from the high side of the range of such figures that various investigators have found together with export-demand elasticities taken from the low side of the range of estimates for these elasticities (i.e., Set V), the figures in Table 10.2 show that aggregative trade and employment effects of a 50 per cent reduction of tariffs are small or moderately favourable. The remainder of the results reported in this paper are based on the Buckler–Almon–Magee elasticity estimates (i.e., Set I).

Some indication of the distribution effects of tariff reductions can be

*Table 10.1: Effects on US trade and employment of a 50 per cent linear tariff reduction*

|  | All industries | Manufacturing |
|---|---|---|
| Change in exports (millions of $) | 1,750 | 1,591 |
| Change in imports (millions of $) | 1,746 | 1,717 |
| Net trade change (millions of $) | 4 | − 126 |
| Export-related employment change (person-years) | 136,000 | 116,400 |
| Import-related employment change (person-years) | − 151,200 | − 148,100 |
| Net change in employment (person-years) | − 15,200 | − 31,700 |

Table 10.2: Aggregate US trade and employment effects of a 50 per cent tariff cut under various trade elasticities

|  | Set I | Set II | Set III | Set IV | V |
|---|---|---|---|---|---|
| Net trade effect (in millions of $) |  |  |  |  |  |
| All industries | 4 | 161 | − 310 | 1,493 | − 2,932 |
| Manufacturing | − 126 | 31 | − 343 | 1,328 | − 2,834 |
| Net employment effect (in person-years) |  |  |  |  |  |
| All industries | − 15,200 | 900 | − 37,300 | 113,300 | − 266,400 |
| Manufacturing | − 31,700 | − 15,600 | − 40,900 | 93,100 | − 251,200 |

obtained by breaking down aggregate employment changes into various skill groups. Dividing net employment changes into fourteen occupational classes yields the following percentage changes in labour requirements: research and development workers at + 0.14; professional and technical workers (production-related) + 0.08; other professional and technical workers 0; management and administrative employees (production-related) − 0.03; other management and administrative employees 0; craftsmen − 0.05; sales workers − 0.03; clerical workers − 0.02; operatives − 0.14; labourers (except farm) − 0.08; service workers − 0.01; private household workers 0; and farm labourers and foremen + 0.45. These figures confirm once again that the basis of the US comparative advantage rests on the existence of a relatively abundant supply of research and development workers (who give the United States a technological jump on other countries), other professional workers and agricultural resources. The demands for other skill groups decline somewhat, the reduction being the largest for semi-skilled (operatives) and non-farm labourers.

While overall trade and employment effects of a 50 per cent tariff cut are small under the most likely sets of trade elasticities, this does not mean that no industry is significantly harmed or benefited from the duty reductions. If one-half of one per cent of an industry's labour force is arbitrarily chosen to divide industries that are or are not significantly affected, the list of industries in which there are employment changes of one-half of one percent of more consists of fifty-four import-sensitive industries and nineteen export-oriented industries. The employment change for the import-sensitive industries is 48,000 and for the export-oriented industries 34,000.

In considering whether to phase cuts in import-sensitive industries over the full ten years permitted by the Trade Act of 1974, an initial question might be whether the annual growth rate for labour in an industry more than offsets the labour-force decline associated with a ten-year phasing arrangement. If it did, there would be no reason for not reducing duties in the industry by the full 50 per cent. If average annual growth rates for labour that prevailed from 1958–71 are representative of the next ten years, the growth factor eliminates unemployment problems caused by the tariff reductions in thirty-four of the fifty-four import-sensitive industries. The remaining twenty consist of such industries as lace goods, tyre cord fabric, cordage and twine, industrial leather, non-rubber footware, glass products, pottery products, lead and zinc, textile machinery, electronic tubes and artificial flowers.

Industries that benefit in employment terms by one-half of one per cent or more include: paperboard mills, computing machines, electrical measuring instruments, semiconductors, aircrafts and aircraft equipment, and scientific instruments.

The regional distribution is also of interest to trade negotiators, and therefore a state-by-state employment impact of a 50 per cent duty reduction has been estimated. The 50 per cent multilateral tariff reduction brings about an employment decline in thirty-four of the fifty states, but these losses are very small. For example, the states in which labour requirements fall by more than 1000 person-years are Illinois, Massachusetts, Michigan, New York and Pennsylvania. In relative terms, employment losses are the highest in four New England states—Massachusetts, Maine, New Hampshire and Rhode Island, whereas the relative employment gains are the greatest in Kansas, Minnesota, North Dakota and South Dakota.

All of the previously reported results are based upon a fixed-exchange-rate model. It is possible to estimate the exchange-rate change required on the part of the United States to eliminate any deficit or surplus pressures on the trade balance as a result of tariff cuts. For elasticity Sets I–III, the required percentage exchange-rate changes needed for a 50 per cent tariff cut on all industries are within a range of $+ 0.003$ to $- 0.688$. The extreme elasticity assumptions used in Sets IV and V yield $+ 2.43$ and $- 2.46$ respectively. There are still, of course, labour-demand effects even though there is no trade-balance impact. These changes are, however, small for all elasticity sets.

## 4 CONCLUSIONS

The main conclusion emerging from the study is that the United States can participate in a substantial tariff-cutting negotiation without causing significant adverse trade and employment effects in the country. Even without taking into account exchange-rate changes, any adverse trade and employment effects are small except under one extreme set of trade elasticities. When exchange-rate variations are taken into account, net aggregate trade changes are eliminated and total employment shifts become minimal, even under the most adverse elasticity assumptions.

Not only are aggregate economic effects of a significant tariff-cutting exercise small, but the effects on individual industries, on various occupational groups and on employment in different states are minimal in most cases. For example, as previously noted, normal industry growth can handle any adverse employment impact, in all but twenty industries, if the reductions are staged over a ten-year period. Employment changes both by skill group and by state are insignificant, especially if the cuts are staged over a ten-year period.

## NOTES

1. If domestic and import products are perfect substitutes, then $e_m = (1 + O_s/O_m)e_d + (O_s/O_m)e_s$, where $c_m$, $e_d$, $e_s$ (all regarded as positive numbers) are, respectively, the elasticities of import demand, domestic demand, and domestic supply and $O_s$ and $O_m$ are the levels of domestic output and imports, respectively. But for most manufactured products, when empirical estimates of $e_m$ and $e_d$ are combined with actual $O_s/O_m$ ratios, the implied $e_s$ associated with these figures is much smaller than the very high values of $e_s$ obtained from direct empirical estimation.

2. Although an infinite import-supply curve is generally assumed, recent evidence seems to indicate that it is upward-sloping for the United States. For example, Peter Clark (The effects of recent exchange-rate changes on US trade balance, Treasury Conference, April 1974) found that a 1 per cent decrease in the US demand for finished manufactures caused foreign producers to reduce their prices by 0.32 per cent. He also found that as foreign demand for US exports increased, there was no change in the dollar price of US exports.

3. In later work a less-than-infinite elasticity of domestic supply will be used for agricultural and mineral products, but at this stage the infinite-elasticity assumption is employed for these products, too.

4. One difference is that domestic production of the domestic good is permitted to vary.

5. The countries covered are: the United States, Japan, Canada, Austria, New Zealand, Finland, Switzerland, Sweden, Australia, Norway and the nine EC members—France, Germany, Italy, Belgium, Luxembourg, the Netherlands, Denmark, the United Kingdom and Ireland.

6. The desired (but unavailable in the required detail) elasticity data are import-demand elasticities for each participating country. Rather than use US import-demand elasticities for all countries, US export-demand elasticities are utilized, since the aggregative results are substantially the same and the different competitive position of an industry on the import versus the export side is taken into account.

7. Some modifications in these coefficients were made after consulting with the Bureau of Labor Statistics (BLS) in the US Department of Labor. The figures also are average rather than marginal labour coefficients, but if short-run supply curves are in fact horizontal, there will be no difference in these two types of coefficients.
8. Employment by state is divided into only nineteen industries.


# REFERENCES

Basevi, Giorgio (1968), The restrictive effect of the US tariff and its welfare value, *American Economic Review* 58 (September): 840–52.
Buckler, Margaret and Clapper Almon (1972), Imports and exports in an input-output model, *American Statistical Association Proceedings*.
Magee, Stephen P. (1970), A theoretical and empirical examination of supply and demand relationships in US international trade, Study for the Council of Economic Advisors, Washington, DC, October.
——. (1973), Prices, incomes and foreign trade, Conference on Research in International Trade and Finance, Princeton University, Working Paper no. 19, Mar. 30–31.
Stern, Robert M. (1964), The US tariff and the efficiency of the US economy, *American Economic Review* 54 (June): 459–70.
——. (1975), Price elasticities in international trade: a compilation and annotated bibliography of recent research, prepared for the Office of the Special Trade Representative, Washington, DC, mimeo, March.
Vaccara, Beatrice and Walter Salant (1960), *Import Liberalization and Employment*, Washington, DC.
Walters, A. A. (1963), Production and cost functions: an econometric survey, *Economica* 31 (Jan–Apr.): 1–66.

# 11 Toward More Efficient Procedures for Multilateral Trade Negotiations*

## 1 EARLY NEGOTIATING TECHNIQUES

The first multilateral tariff negotiation occurred in 1947, while international discussions were still going on over the specific provisions to be included in the ill-fated ITO. Political leaders in most countries wanted to reduce the high tariff barriers erected during the early 1930s as soon as possible, and therefore decided not to wait until the ITO was approved. Fortunately, as part of the agreement reached, the GATT, the negotiators approved most of the articles in the commercial policy part of the ITO draft that covered 'good' international behaviour with regard to various non-tariff trade matters.

The negotiating technique followed initially was similar to that developed by US negotiators in the 1930s and early 1940s under the Trade Agreements Act of 1934. It was shaped by the need to satisfy several constraints. First, unilateral tariff cuts were ruled out on the grounds that the already unfavourable unemployment situation of the 1930s would be exacerbated. This meant that bilateral or multilateral negotiations were necessary to achieve the politically required rough balance of changes in the value of total exports and imports. A multilateral approach in which the participants would follow a simple tariff-reducing rule was considered but it was rejected on grounds that it paid insufficient attention to the problems of individual import-sensitive industries (Hawkins and Norwood, 1963, p. 75). A multilateral approach based on item-by-item negotiations was also ruled out as being impractical due to the complexity of negotiating simultaneously with many countries on many items (Hawkins and Norwood, p. 74).

Another important constraint was that the negotiating procedure had to be consistent with the most-favoured-nation (MFN) principle adopted by the United States in 1923 and firmly held by the architects of the trade

* From *Aussenwirtschaft (The Swiss Review of International Economic Relations)* 41, Jahrgang–Heft II/III (September 1986): 379–94.

liberalization movement. But this requirement, coupled with a bilateral, item-by-item approach raised the 'free-rider' problem. If two countries, A and B, reciprocally cut their duties on many items and extended these cuts to all countries, other nations that export the same products to A and B would be reluctant to cut their own duties on items of export interest to A and B, since they already would enjoy greater market access to these two countries. The solution devised to meet this negotiating problem was to utilize the principal-supplier rule, under which two countries exchange offer and request lists on tariff items for which each is *the* (or at least *a*) principal export supplier of the other country. This supposedly enables the MFN principle to be followed by all countries and yet still keeps to acceptable levels the 'free rides' gained by those that do not want to make major concessions themselves. These latter countries do not receive concessions on their major export products.

It was recognized that this technique did not fully resolve the free-rider problem, however. Suppose a small country was heavily reliant on one or two items for most of its export earnings from large countries but was not the principal supplier of these items to the large countries. After the large countries negotiated with their principal suppliers of these goods, the small country would have little incentive to open up its own markets to the large countries. One method used by large countries to deal with this problem was to cut their duties somewhat in negotiations with their principal suppliers, but then cut these duties still further in negotiations with non-principal suppliers for whom concessions on the items are important. The cuts were, of course, always extended to all countries each time. Another technique sometimes followed when there were distinguishable country differences in the quality of a product covered by a single tariff rate was to establish separate tariff lines for each variety and then negotiate separately with the principal supplier of each.

Following the principal-supplier rule and at the same time requiring at least a rough balance of concessions bilaterally limited the scope of the negotiations. Mutual concessions tended to be made on lists of items whose total export values were approximately the same. Consequently, in situations where the export values of principally supplied items differed significantly between two countries, tariff-reducing negotiations were never held on some items. Of course, one way this can be handled is for each country to cut duties on all principally supplied items but for the larger exporter in value terms to cut duties by a smaller percentage. But even if this is followed, the resulting cuts are likely to be less than what is politically possible.

The five multilateral negotiations held from 1947 until the Kennedy Round in 1962 were essentially a series of simultaneous bilateral negotiations.[1] Country teams were formed to exchange offer and request lists with each other and conduct reciprocal negotiations. Participants were expected to take into consideration the indirect benefits they received from the negotiations between other governments in determining when a balance of concessions with their trading partners had been reached. This was done after a series of tentative pairwise agreements had already been reached and thus did not significantly alter the essentially bilateral nature of the negotiations. The main multilateral feature of the negotiation was that the agreements between the various pairs of countries were combined into a single agreement between all the participants at the end of the negotiations.

Using a linear programming approach applied to actual 1964 trade and tariff data for dutiable imports of non-agricultural goods and assuming a reasonable set of import-demand elasticities, Baldwin and Lage (1971) compared the trade-expansionary effects of a maximum 50 per cent cut from a bilateral versus a multilateral balancing requirement for a group of six major participants in the Kennedy Round, namely, the United States, the EEC, the United Kingdom, the European Free Trade Association (EFTA), Japan and Canada. They found that if a multilateral approach had been followed, using the constraint that the change in a group's total imports from the others cannot exceed its change in total exports to the others by more than 20 per cent, the maximum increase in world trade would have been $5.91 billion. With the constraint that no group's change in imports from any other group could exceed its change in exports to that group by more than 20 per cent, the maximum increase in world trade permissible under these conditions would have been only $0.35 billion. As might be expected, a bilateral balancing requirement significantly limits the permissible increase in world trade.

## 2   THE KENNEDY AND TOKYO ROUNDS OF NEGOTIATIONS

### 2.1   Tariff-Negotiating Strategies and Methods in the Kennedy Round

One criticism of the item-by-item approach, the validity of which became more and more apparent during the negotiations of the 1950s, is that the difficulties faced by each individual industry tend to receive too much attention compared with the potential national benefits of broad duty reductions. Adjustments in economically inefficient but politically powerful sectors tend to be postponed indefinitely so that protection remains high in a number of important industries.

The extent of duty cuts in the four GATT tariff-reducing rounds that followed the 1947 negotiations illustrates the difficulty of going much beyond duty-cutting in industries not faced with significant import competition. In most industrial countries at the end of World War II there were still many high-duty sectors that had received their protection as a consequence of the general protectionist trend of the 1930s rather than because of any import competition problem they faced. In the initial postwar trade-liberalizing negotiations, it was not difficult politically to reduce these duties significantly. The average cut in all US duties in the 1947 negotiations was 21.1 per cent. It was difficult politically to continue this pace of liberalization. In the next four rounds between 1949 and 1962 the average US cuts amounted to only 1.9, 3.0, 3.5 and 2.4 per cent, respectively.

After the EEC adopted a common external tariff schedule by averaging the tariffs of its six members, Community trade officials became increasingly concerned about the difference between their industry profile of tariffs and the duty profiles of the United States, Japan and the United Kingdom. The averaging process tended to yield a pattern of Community tariff rates that was mainly in the 10 to 20 per cent range, whereas many US, Japanese and UK tariffs remained above 30 per cent. There was concern that this divergent structure would cause a significant amount of trade to be diverted from these other major import markets to the Community. Thus, Community trade officials favoured a negotiating approach that would bring about significant cuts in the high-duty items of the United States, Japan and the United Kingdom. To implement this objective, the EEC proposed an across-the-board tariff cut of 20 per cent at the outset of the Dillon Round in 1960.

The United States did not accept the Community's formula approach in the Dillon Round, but in the Kennedy Round (1962–7), American officials did move to a position of favouring a general tariff-cutting rule rather than an item-by-item approach. President Kennedy wanted a deep average cut in tariffs for both international political and domestic economic reasons. He believed that such a cut would not only strengthen political ties among the nations of the non-communist world but would reduce the degree of trade diversion away from American suppliers and to suppliers within the Community that was being brought about by the elimination of duties within the Community. Consequently, US trade negotiators proposed an across-the-board 50 per cent reduction at the outset of the Kennedy Round in 1962.

By this time, however, the Community did not want just a uniform percentage cut in all manufacturing tariffs but a cutting rule that would bring about a larger percentage reduction in high-duty items than in low-duty items. Community negotiators countered the US proposal for a 50 per cent general cut with one based on the concept of *écrêtement* or 'depeaking' that would reduce tariffs on manufactured goods by 50 per cent of the *difference* between their existing levels and 10 per cent. Duties on semimanufactures and raw materials were to be cut 50 per cent of the difference between their existing rates and 5 per cent and zero respectively.[2]

The United States vigorously opposed the Community's depeaking proposal on the grounds that there would be an average cut of only about 15 per cent, even before any exceptions. The US proposal for a 50 per cent cutting rule was finally accepted but with the qualification that in cases where there were 'significant disparities in tariff levels' the tariff rules would be based upon 'special rules of general and automatic application'.[3] The term 'significant' was defined as 'meaningful in trade terms', and the purpose of the special rules was to 'reduce such disparities'.

Despite lengthy negotiations, the participants were unable to agree on a simple formula that would reduce tariff disparities. The Community's suggestion was to define a disparity as existing for a country if the duty on a manufactured item in one or more of the so-called reference countries, namely, the United States, the United Kingdom and Japan, was at least twice as high as the duty on the same item in the country and at the same time exceeded this latter duty by at least ten percentage points. On items satisfying these criteria the reference country would cut its duties by 50 per cent while the country claiming the disparity would cut its duty on the item by only about 25 per cent.

The problem with this proposal was that it tended to hurt third countries. Take the case of watches. US tariffs on watches were over 50 per cent whereas watch duties in the EEC were around 15 per cent. Furthermore, Switzerland, which was the major watch exporter, maintained duties of only about 5 per cent. Thus, both the Community and Switzerland could claim a disparity against the United States and thereby only cut their watch duties by 25 per cent. But this would mean that Switzerland would only gain a 25 per cent cut in one of its major export markets, namely, the EEC. Without such a rule the Swiss would receive a 50 per cent cut from the EEC as well as from the US. Because of the opposition of such third countries to the Community's proposal, a general disparities rule was never adopted. Instead, the EEC dealt with major disparities bilaterally on a case-by-case basis.

A key feature of the Kennedy Round was that trade ministers agreed at the outset there would be 'a bare minimum' of exceptions to the linear cutting rule. At the time that the 50 per cent cutting rule was being agreed on, tough political decisions were being made within each country on the particular items to be excepted. In the United States, for example, President Kennedy gave approval to the exceptions list near the beginning of the negotiations. Each country also had to justify any exceptions at the time it submitted its list of items on which it was willing to make cuts. Consequently, the initial exceptions were quite modest for most countries and mainly confined to declining industries or ones where national security considerations seemed important.

There was, however, another constraint that had to be satisfied for each participant, namely the achievement of reciprocity. While not explicitly stated, it seemed to be accepted that reciprocity between two countries would be achieved if both countries cut all duties by the full formula. Exceptions to the full cut gave others the right to consider pullbacks from their initial offers if they did not think a balance of concessions had been achieved.

Once each country tabled its exceptions, the process of achieving reciprocity proceeded in a manner similar to the old item-by-item method. After examining other countries' exceptions lists, each of the participants that had accepted the formula approach prepared request lists of products on which they asked for greater tariff reductions from various other participants. They also prepared and circulated indicative lists of items on which they would withdraw their initial offers either partially or fully if their requests for further concessions were not satisfied. Some further liberalizing offers were forthcoming in the Kennedy Round as a result of this negotiating process. The United States, however, had tabled a smaller exceptions list than the EEC or Japan, and US negotiators felt that these participants had to be much more forthcoming for a satisfactory balance of concessions to be reached.

Further significant liberalization did not occur and after presenting its indicative withdrawal list in November 1966, the United States in March 1967 formally withdrew many items from its list of products subject to the full 50 per cent cutting rule. For example, the initial set of offers included a 50 per cent cut on all cotton textiles, but because others did not offer to cut to this extent in this sector, the US announced it was reducing the cuts in this area to about 20 per cent. Reductions in initial offers were also made on man-made fibres, steel, machinery, electronic products and agricultural goods. After others responded to US withdrawals, the US removed still more items from its offer list when it presented its final offers in May 1967. About 10 per cent of all dutiable items were withdrawn from the US offer list during the final stages of the negotiations.

## 2.2 The Tokyo Round
The Tokyo Round of tariff negotiations differed in a number of important respects from the Kennedy Round. First, the United States

agreed to a duty-cutting rule that reduced higher duty rates by a greater percentage than lower rates. Initially, the United States suggested a uniform 60 per cent cutting rule, but in the face of considerable resistance to this formula by the Community and other participants, American negotiators formally proposed a rule that gave a modest degree of harmonization up to 6.67 per cent and then became linear at 60 per cent thereafter. The EEC harmonization proposal was to cut each duty by a percentage equal to the level of the duty rate itself. This process was to be repeated four times. The Japanese and Canadians also proposed cutting rules that reduced high duties more in percentage terms than low ones.

As in the Kennedy Round, the United States objected vigorously to the EEC formula on the grounds that the modest level of average duty reduction it produced (about 25 per cent) was hardly worth the effort of a major multilateral negotiation. The Community was equally adamant that the US formula would not produce tariff harmonization.[4] Discussions among the major participants led to agreement on the need for a cutting rule that produced a significant degree of both tariff harmonization and average duty reduction. The compromise formula accepted was proposed by the Swiss. Each duty rate would be cut by a rate equal to $x/(x + 0.14)$, where $x$ is the existing rate of duty. A 14 per cent duty would, for example, be cut by 50 per cent.[5]

Another important feature of the Tokyo Round was that the duty-cutting formula was negotiated mainly by the trade ministers from the various countries and did not involve detailed high-level political decisions concerning just what the exceptions to the cutting rule would be. Indeed, the ministerial meeting opening the negotiations did not resolve to minimize exceptions to the extent that the conference opening the Kennedy Round had. As a consequence, in a country such as the United States the internal negotiations over the tariff-cutting rule were quite separate from those over the particular items to be excepted from full cuts.

In making its initial offer the EEC applied the Swiss formula to all dutiable manufactured items. In contrast, the original offers of the United States and other industrial nations included a significant number of exceptions (e.g., the United States excluded all footwear from cuts). The United States as well as Japan and Canada also offered many greater-than-formula cuts in order to obtain the overall average cut of about 40 per cent that had been agreed by some participants. In making these greater-than-formula cuts, US negotiators stated that they would be implemented only if other countries made equivalent concessions. The EEC responded by stating that it would not give credit in its reciprocity calculations for such cuts that often worked against the harmonization objective. Consequently, in April 1978, only three months after making its initial offers, the EEC announced a list of tentative withdrawals aimed at yielding a better balance of concessions. Community negotiators did emphasize, however, that they would restore items to the list if other countries were more forthcoming.

Apparently, there was not sufficient improvement in the offers of others, and in July 1979 the Community made these withdrawals part of their formal offer list. A rough comparison of the Community's initial and July offers indicates that about 20 per cent of all its tariff items were withdrawn from full formula cuts at this time. In February 1979, the United States announced it would withdraw its greater-than-formula reductions at the end of the month and did so with regard to most cuts when other countries failed to come up with satisfactory additional cuts. In making its final offers in March 1979, the EEC exempted another 15 per cent of its tariff items from full formula cuts. The United States also pulled back still more in its final offers announced in April 1979.

## 2.3 Non-tariff Negotiations

Although US trade officials had the authority to negotiate on non-tariff trade barriers or distortions during the Kennedy Round, they made only conservative use of this authority. Negotiations in the tariff area, particularly on the disparities issue, were so time consuming that little time was left for non-tariff discussions. The main accomplishments in the non-tariff area were the negotiation of an antidumping code, agreement on the abolition of the US practice of valuing certain chemical products for customs purposes at their ASP rather than at their foreign price, and elimination of the discriminatory elements of certain road-use taxes in Europe. These agreements were never implemented, however, because the US Congress thought that the executive branch had usurped the right of Congress to make laws on such matters.

In contrast, NTB negotiations were a major part of the Tokyo Round. Committees were established to negotiate new codes of 'good' international behaviour with regard to subsidies, government procurement procedures, safeguards, customs valuation practices and technical barriers to trade. Any participant interested in these subjects could take part in the committee deliberations. There was considerable hope initially that sectoral negotiations covering all forms of trade-distorting measures in a particular industry would take place on a widespread basis but, in manufacturing, sectoral negotiations proved successful only in the aircraft industry.

One major objective of the United States was to curtail the use of government subsidies. US industry officials believed that the far greater use of subsidies by foreign governments gave foreign exporters an unfair advantage not only in their own and US markets, but in third markets as well. In contrast, other countries, such as the members of the EEC, favoured the continued use of subsidies to promote economic adjustment as well as other social and economic goals. Due to such basic differences in views, the codes finally agreed on were very broadly worded and often included the language proposed by the disagreeing participants. Thus, depending on what part of the code was referred to, each participant could claim its viewpoint was upheld by the code. Since the dispute-settlement part of each code was weak, the actual manner in which the codes have operated has done little to strengthen international discipline in the NTB field.

Negotiations over NTBs were most successful when they went beyond general declarations of good intentions and resulted in specific trade-liberalizing concessions by the participants. The government procurement code provides a good example of this. After agreeing on the desirability of denying preferential treatment to domestic suppliers on non-military government contracts, the signatories negotiated on the particular agencies and products to be subject to non-discriminatory bidding practices. The countries involved evaluated the degree to which the offers of other countries gave them reciprocity and, as in the case of tariff negotiations, then pressed for further offers or threatened to reduce the list of their agencies that would not discriminate against foreign suppliers unless additional offers were forthcoming.

## 3   IMPROVING PROCEDURES FOR A NEW GATT NEGOTIATING ROUND

### 3.1   Tariffs and Non-tariff Import Barriers

The extent of multilateral tariff reductions has been significantly limited not only because of industry-specific domestic political pressures for protection based on such reasons as national security or adjustment difficulties, but because of national negotiating objectives dealing with overall reciprocity and desired shifts in the level and profiles of other countries' tariff rates. The shift to a formula approach, while still permitting formula exceptions, represented an effort to implement general negotiating objectives relating to tariff levels and profiles more fully and at the same time to satisfy politically powerful domestic sectoral demands for protection and achieve reciprocity. Yet, especially in the Tokyo Round where decisions concerning average tariff levels and profiles were first negotiated, then national decisions covering exceptions undertaken, and finally national judgements concerning reciprocity made, the outcome that emerged seemed to be much inferior to the optimum outcome that would satisfy each country's concerns with regard to all these elements in its objective negotiating function.

Using a game-theoretic approach, Baldwin and Clarke (1984) found that the Swiss formula produced a reasonably good compromise between the desire of the United States for a deep average cut in EEC tariffs and the EEC's desire for a significant reduction in the variance of US tariff rates. EEC rates would have declined by an average of 39 per cent under the Swiss cutting rule rather than by the 60 per cent proposed by the United States, while the variance in US rates would have been reduced even slightly more under this formula than under the cutting scheme proposed by the Community.[6] But after US exceptions were introduced and subsequent pullbacks by the EEC and the US took place, the outcome was quite unsatisfactory. The actual average cut in EEC duties was only 26 per cent, and the actual reduction in the variance in US tariffs was only 34 per cent in contrast to a variance reduction of 87 per cent given by the Swiss cutting rule.

Thus, it appears that failing to integrate better the formula negotiations, the process of determining exceptions and the attainment of reciprocity necessarily led to an inefficient negotiating outcome. Since the same type of negotiating game has been played several times by the main participants, all should understand what types of industries are most likely to be excepted by the various participants and how this is likely to affect the industry pattern of cuts as well as the average depth of tariff cuts. If such consequences are recognized at the time negotiations on a cutting rule are taking place, it may be possible to select a rule that better achieves the objectives of all. Similarly, the nature of withdrawals on reciprocity grounds should not come as a great surprise to any participant, given the long experience each has had with the others. Taking account of likely reciprocity-seeking behaviour by other countries may lead a participant to modify its exceptions list and the type of cutting formula it initially seeks in order to satisfy more fully its own objective function, taking account of all elements of the negotiations.

The argument that the negotiations would simply be too complex and cumbersome in the absence of a sequential procedure no longer has much force, given the negotiating experience of the participants and, in particular, the existence of high-speed computers that can easily process the large amounts of data needed to develop information about the many interrelationships. But having knowledgeable negotiators and an easily accessible data base that provides trade and tariff data on other participants is not in itself enough. Pressure must also be applied to the negotiators to come up with more efficient results. There is an unfortunate tendency for negotiators to not try as hard as they might to improve everyone's position, once they think they have reached a compromise that they can declare represents a successful negotiation from an international political and domestic economic viewpoint.

One source of pressure for more efficient negotiating outcomes could be the smaller industrial countries that have long recognized the benefits of lower protection levels in the large industrial countries. The role of these countries in preventing the disparities issue from becoming a significant derogation to the 50 per cent cutting rule during the Kennedy Round and in achieving a tariff-reducing rule in the Tokyo Round containing both significant harmonization and cutting elements was very important. These countries could also be mobilized to reduce the disintegration in the negotiations that seems to occur once a minimal success point is reached. A GATT negotiating committee could be formed to oversee the process by which country-specific requests for further improvements and threats of further withdrawals on reciprocity grounds are handled. It presumably would rely heavily on the Secretariat which would maintain a comprehensive data bank and suggest possible compromises to the participants that would meet their particular concerns but also benefit other participants to a greater extent.

Such a group, along with the Secretariat, should also try to achieve a broader and more flexible view on the concept of reciprocity. Pullbacks on reciprocity grounds should be subject to a justification and consultation process, just as exceptions to the 50 per cent cutting rule were in the Kennedy Round. Account should also be taken not just of bilateral benefits between principal suppliers but of indirect benefits resulting from cuts by other participants. It has long been recognized that these benefits should be counted, but the complexity of the negotiations prevented participants from doing so. With computers and a comprehensive GATT data base available to all participants, such calculations could be easily carried out by individual countries or by the Secretariat for these countries. Furthermore, rather than pulling back offers on the grounds that reciprocity has not been achieved, countries should be urged to consider such alternatives as staging their cuts over a longer period than their trading partners, pressing for agreements on future reciprocity-yielding cuts by other countries within a given time period, saving the unfavourable balance for use in future negotiations, and proceeding with the cuts but making it clear that they may have to be withdrawn if injury-causing import increases occur as a result.

High-speed computers and a comprehensive data base will enable the next negotiation to proceed in a manner that is less likely to result in an inefficient negotiating outcome than in the last two rounds. After agreeing in broad terms at a ministerial conference about the nature of the negotiations, for example, that a significant average cut will be sought that includes a major effort to reduce pockets of high tariffs and easily quantifiable non-tariff protection, trade officials can initiate the negotiations by presenting country-specific request lists for reducing particular tariff and non-tariff barriers. The items on which each country will request concessions from others will tend to be those on which domestic export interests believe a significant increase in foreign sales can occur if foreign barriers are lowered. Consequently, in considering whether concessions can be made on items requested by other countries, trade officials will be able to balance politically important export interests against politically important import-competing sectors. In recent negotiations trade officials have had to press within the government for liberalizing concessions by import-competing sectors without having specific export interests as allies in the political bargaining process. Moreover, once the list of exceptions has been agreed on domestically, it is very difficult to reduce the number of items covered, even though a foreign concession is offered that not only makes such concessions worthwhile in national welfare terms but would make additional liberalization politically feasible in the absence of such an agreement.

What if a particular participant decides not to be as forthcoming in its requests and possible offers as most of the other participants? Will this not reduce the level of concessions for all to the level of the country least desirous of liberalization? If the country is small, the problem can usually be handled by isolating it through the use of the principal-supplier rule or by subdividing tariff categories. If the country is a major trading power, the problem is more serious, but the procedure used to try to make it more forthcoming in the negotiations can be the same one that has proved successful under the formula approach. With a mechanism that measures the benefits to all countries (and not just principal suppliers) of tariff concessions by a major trading power, the weight of the entire negotiating community can be brought to bear on the country favouring only a modest average reduction. Just as when broad tariff-cutting rules are being negotiated, the possibility of failure of the negotiations can be laid at the doorstep of such a country. If past experience is relevant, this pressure is likely to produce a more trade-liberalizing response.

Both goods and services should be covered in the negotiation, since there are important concession-balancing opportunities between goods and services. For example, if a developing country agrees to allow a certain number of additional foreign banks or insurance companies to operate in the country, it could be granted an increase in its foreign textile and apparel quotas or reduced tariffs on such labour-intensive items as jewelry, musical instruments and sporting goods. Such trade-offs as liberalizing bidding on government contracts for a country in return for easing its domestic content requirements for foreign firms should also be explored.

## 3.2 Unfair Trade Practices
Although there is a need to reduce the many tariffs and easily

quantifiable NTBs that significantly restrict trade in goods and services, much of the pressure for further negotiations in recent years has been directed at reducing the use of so-called 'unfair' trading practices such as domestic subsidies that artificially promote a country's exports or reduce its imports. As noted earlier, negotiations in such areas as domestic subsidies have not been very successful. When there is no initial agreement concerning what 'good' behaviour should be, negotiations on codes of good behaviour lead to vaguely worded rules that are difficult to implement, particularly when the dispute-settlement procedures and enforcement mechanisms are weak. This has been the case with the GATT.

What is needed in this area are comprehensive negotiations conducted in a manner similar to those for tariffs or for the particular products and agencies covered by the government procurement code. The aim for subsidies should be to phase out particular subsidies gradually, bind their levels for a specified period of time, or introduce export taxes to offset the export-subsidizing element of domestic aids. The incentives to bring another country to the bargaining table would be not only the willingness to reduce one's own subsidies but the threat of carrying out the countervailing duty procedures permitted under current GATT rules. Prime attention should be given to industry-specific subsidies, since these are not only the easiest to identify but are the type of subsidies that raise the greatest objections on the part of foreign producers.

Each country would first undertake a comprehensive evaluation of the subsidizing practices of other countries that it believes are causing material injury to its industries. It would then make specific requests of other countries concerning the reduction or offset of injury-causing subsidies. At the same time the country would announce the countervailing duty action it was prepared to initiate domestically if bilateral or multilateral negotiations were not successful. If past experience is any guide, most countries will enter into serious negotiations aimed at preventing the imposition of countervailing duties against their exports. Countries that believe their subsidies do not violate GATT rules could announce that they would either request the formation of a GATT panel of experts to make a decision on their contention or they would take appropriate unilateral action. With a large number of panel requests, significant progress could be made in establishing precedents and procedures in the panel decision-making process in the GATT. Other allegedly unfair trading practices, such as various domestic rules that discriminate against foreigners, are more difficult to handle, but the same general procedure could be tried. In these cases the threat of retaliatory discriminatory action would also be used to bring countries to the bargaining table.

The possible danger of a comprehensive negotiation on unfair trading practices is that the entire liberal international trading order could unravel, but this is just what is happening under the piecemeal approach now being followed on the subsidy problem. If the current trend toward the breakdown of international trading discipline continues, many of the benefits of postwar international cooperation on trade matters are likely to be lost. If the entire problem is faced at one time, the need to preserve the existing order becomes more apparent to all and multilateral forces are likely to be marshalled for reaching a compromise that will permit more open trade within a framework that is regarded as fair.

## NOTES

1. *See* Catudal (1958).
2. Agricultural products were not covered by the formula.
3. Ministerial Resolution (1963), *Bulletin*, US Department of State, 24 June.
4. Community officials stated that their objective was to reduce the differences in tariff structures or profiles among trading partners by cutting high duties by a greater percentage than low duties. They stressed that they did not seek to equalize customs duties for the same products.
5. Some countries used 0.16 or 0.15 for the constant term in the formula.
6. These calculations are obtained by applying the formulas to the tariff and trade data for twenty-two sectors given in Alan V. Deardorff and Robert M. Stern, *An Economic Analysis of the Effects of the Tokyo Round of Multilateral Trade Negotiations on the United States and the Other Major Industralized Countries*, MTN Studies 5, Committee on Finance, US Senate, Committee Print, CP 96−15, pp. 26−30 and p. 149.

## REFERENCES

Baldwin, Robert E. and Gerald M. Lage (1971), A multilateral model of trade-balancing tariff concessions, *The Review of Economics and Statistics* 53 : 237−45.
——. and Richard N. Clarke (1987), Game-modelling multilateral trade negoti-ations, *Journal of Policy Modelling*, 9(2): 257−84.
Catudal, Honore M. (1958), How a trade agreement is made, *Bulletin*, US Department of State, Washington, DC.
Deardorff, Alan V. and Robert M. Stern (1979), *An Economic Analysis of the Effects of the Tokyo Round of Multilateral Trade Negotiations on the United States and the Other Major Industrialized Countries*, MTN Studies 5, Com-mittee on Finance, US Senate, Committee Print, CP 96−15.
Hawkins, Harry C. and Janet L. Norwood (1963), The legislative basis of United States commercial policy, In *Studies in United States Commercial Policy*, ed. William B. Kelly Jr, Chapel Hill: University of North Carolina Press.

# PART V
## Policy Issues and Trade Strategies

# 12 The New Protectionism: A Response to Shifts in National Economic Power*

## INTRODUCTION

The international trading economy is in the anomalous condition of diminishing tariff protection but increasing use of non-tariff trade-distorting measures. The former trend is the result of the staged tariff cuts agreed on in the GATT-sponsored Tokyo Round of multilateral negotiations concluded in 1979. The latter trend is taking place largely outside the framework of GATT and threatens to undermine the liberal international trading regime established after World War II.

This paper relates the new non-tariff protectionism to significant structural changes in world industrial production that have brought about a decline in the dominant economic position of the United States, the concomitant rise to international economic prominence of the European Economic Community and Japan, and the emergence of a group of newly industrializing countries (NICs). The first two sections describe the rise of the United States to a dominant position in international economic affairs in the immediate postwar period and indicate the types of 'hegemonic' actions it took. 'Shifts in international economic power' explains how changes in trade, finance, and the energy situation have led to modifications in national trade policy behaviour, particularly on the part of the United States. We then speculate about the nature of the international regime that is evolving under the present pattern of economic power among nations. The paper's final section is a summary and conclusion.

## THE RISE IN US HEGEMONY

The role of the United States in the evolution of the modern trading system has been central. Although this country became an important

* Reprinted by permission of the publisher, from Dominick Salvatore (ed.) (1986), *The New Protectionist Threat to World Welfare*, Amsterdam: North-Holland. Copyright (c) 1986 by Elsevier Science Publishing Co., Inc.

trader on the world scene after World War I, it gave little indication at the time of a willingness to assume a major international leadership role. The American share of the exports of the industrial countries rose from 22.1 per cent in 1913 to 27.8 per cent by 1928 (Baldwin, 1958), but during this period the United States chose political and economic isolation, rejecting membership in the League of Nations and erecting in 1930 the highest set of tariff barriers in its peacetime history. The failure of the London Economic Conference of 1933 due to the inward-looking economic position of the United States marks the low point of US internationalism in the interwar period.

A major policy reorientation toward participation in international affairs began to occur in the United States during the late 1930s and especially in World War II. More political leaders and the electorate generally began to accept the view of key policy officials in the Roosevelt administration that continued isolationism would bring not only renewed economic stagnation and unemployment to the American economy but also the likely prospect of disastrous new worldwide military conflicts. Consequently, active participation in the United Nations was accepted by the American public, as were the proposals to establish international economic agencies to provide for an orderly balance-of-payments adjustment mechanism for individual nations and to promote reconstruction and development. International trade had long been a much more politicized subject, however, and all that was salvaged (and then only by executive action) from the proposal for a comprehensive international trade organization was the GATT.

The economic proposals initiated by the United States were not, it should be emphasized, aimed at giving this country a hegemonic role. They envisioned the United States as one of a small group of nations that would cooperate to provide the leadership necessary to avoid the disastrous nationalistic policies of the 1930s. The envisioned leadership group included the United Kingdom, France, China and, it was hoped, the Soviet Union.

Hegemony was thrust upon the United States by a set of unexpected circumstances. First, the failure of the United Kingdom to return to anything like its prewar position as a world economic power was unforeseen. US officials thought, for example, that the US loan of $3.75 billion to the United Kingdom in 1946 would enable that country to restore sterling convertibility and to return to its earlier prominent international role, but the funds were quickly exhausted and it was necessary to restore exchange control. The 1949 devaluation of the pound was equally disappointing in its failure to revitalize the country. Economic reconstruction in Europe also proved much more costly than envisioned. The resources of the International Bank for Reconstruction and Development proved much too small to handle this task and massive foreign aid by the United States became necessary. Meanwhile the US economy grew vigorously after the war rather than, as many expected, returning to stagnant conditions.

The failure of either China or the USSR to participate in the market-oriented international economy placed an added leadership burden on the United States. But perhaps the most important factor leading to US hegemony was the effort by the Soviet Union to expand its political influence into Western Europe and elsewhere. American officials believed they had little choice from a national viewpoint but to assume an active political, economic and military leadership role to counter this expansionist policy, an action that most non-communist countries welcomed.

## HEGEMONIC BEHAVIOUR

The significant expansion of productive facilities in the United States during the war, coupled with the widespread destruction of industrial capacity in Germany and Japan, gave American producers an enormous advantage in meeting the worldwide pent-up demands of the 1940s and 1950s. The US share of industrial-country exports rose from 25.6 per cent in 1938 to 35.2 per cent in 1952 (Baldwin, 1958). (The combined share of Germany and Japan fell from 24.0 per cent to 11.4 per cent between these years.) Even in a traditional net import category like textiles, the United States maintained a net export position until 1958.

Static trade theory suggests that a hegemonic power will take advantage of its monopolistic position by imposing trade restrictions to raise domestic welfare through an improvement in its terms of trade. However, like the United Kingdom when it was a hegemonic nation in the nineteenth century, the United States reacted by promoting trade liberalization rather than trade restrictionism. A restrictionist reaction might have been possible for a highly controlled, planned economy that could redistribute income fairly readily and did not need to rely on the trade sector as a major source of employment generation or growth, but the growth goals of free-market firms, together with the nature of the political decision-making process, rule out such a response in modern industrial democracies.

Industrial organization theory emphasizes that firms in oligopolistically organized industries take a long-run view of profitability and strive to increase their market share. By doing so, they try both to prevent new competitors from entering the market, possibly causing losses to existing firms, and old competitors from increasing their shares to the point where others might suffer progressive and irreversible market losses. US firms organized in this manner seized the postwar competitive opportunities associated with American dominance to expand overseas market shares through both increased exports and direct foreign investment. The desire of US political leaders to strengthen non-communist nations by opening up American markets and providing foreign aid complemented these goals of US business, and business leaders actively supported the government's foreign policy aims. Even most producers in more competitively organized and less high-technology sectors such as agriculture, textiles and miscellaneous manufactures favoured an outward-oriented hegemonic policy at this time, since they too were able to export abroad and were not faced with any significant import competition.

The United States behaved in a hegemonic manner on many occasions in the 1950s and early 1960s. As Keohane (1984, ch. 8) emphasizes, in doing so, it did not coerce other states into accepting policies of little benefit to them. Instead, the United States usually proposed joint policy efforts in areas of mutual economic interest and provided strong incentives for hegemonic cooperation. In the trade field, for example, US officials regularly pressed for trade-liberalizing multilateral negotiations and six such negotiations were initiated between 1947 and 1962. But the United States traded short-term concessions for possible long-run gains, since the concessions by most other countries were not very meaningful in trade terms due to the exchange controls they maintained until the late 1950s. The US goal was to penetrate successfully the markets of Europe and Japan as their controls were eased and finally eliminated.

One instance in which the United States did put considerable pressure on its trading partners to accept the American viewpoint was in the Kennedy Round of multilateral trade negotiations. At the initial ministerial meeting in 1963, US trade officials—with President Kennedy's approval—threatened to call off the negotiations unless the EC accepted the American proposal for a substantial, across-the-board tariff-cutting rule. Members of the Community had regained much of their economic vitality and the United States wanted economic payment for its earlier unreciprocated concessions and its willingness to support a customs-union arrangement that discriminated against the United States.

In the financial area the $3.75 billion loan to the United Kingdom in 1946, the large grants of foreign aid after 1948 under the Marshall Plan, and the provision of funds to establish the European Payments Union in 1948 are examples of hegemonic leadership by the United States. American leaders envisioned the postwar international monetary regime to be one with fixed and convertible exchange rates in which orderly adjustments of balance-of-payments problems would take place. When the IMF proved inadequate to cope with the magnitude of postwar payments problems, the United States provided financial aid until the affected countries were strong enough economically for the IMF to assume its intended role. A US hegemonic role was also exercised in the energy field, as American companies, with the assistance of the US government, gained control over Arab oil during the 1940s and 1950s.

## SHIFTS IN INTERNATIONAL ECONOMIC POWER

### Trade Competitiveness

The hegemonic actions of the United States, aimed at maintaining the liberal international economic framework established largely through its efforts and at turning back the Soviet Union's expansionism succeeded very well. By 1960 the export market shares of France, Germany, Italy and Japan had either exceeded or come close to their prewar levels. Among the industrial countries only the United Kingdom failed to regain its prewar position by this time. The restoration of peacetime productive capabilities in these countries meant that the exceptionally high market shares of the United States in the early postwar years declined correspondingly. The 35.2 per cent US export share of 1952 had dropped to 29.9 per cent by 1960, a figure that was, however, still higher than its 1938 share of 25.6 per cent (Baldwin, 1962).

For manufactured products alone, the picture is much the same. The US world export share decreased from 29.4 per cent in 1953 to 18.7 per cent in 1959, while the shares of Western Europe and Japan rose from 49.0 per cent to 53.7 per cent and from 2.8 per cent to 4.2 per cent respectively (Branson, 1980). The export market share of Western Europe remained unchanged in the 1960s, but the Japanese share continued to rise and reached 10.0 per cent in 1971. At the same time the US share of world exports of manufactures fell to 13.4 per cent by 1971.

While aid from the US government played an important part in restoring the trade competitiveness of the European countries and Japan, the governments of these nations themselves were the prime driving force for revitalization. The French government, for example, formulated an industrial modernization plan after the war and two-thirds of all new investment between 1947 and 1950 was financed from public funds. Similarly, the British government under the Labour Party created an Economic Planning Board and exercised close control over the direction of postwar investment, while even the relatively free-market-oriented German government channelled capital into key industries in the 1950s. Government investment aid to the steel, shipbuilding and aircraft industries and the use of preferential governmental policies to promote the computer sector are other examples of the use of trade-oriented industrial policies in Europe during this period.

Japan is perhaps the best-known example of the use of government policies to improve international competitiveness. During the 1950s and 1960s the Japanese government guided the country's industrial expansion by providing tax incentives and investment funds to favoured industries. Funding for research and development in high-technology areas also became an important part of the government's trade policy in the 1970s. Governments of newly industrializing developing countries use industry-specific investment and production subsidies to an even greater extent than any of the developed nations in their import-substitution and export-promotion activities.

Not only had the prewar export position of the United States been restored by the late 1960s, but the period without significant import pressures in major industries with political clout had come to an end. Stiff competition from the Japanese in the cotton textiles industry was evident by the late 1950s, and the United States initiated the formation of a trade-restricting international cotton textile agreement in 1962. A broad group of other industries also began to face significant import competition in the late 1960s. The products affected included footwear, radios and television sets, motor vehicles and trucks, tyres and inner tubes, semiconductors, hand tools, earthenware table and kitchen articles, jewelry and some steel items.

Trade-pattern changes in the 1970s and early 1980s were dominated by the price-increasing actions of the Organization of Petroleum Exporting Countries (OPEC). This group's share of world exports rose from 18.2 per cent in 1970 to 27.3 per cent in 1980 (Economic Report of the President, 1985). By 1984 OPEC's share, however, had fallen to 23.5 per cent as the power of the cartel declined. During this period the US export share fell from 13.7 per cent to 10.9 per cent, while that of the EC dropped from 36.1 per cent to 30.7 per cent. Japan, however, managed to increase its share from 6.1 per cent to 8.4 per cent. The latter figures reflect Japan's continued strong performance in manufacturing; its share of industrial countries' manufacturing exports rose from 9.9 per cent in 1971 to 15.3 per cent in early 1984 (US Department of Commerce, 1985).

The 1970s and early 1980s were a time of relative stability in the US manufacturing export share, with this figure rising slightly—from 19.6 per cent in 1971 to 20.1 per cent in 1984. In contrast, the EC's manufacturing export share declined from 59.9 per cent in 1971 to 54.6 per cent in 1984. Another major development of this period was the increase in the manufacturing export share of the developing countries from 7.1 per cent in 1971 to 11.0 per cent in 1980.

An important feature of the shifts in trading patterns of industrial countries in the 1970s and 1980s has been that not only have labour-intensive sectors like textiles, apparel and footwear continued to face severe import competition but that large-scale oligopolistically organized industries such as steel, automobiles and shipbuilding have had to contend with such competition. Machine tools and consumer electronic goods have also come under increasing import pressure.

The decline in the dominance of the United States in trade policy matters became apparent in the Tokyo Round of multilateral trade negotiations as well as when the United States proposed a new negotiating round in 1982. As it had in the Kennedy Round, the United States proposed an across-the-board linear tariff-cutting rule at the outset of the Tokyo Round, whereas the EC again proposed a formula that cut high tariff rates by a greater percentage than low duties. This time the United States did not prevail. The other industrial nations treated both the United States and the Community as major trading blocs whose negotiating objectives must be satisfied. The result was a compromise duty-cutting rule that met the US desire for a deep average cut and at the same time produced the significant degree of tariff harmonization sought by the EC. At the 1982 GATT ministerial meeting the United States again called for a new multilateral exercise that included as major agenda items negotiations aimed at reducing export subsidies in agriculture and barriers to trade in services. The Community and the developing countries both rejected the US proposals, and it has become clear that the United States can no longer determine the pace at which such negotiations will be held.

## International Financial and other Economic Changes

As a decline in the dominant trade-competitive position of the United States became increasingly evident in the 1960s, both the United States and many other countries became dissatisfied with the US role in international monetary affairs. Since the supply of gold in the world increases only slowly, the demand for additional international liquidity that accompanied the rapid growth in world trade had to be met by greater holdings of dollars, the other official form of international reserves. As these holdings grew, a number of countries became concerned about the freedom from monetary and fiscal discipline that such an arrangement gave the United States and they resented the seigniorage privileges it granted. The United States also became increasingly dissatisfied with its inability to change the exchange rate of the dollar as a balance-of-payments adjustment means. Another indication of the decline in US hegemony was the creation in 1969 of a new form of international liquidity in the IMF: Special Drawing Rights (SDRs), designed to reduce the dependence of the international economy on the dollar.

The shift to a flexible exchange-rate system in 1971, however, was the clearest manifestation of the decline in US dominance in the monetary field. Although the results of this action have not given countries the expected degree of freedom from US financial influence, the role of the dollar as a reserve and vehicle currency has declined. Another institutional change directed at reducing the monetary influence of the United States was the formation of the European Monetary System in 1979.

The difficulties faced by the industrial nations in the energy field as a consequence of the success of OPEC have already been mentioned, but the importance of this shift in economic power is hard to exaggerate. This development was an especially devastating blow to the international economic prestige of the United States.

## TRADE POLICY RESPONSES TO THE REDISTRIBUTION OF NATIONAL ECONOMIC POWER

The non-hegemonic members of the international trading regime (i.e., countries other than the United States) responded to the inevitable industry disruption caused by the shifts in comparative cost patterns in a manner consistent with their earlier reconstruction and development policies. With the greater postwar emphasis on the role of the state in maintaining full employment and providing basic social welfare needs, these governments intervened to prevent increased imports and export market losses from causing what they considered to be undue injury to domestic industries. Assistance to industries such as steel and shipbuilding injured by foreign competition in third markets took the form of subsidies. These included loans at below-market rates, accelerated depreciation allowances and other special tax benefits, purchases of equity capital, wage subsidies and the payment of worker social benefits. Not only had such activities been an integral part of the reconstruction and development efforts of the 1940s and 1950s, but the provisions of the GATT dealing with subsidies other than direct export subsidies also did not rule out such measures.

Because of the difficulties of modifying the tariff-reducing commitments made in earlier multilateral trade negotiations, import-protecting measures generally did not take the form of higher tariffs. By requiring compensating duty cuts in other products or the acceptance of retaliatory increases in foreign tariffs, increases in tariffs could have led to bitter disputes and the unravelling of the results of the previous negotiations. Therefore, to avoid such a possibility, governments negotiated discriminatory quantitative agreements outside the GATT framework with suppliers who were the main source of the market disruption. For example, quantitative import restrictions were introduced by France,

Italy, the United Kingdom and West Germany on Japanese automobiles as well on radios, television sets and communications equipment from Japan, South Korea and Taiwan (Balassa and Balassa, 1984). Flatware, motorcycles and videotape recorders from Japan and the NICs of Asia were also covered by such import restrictions of various European countries. In the agricultural area, which had been excluded from most of the rules of the GATT, governments did not hesitate to tighten quantitative import restrictions (or restrictions like those under the EC's Common Agricultural Policy that have the same effect) or provide subsidies to handle surpluses produced by high domestic price-support programmes.

In the United States the disrupting effects of the postwar industry shifts in competitiveness throughout the world produced basic policy disputes that continue today. Except for the politically powerful oil and textile industries, until the late 1960s import-injured industries were forced to follow the administrative track provided for import relief under the escape-clause provision of the GATT. Moreover, many of the industry determinations by the ITC were rejected at the presidential level on foreign policy grounds—the need for the hegemonic power to maintain an open trade policy. Industry subsidies provided by foreign governments, though subject to US countervailing duty laws, were largely ignored by the executive branch for the same reason.

The official position of the United States began to change under the strong import pressures of the late 1960s. As their constituents described the competitive problems they were facing, fewer members of Congress accepted the standard argument that a liberal US trade policy was essential to strengthen the free world against communism. The intensity of congressional views on trade issues is indicated by their rejection of President Lyndon Johnson's 1968 request for new trade authority and by the near-approval in 1970 of protectionist legislation. The growing unwillingness of US allies to accept the unquestioned leadership of the United States in international political, military and economic affairs also caused officials in the executive branch to question the traditional American position on trade policies.

The view that gradually gained the support of the major public and private interests concerned with trade matters was that much of the increased competitive pressure on the United States was due to unfair foreign policies such as government subsidization, dumping by private and public firms, preferential government purchasing procedures, and discriminatory foreign administrative rules and practices relating to importation. This argument had appeal for several reasons. No new legislation was required to provide import relief; stricter enforcement of long-existing domestic legislation seemed to be all that was necessary.

After a material-injury clause was introduced into the US countervailing duty law in 1979, these laws also were consistent with the provisions of the GATT dealing with unfair trade practices. Consequently, stricter enforcement of US unfair trade laws was unlikely to lead to bitter trade disputes with other countries. By placing the blame for their decline in competitiveness on unfair foreign actions, US managers and workers could avoid the implication that the decline might be due to a lack of efficiency on their part. Finally, government officials could maintain that the United States was still supporting the rules of the liberal international regime that the country had done so much to fashion.

The emphasis on the greater need for fair trade is evident in the 1974 legislation authorizing US participation in the Tokyo Round of multilateral negotiations. In reshaping the proposal of the president, the Congress stressed that the president should seek 'to harmonize, reduce, or eliminate' NTBs and tighten GATT rules with respect to fair-trading practices. Officials in the executive branch supported these directives not only on their merits but also because they deflected attention from more patently protectionist policies.

The new codes that were approved in the Tokyo Round by no means fully satisfied those who stressed the need for fairer trade, but their provisions and the attention that the subject received established the framework for many US trade policy actions that have followed the conclusion of these negotiations. There has been a marked increase recently in the number of antidumping and countervailing duty cases, determinations in such cases rising between 1981 and 1983 from 21 to 50 in the United States and from 31 to 58 in the EC (Moore, 1985). Another indication of the greater use of these statutes to gain import protection is the increased number of ITC injury findings in antidumping cases, from 8 in the 1961–4 period to 32 between 1980 and 1983. The most important protectionist action taken by the United States since the late 1960s—the gradual tightening of controls over steel imports—has also been justified mainly on the grounds of unfair trade practices by foreign producers. For example, the TPM introduced by President Carter in 1978 that in effect established minimum import prices for steel was designed to offset foreign dumping. When a series of voluntary export-restraint agreements with leading steel-exporting nations was concluded in late 1984, a spokesperson for the US Trade Representative stated: 'We are responding to unfair trade in the US; defending yourself against unfair trade is not, in our opinion, protectionism' (*New York Times*, 19 December 1984).

The unfair trade argument has been used in support of most other trade-restricting or trade-promoting actions taken by the United States in recent years. The textile and apparel sectors have been described by government officials as 'beleaguered' by disruptive import surges, justifying more restrictive import controls. Similarly, when temporary orderly marketing agreements (OMAs) were negotiated in the 1970s with selected East and South east Asian countries, the implication conveyed was that these were responses to unfair export activities of these nations. Even the Japanese voluntary export restraints on automobiles were sometimes justified by American industry and government officials on the grounds that industry's competitive problem was in part due to the unfair targeting practices of the Japanese government. On the export-promoting side, it is routinely claimed that subsidized export credits through the Export–Import Bank and special tax privileges to exporters establishing foreign sales corporations are necessary to counter unfair foreign practices in these areas. In short, fair-trade arguments using such phrases as the need for 'a level playing field' or 'to make foreign markets as open as US markets' have become the basic justification for the greater use of trade-distorting measures by the United States.

## THE FUTURE OF THE INTERNATIONAL TRADING REGIME

The United States fared well economically in its hegemonic role; American exporters and investors established substantial foreign market positions from which they are still benefiting greatly. The open trade policy that US officials were able to maintain for so long also promoted growth and resource-use efficiency and thus extended the period of US economic dominance. But the postwar recovery of Europe and Japan and the emergence of the NICs brought an inevitable relative decline in US economic and political power. The comparative economic position of Western Europe also receded from its postwar recovery level as Japan and the NICs grew more rapidly. The outcome has been an increase in industrial-country protection that takes the form of non-tariff trade-distorting measures.

No country or country group is likely to assume a dominant role in the world economy during the rest of the century. Japan would seem to be the most likely candidate for this leadership role with its highly competitive industrial sector, but it appears to be too small economically to be a hegemonic power. Moreover, like the United States in the 1920s, Japan is still quite isolationist. Government officials and businesspeople are conditioned by the disastrous outcome of the country's expansionist efforts in the 1930s and 1940s and by its past history of inwardness. Furthermore, when a potential hegemonic nation first demonstrates its competitive strengths over a wide range of products, certain traditional sectors (such as agriculture) that are faced with difficult adjustment problems tend to be able to prevent the national commitment to trade openness required of a dominant economic power. This occurred in the early stages of both the British and the American rise to economic dominance and is now keeping Japan from making a commitment to openness commensurate with its competitive abilities. In addition, Japanese consumers have not yet developed the taste for product variety needed to make Japan an important market for foreign-manufactured goods. The EC possesses the size and resources to be the dominant economic power, but the economic diversity among its members and the severe structural adjustment problems faced by almost all of them preclude a hegemonic role for this economic bloc.

The United States remains the country most able to identify its trading interests with the collective interests of all. However, a number of the industries that were the most competitive internationally during the rise of US hegemony have become victims of their success. The high profits these oligopolistically organized industries were able to maintain provided the investment funds needed to take advantage of the expanding market opportunities at home and abroad. But their economic structures were also favourable to the development of powerful labour unions that wished to share these profits through higher wages. The outcome was wage increases in these industries that far exceeded wage increases in manufacturing in general. As other countries developed their productive capabilities, these American industries found themselves penalized by above-average labour costs and an institutional framework that made it very difficult to adjust to the new realities of international competition. Also, management in some of these industries failed to keep up with the most advanced practices. Another important feature of these industries is their ability to obtain protection by exerting political pressure at the congressional and presidential levels, if they fail to gain it through administrative routes involving the import-injury, antidumping and countervailing duty laws.

As a consequence of these developments, protectionism has gradually spread in the United States as such industries as steel and automobiles have come under severe international competitive pressures. European governments are faced with even stronger protectionist pressures for similar reasons and have also moved toward more restrictive import policies. Mancur Olson (1983) has argued that organized common-interest groups such as these industries tend to delay innovations and the reallocation of resources needed for rapid growth.

There seems to be no reason why the recent trend in non-tariff protectionism at the industry-specific level will not continue in the United States and Europe and become more important in Japan. But one should not conclude from this that the present international trading regime will turn into one where protectionism is rampant. There are—and will continue to be—dynamic, export-oriented industries in the older industrial countries that will seek access to foreign markets and see the relation between this goal and open markets in their own country. Moreover, such industries will have considerable political influence, as US high-technology and export-oriented service industries have demonstrated. These sectors will continue to provide the United States, Western Europe and Japan with the economic power that makes international openness a desirable trade policy objective, and none of these trading blocs is likely to adopt a policy of general protection.

But will not creeping protection at the industry level eventually bring a *de facto* state of general protection? This is, of course, a real possibility, but this conclusion need not follow because protection usually does not stop the decrease in employment in declining industries. Even politically powerful industries usually have only enough political clout to slow down the absolute fall in employment. Furthermore, while employment tends to increase due to the fall in imports from the countries against which the controls are directed, offsetting forces are also set in motion. These include a decrease in expenditures on the product as its domestic price tends to rise; a shift in expenditures to non-controlled varieties of the product, to either less or more processed forms of the good and to substitute products; a redirection of exports by foreign suppliers to more expensive forms of the item; and, if the import controls are country-specific, an increase in exports by non-controlled suppliers. Also, the larger industry profits associated with the increased protection are likely to be used to introduce labour-saving equipment at a more rapid pace than previously.

The continued decline in employment after increased protection is well documented from histories of protection in particular industries (e.g., United States International Trade Commission, 1982). In the European Community and the United States, even such politically powerful industries as textiles and apparel and steel have been unable to prevent employment from falling despite increased import protection.

There are many factors that determine an industry's effectiveness in protection seeking. Its size in employment terms is one important factor. With declining employment, an industry faces diminution of its political power because of the fall in its voting strength and attendant decrease in its ability to raise funds for lobbying purposes. The decline in the political power of the US agricultural sector as the farm population has declined is an example that supports this hypothesis. It seems likely that highly protected industries such as textiles and apparel will gradually lose their ability to maintain a high degree of import protection. Consequently, in older industrial nations the spread of protection to sectors in which NICs gradually acquire international competitiveness may be offset by a decrease in protection in currently protected sectors. Counter-protectionist pressures also build up as industry-specific protection spreads. The stagnating effect of this policy becomes more obvious, as do the budgetary and economic-efficiency costs. A state of affairs may thus be reached in which protectionism will not increase on balance in the current group of industrial countries, or only at a very slow rate. Meanwhile, export-oriented high-technology and service sectors will encourage continued international cooperation to maintain an open trading regime.

Even if this sanguine scenario takes place, the international trading regime is likely to operate quite differently than it did in the years of US dominance. Industrial countries will seek short-run economic reciprocity in their dealings with each other. In particular, the United States will no longer be willing to trade access to its markets for acquiescence to US political goals and the prospect of long-term penetration of foreign economic markets. The developing countries and nations with special political relationships with particular major trading powers will probably continue to be waived from the full-reciprocity requirement but their trade benefits from this waiver will be closely controlled. Greater emphasis will be placed on bilateral negotiations to reduce non-tariff trade distortions, though the negotiations may still take place at general meetings of GATT members. The articles and codes of the GATT will provide the broad framework for the negotiations, but the variety and discriminatory nature of non-tariff measures make true multilateral negotiations too cumbersome. Bilateral negotiations will also be used to a greater extent in handling trade disputes. The GATT dispute-resolution mechanism will be utilized by smaller countries in their dealings with the larger trading nations and by the larger nations to call attention to actions by one of their members that are outside of generally accepted standards of good behaviour. These means of settling disputes do not differ essentially from the practices followed throughout the history of the GATT.

Greater discrimination in the application of trade restrictions and in the granting of trade benefits is another feature of the emerging international trading regime. The safeguard provisions of the GATT, for example, will probably be modified to permit the selective imposition of quantitative import controls on a temporary basis. It will be justified, at least implicitly, on the grounds that injury-causing import surges from particular suppliers represent a form of unfair competition and thus can be countered with discriminatory restrictions under GATT rules. More state assistance for the development and maintenance of high-technology and basic industries will be another characteristic of the international trading order likely to evolve during the rest of the century. The governments of both industrial and developing nations will continue to insist on domestic subsidies to develop a certain minimum set of high-technology industries and to maintain a number of basic industries on the grounds that these are needed for a country to become or remain a significant economic power.

The international trading regime described above is not one that will gain favour with economists. It will not yield the degree of economic efficiency or economic growth that economists believe is achievable in an open, non-discriminatory trading order. But this is an essay on the probable nature of the future international trading order, not the one economists would most like to see evolve. Free trade is not a politically stable policy in an economic world of continuing significant structural shifts involving severe adjustment problems for some politically important sectors and the demands of infant industries for special treatment. But neither is general import protectionism a politically stable state of affairs in modern industrial democracies with dynamic export sectors. Stable conditions in this type of world economy involve openness in some industries and protection in others, with the industries in each category changing over time. The particular mix of openness and import protection can vary significantly, depending on such factors as the country distribution of economic power and the pace of structural change. The present situation, in which there are three major industrial trading powers and a rapid rate of new technology development and international transfer of old technologys suggests that the currently evolving trading regime will be characterized by more government control and private cartelization than has existed throughout most of the postwar period.

## SUMMARY AND CONCLUSION

The new protectionism threatening the international trading regime is related to significant structural changes in world production that have brought about a decline in the dominant economic position of the United States, a concomitant rise of the EC and Japan to international prominence and the emergence of a highly competitive group of newly industrializing countries.

The trading regime expected to develop after World War II involved the major economic powers' sharing responsibility for maintaining open and stable trading conditions. But the unexpected magnitude of the immediate postwar economic and political problems thrust the United States into a hegemonic role. US economic dominance manifested itself in the trade, finance and energy fields and enabled American producers to establish strong export and investment positions abroad. Yet, by facilitating the reconstruction and development of Western Europe and Japan as well as the industrialization of certain developing countries, US hegemonic activities led eventually to a marked decline in the American share of world exports and a significant rise of import competition in both labour-intensive sectors and certain oligopolistically organized industries. These developments significantly diminished the leadership authority of the United States.

Most industrial countries responded to the inevitable market disruptions associated with these shifts in comparative advantage by providing extensive government assistance to injured industries in the form of subsidies and higher import barriers. Such behaviour was consistent with the extensive role the governments of these countries played in promoting reconstruction and development. For the hegemonic power, the United States, the policy adjustment has been more difficult. Government and business leaders have gradually adopted the view that unfair foreign trading practices are the main cause of the country's competitive problems. By focusing on more vigorous enforcement of US statutes and GATT rules on fair trade, they are able to press for import protection and still maintain their support for the type of open trading regime the United States did so much to establish after World War II. Attention has been diverted from the role that high labour costs and inefficient managerial practices in certain industries play in explaining these problems.

No other trading bloc seems able or prepared to become a hegemonic power, but free trade is not a politically stable policy in a dynamic economic world in the absence of such leadership. Without the foreign policy concerns of the dominant power, domestic sectors injured by import competition and the loss of export markets are able to secure protection or other forms of government assistance through the political process in industrial democracies. Nevertheless, these industries are unlikely to be able to stop market forces from preventing the decline in employment in the industries and thus an erosion of their political influence. General protectionism is also not a politically stable policy in a rapidly changing economic environment. Politically important export industries that can compete successfully abroad will press for the opening of foreign markets and they realize the need to open domestic markets to achieve this result.

While it is possible that particular instances of protectionism will continue to spread and bring about an essentially closed international trading order, a more sanguine outcome, involving the support of the three major trading powers (the United States, the EC and Japan) seems possible. This is the emergence of a regime characterized by more trade-distorting government interventions than at the height of American hegemony and by the existence of a significant group of government-assisted industries. But while new industries will be added to this group, assistance will be withdrawn from others as they lose political influence so that, on balance, the list does not increase over time or does so only very slowly. Such a regime will not yield the growth and efficiency benefits of an open-trading system, but at least it will not lead to the disastrous economic and political consequences brought about by the type of trading order that prevailed in the 1930s.


# REFERENCES

Balassa, Bela and Balassa, Carol (1984), Industrial protection in the developed countries, *The World Economy* 7: 179–96.

Baldwin, Robert E. (1958), The commodity composition of trade: selected industrial countries, 1900–1954, *The Review of Economics and Statistics* 40: 50–68.

——. (1962), Implications of structural changes in commodity trade, in *Factors Affecting the United States Balance of Payments*, Part 1, Washington, DC: Joint Economic Committee, 87th Congress, 2nd Session.

Branson, William (1980) Trends in US international trade and investment since World War II, In *The American Economy in Transition*, ed. Martin Feldstein, Chicago: University of Chicago Press.

*Economic Report of the President* (1985), Washington, D.C: US Government Printing Office.

Keohane, Robert O. (1984), *After Hegemony: Cooperation and Discord in the World Political Economy*, Princeton, N. J.: Princeton University Press.

Moore, Michael (1985), Import relief from fair and unfair trade in the United States and the European Community, Madison, Wis.: Department of Economics, University of Wisconsin.

Olson, Mancur (1983), The political economy of comparative growth rates, In *The Political Economy of Comparative Growth Rates*, ed. Dennis C. Mueller, New Haven: Yale University Press.

US Department of Commerce (1985), *United States Trade: Performance in 1984 and Outlook*. Washington, DC: US Department of Commerce, International Trade Administration.

US International Trade Commission (1982), *The Effectiveness of Escape Clause Relief in Promoting Adjustment to Import Competition*, USITC Publication 1229, Washington, DC: US International Trade Commission.

# 13 Responding to Trade-Distorting Policies of Other Countries*

Continuing dissatisfaction on the part of the United States with the rules and dispute-settlement procedures of the GATT has recently focused attention on the various steps that individual nations can take to reduce, deter or offset the trade barriers and 'unfair' trade practices of other countries. This paper briefly considers from an economic viewpoint the appropriateness of alternative responses to such trade-distorting measures. The first section examines the social welfare standards that are implicit both in the articles of the GATT and most national trade legislation, and explains the currently permitted responses to foreign trade-distorting practices in terms of these standards. The next section considers the effectiveness of the responses allowed under present GATT rules, particularly those relating to increases in tariffs and subsidies by other countries. The final section proposes certain changes in these response rules that are aimed at improving the prospects for the continuance of an open international trading regime.

## 1

Economists evaluate trade policies mainly in terms of their effects on allocative efficiency and thus real income at a national or world level. They generally assume that internal redistributive goals are met through non-trade tax and expenditure policies. Those who frame national trade legislation and the rules of such international organizations as the GATT adopt a more complicated set of standards. While they believe in general that a liberal international trading regime is desirable because of its long-run real income benefits, they are also greatly concerned with the short-run redistributive implications of shifts in trading patterns. In particular, as W. M. Corden (1974, p. 107) has noted, they tend to hold

---

* From *American Economic Review* 74, no. 2 (May 1984): 271-6 (with T. Scott Thompson).

the view that it is undesirable to permit changes in the pattern of foreign trade to reduce substantially and rapidly the real income of any significant group in the economy. Since the consumption impact of most shifts in trading patterns is spread thinly over many individuals, whereas the production effect is concentrated upon a relatively small group, this viewpoint imparts a bias in favour of producers into national and international trading rules.

In the minds of most policymakers, the degree of undesirability of an income reduction to a particular sector depends not only on the magnitude and rapidity of the decline, but also on its cause and the nature of the affected economic sector. If, for example, the income loss is due to the deliberate action of a foreign government rather than to a basic shift in comparative advantage brought about by free-market forces, national and international trading rules permit a country to respond under a weaker standard of injury, for example, 'material' rather than 'serious' injury. A decline in income resulting from increased foreign competition is also regarded as more actionable if the injured industry is an import-competing one rather than an export sector. For example, the GATT permits a country to impose countervailing duties against subsidized imports if it determines that they are causing, or threatening to cause, material injury to a domestic industry. When an export industry is injured by foreign subsidization, under GATT rules the adversely affected country can only undertake counter-measures if authorized by the GATT Subsidies Committee.

Present international and domestic trading rules are also based upon a particular view of the way in which economies adjust to change. Increases in imports are regarded as tending to cause injurious short-run reductions in income and employment in import-competing domestic sectors. In contrast, export increases caused by foreign duty reduction bring about income and employment gains to export sectors. Consequently, negotiators regard their duty reductions as 'concessions' to foreigners that must be balanced by comparable reductions in foreign tariffs for it to be worthwhile to reduce their own trade barriers.

Under this framework of thinking, when a country raises a tariff that it had previously cut as part of a formal trade negotiation, GATT rules and practices specify that this country must either reduce tariffs on other items in order to maintain the existing balance of concessions, or else be willing to accept comparable duty increases on other items by its trading partners. The purpose of permitting foreign countries to raise their duties under these circumstances seems to be to discourage such initial tariff increases, since if the objective had been to offset any injury in the affected foreign export sector, the GATT would have allowed foreigners to subsidize exports from this sector.

The GATT rules relating to permitted responses to domestic subsidies by a country are based on a somewhat different line of thinking. When a domestic subsidy increases a country's exports and thereby causes material injury to an import-competing sector abroad, the foreign country is permitted to impose a countervailing duty equivalent to the subsidy. The purpose here appears to be to offset the injury in the particular industry rather than to deter the domestic subsidization. As already noted, when the subsidization reduces imports into the country from foreigners, a unilateral response on the part of foreigners is not permitted. The subsidizing country, however, must undertake consultations with another GATT member that believes the subsidy either causes injury to its domestic industry or nullifies or impairs its GATT benefits. If a mutually acceptable solution is not reached, the GATT Subsidies Committee may appoint a panel of experts to assess the situation. The Committee may then authorize 'such countermeasures as may be appropriate'.


2.

How well have the responses sanctioned by the GATT to foreign trade-distorting measures worked in practice? As far as tariffs are concerned, the evaluation must be that GATT procedures and rules have worked quite well. The preferred GATT procedure of reacting to foreign tariffs by offering to undertake a multilateral tariff-reducing negotiation has been utilized on a regular basis since the end of World War II, and has resulted in significant reductions in the level of import duties maintained by GATT members. Furthermore, large countries in general have not tried to exploit their power to improve their terms of trade nor to impose profit-shifting tariffs under imperfectly competitive international market conditions. As the traditional terms-of-trade literature and recent analyses of trade policy under imperfect competition have shown, (for example, James Brander and Barbara Spencer, 1982a), it is usually in the national interest of a country to introduce tariffs if foreign governments do not respond in kind. Moreover, even if other governments do retaliate, a particular country may end up better off than under free trade, but potential world income is reduced in the process. Just why tariff increases based on this nationalistic motivation have not been more widespread is not entirely clear. In part, it may be due to the acceptance of the view, based on the experience of the 1930s, that all countries eventually lose in a retaliatory tariff war.

There are, however, certain developments that threaten the effectiveness of GATT procedures for achieving a continued liberalization of world trade. One is the breakdown of the so-called 'escape clause' or safeguards provisions (Article 19) of the GATT. According to this article (and also US trade law), the level of protection for a domestic industry can be raised if increased imports cause or threaten to cause serious injury to the industry. In recent years, many governments have avoided the obligation of compensating other countries with reductions in protection on other product lines (or risk retaliation) by negotiating orderly marketing agreements or voluntary export restraints outside of the GATT framework with the particular countries that are the main source of the increased imports. The agreements generally take the form of quantitative restrictions, and compensation is not provided to the restricting countries. The latter are persuaded to accept the arrangements because they usually receive the windfall gains associated with the quotas and are also threatened with more severe restrictions if they do not cooperate. Other exporting countries are generally quite satisfied, since they can often capture part of the market lost by the export-restricting countries. From an economic viewpoint the outcome is a greater distortion of world production than if the degree of protection had been increased on a MFN basis.

A second disturbing development is the failure to maintain the downward trend in protection in certain important sectors. For example, many countries continue to restrict severely imports of agricultural and textile products. Some trade policy leaders in the United States believe that the failure of certain countries to reduce tariffs in key sectors and their greater use of non-tariff measures to offset previous tariff concessions have resulted in a situation in which US markets are much more open to other countries than foreign markets are to US goods and services. They argue that a new concept of reciprocity should be introduced into US trade law whereby the United States would be able to raise its trade barriers against foreign countries that failed to grant access to their markets to the same extent that the United States does to its markets.

The greater use in recent years of non-tariff measures to influence the volume and composition of trade has also reduced the effectiveness of GATT procedures for liberalizing world trade. It has turned out to be much more difficult to undertake successful multilateral negotiations that reduce the use of these measures than to cut tariffs. For example, despite the success in negotiating a new subsidies code during the Tokyo Round, there is still much dissatisfaction in some countries over the way in which the GATT subsidy rules are operating. The US trade officials and industry representatives, in particular, maintain that more extensive subsidization by other governments gives industry in these countries an

unfair advantage over American firms. They argue that the US government has ignored this subsidization far too long and should now adopt
an aggressive policy of countervailing such subsidies with import duties
and equivalent subsidies for US exports to third-country markets. The
aim of some who favour this approach is to force other countries to the
negotiating table for the purpose of formulating tighter GATT subsidy
rules, while the purpose of others is simply to outdo these countries at the
subsidies game by using the superior resources and market power of the
United States.

Some countries maintain that the United States is improperly adopting
this aggressive policy to mask its decline in competitiveness and unwillingness to adjust to the new realities of comparative advantage. They
claim that many of their subsidies are aimed at offsetting market
distortions or at easing adjustment problems, and therefore should not
be countervailed. Whatever the merits of the various arguments, it is
clear that a trade policy disequilibrium situation exists, in which retaliatory episodes of countervailing duties or subsidies may become much
more frequent than in the recent past.

Recent analyses of optimal trade policies under imperfectly competitive market conditions strengthen the view that this type of governmental
behaviour may become more prevalent. Writers such as Brander and
Spencer (1982b) demonstrate, for example, that under some imperfectly
competitive circumstances, a country can increase its economic welfare
by capturing larger market shares in oligopolistic international markets if
its government subsidizes exports or production. It is also in the interest
of other governments whose firms are competing in these markets to
follow suit and subsidize the exports or production of their firms.


3


The developments described above indicate the need for new international efforts to agree on appropriate responses to trade-distorting
policies of other countries. With regard to safeguards procedures and the
compensation issue, it is quite possible that countries will over time
become dissatisfied with the use of procedures outside of the GATT
framework involving quantitative restrictions and the abandonment of
the MFN principle as they gain more experience with their ineffectiveness
and the political ill will they generate. Unfortunately, it may take a
number of years for the drawbacks of discrimination to be fully
appreciated by the trading community. One meritorious proposal aimed
at encouraging countries to follow the MFN principle in their current

safeguards actions is to eliminate the compensation requirement, provided the protection is limited in duration, say, three to five years, and decreases over the period. Other countries would be able to demand compensation or be permitted to retaliate if the protection extended beyond the period.

Changes in safeguards procedures are also needed to encourage governments to employ tariffs rather than quantitative restrictions for protective purposes. Representatives of injured industries generally prefer import quotas over tariffs because their effect in restricting the value of imports is more certain. They often do not appreciate the fact that the tendency for foreign suppliers to shift toward higher unit-value of imports is more certain. They often do not appreciate the fact that the tendency for foreign suppliers to shift toward higher unit-value varieties of the protected products creates the same type of uncertainty as the lack of precise knowledge concerning the elasticity of import demand. From a national viewpoint, the main drawback of quantitative restrictions administered by the exporting countries is the transfer to foreigners of all or part of the revenue equivalent to what would be collected from a tariff.

As a means of overcoming the objection to the use of tariffs to provide temporary protection, a fast-track procedure should be established whereby after an affirmative import-injury determination has been made, tariffs could be increased quickly if the value of imports fails to decline to the level deemed necessary by the government to help the industry to adjust in the allotted time period. Utilizing the tariff revenues generated from the temporary protection for adjustment assistance purposes in the injured industry, as suggested by Gary Hufbauer and Howard Rosen (1986), would also help to encourage the use of tariffs in preference to quotas. This proposal additionally has appeal on equity grounds, since domestic consumers who benefit from the injury-causing imports would be required to give up a portion of these benefits to finance the costs of adjusting to the imports.

Ascertaining reciprocity by whether levels of protection between two countries are the same rather than, as has been traditional, by whether changes in the levels of protection between two countries are the same would be a major departure from the procedures followed thus far in the post-World War II liberalization of world trade. Multilateral negotiations would be replaced by bilateral negotiations that could result in a different level of protection against each country for any particular product. Not only would this significantly increase the distortion of world trade, but the outcome of such time-consuming negotiations could in many instances be levels of protection that prove ineffective due to shifts in supply sources and in the production stages at which goods are traded.

Those proposing a new reciprocity concept seem to be mainly concerned with what they regard as the absence of a balance of trade concessions between the United States and Japan. However, this issue can be settled within the present framework of the GATT. Specifically, if US officials believe that Japan or any other country has nullified or impaired the trading benefits accruing to the United States from prior cuts in US and Japanese tariffs by introducing offsetting non-tariff measures, they can bring a GATT Article 23 action against Japan. Under this procedure, failing a satisfactory resolution of the dispute through consultation between the two countries, the members of the organization rule on the matter after receiving the report of a panel of experts. Since other countries would undoubtedly utilize the Article 23 dispute-settlement procedure should the United States unilaterally adopt the new reciprocity concept, there seems little reason for the United States not to follow this route itself unless it is prepared at this stage to risk the complete breakdown of the present international trading regime.

Changes in the GATT as well as national rules dealing with the responses of governments to subsidization by other countries are very much needed. There is insufficient distinction between subsidies that tend to raise potential real income in the world and those that achieve some national aim at the cost of worsening the allocation of world resources. There is also inadequate recognition under existing rules of the appropriateness of using subsidies temporarily to facilitate adjustment in industries injured by trade-related causes. Furthermore, greater agreement is needed in distinguishing between subsidies that are sufficiently general to be unlikely to cause material injury to a particular industry and those that are countervailable because they do cause such injury.

As economists have long pointed out, the existence of market failures due to production and consumption externalities calls for the use of production and consumption subsidies (or taxes) as first-best policies to offset these market distortions. For example, as Paul Krugman (1983) points out, there is a case for providing government support for R-and-D-intensive, technologically progressive industries because investment in knowledge in these sectors produces knowledge benefits in other firms and sectors. Instead of reacting to such subsidization by imposing countervailing duties, other countries should consider whether research-oriented subsidies are also appropriate for their own R-and-D-intensive industries. All subsidies of this sort should be fully reported and justified in the GATT and be subject to panel determinations as to whether they do in fact operate in the direction of raising real income levels for all countries. Furthermore, in judging the merits of this type of subsidization, the GATT should only accept first-best policy offsets to market failures. Otherwise, not only is the direction of the real income change uncertain under second-best policies, but countries may be encouraged to settle for policies that are inferior in terms of the long-run income goals of the community of trading nations.

Current international tensions over subsidization could also be eased considerably if subsidies to some industries were placed within the safeguards framework of the GATT. There seems little reason for not allowing temporary production subsidies to industries seriously injured by increased imports in the same way that temporary tariff increases are permitted for such industries. Furthermore, export-oriented industries seriously injured because of the penetration of other countries into their third-country export markets should be permitted to receive temporary subsidies without being countervailed. As when tariffs are employed, the circumstances for such aid should be fully reported and justified in the GATT and strictly limited in duration.

Some progress has recently been made in deciding upon what types of government subsidies should not be countervailable because of their generality. For example, the Office of International Trade Administration in the US Department of Commerce has proposed not countervailing against subsidies generally available to all industries and regions or directed at a broad productive factor or intermediate input. More detailed studies of the allocative effects of such subsidies are needed before clear international rules on these matters can be agreed on.

The general objective of the international trading community should be to establish a self-enforcing behaviour framework in which responses by individual members discourage any single member from pursuing actions that distort the allocation of world resources. In a world of large trading powers and imperfectly competitive product markets, the ability to take credible counteraction is essential. This should include actions to offset trade-distorting policies directed at both a country's domestic and export markets. If broad agreement on such a framework is to be reached, it must be recognized both that some government policies with significant trade effects can improve the allocation of world resources and that governments are often forced to utilize second-best measures for adjustment purposes. Countervailing actions should not be automatic under these circumstances. Because of the use of trade policies for such purposes, there will remain a need under any self-enforcing framework for a quasijudicial means for settling trade disputes among countries. Therefore, another much-needed change is to improve the GATT dispute-settlement process by insulating it from the short-run interests of the disputants and raising the level of competence of the panels involved in the decision-making process.

# REFERENCES

Brander, James A. and Barbara J. Spencer (1982a), Tariff protection and imperfect competition, In *Monopolistic Competition in International Trade*, ed. H. Kierzkowski, Oxford: Oxford University Press.

——. and ——. (1982b), International R & D rivalry and industrial strategy, *Review of Economic Studies*.

Corden, W. M. (1974), *Trade Policy and Economic Welfare*, Oxford: Clarendon Press.

Hufbauer, Gary C. and Howard Rosen (1986), *Trade Policy for Troubled Industries*, Policy Analyses in International Economics, no. 15, Washington, DC: Institute for International Economics.

Krugman, Paul (1983), International competition and US economic growth, Discussion Paper, Washington, DC: Urban Institute, September.

# 14   GATT Reform: Selected Issues*

## 1   INTRODUCTION

There is general dissatisfaction in both developed and developing
countries with the operation of the global trading regime. In particular,
there is much criticism of the international organization that was
established in 1948 to provide a set of rules of 'good' international
trading behaviour, to sponsor multilateral trade-liberalizing negotiations, and to help resolve disputes among its members, the GATT.

Not only has this institutional mechanism been unable to prevent a
significant increase in the use of non-tariff trade-distorting measures in
recent years, but more and more trade policy actions are being taken
outside of the GATT framework. Nogues, Olechowski and Winters
(1985) estimate that 27.1 per cent of the total imports of the industrial
countries are now covered by non-tariff barriers (36.1 per cent for
agricultural products and 16.1 per cent for manufactured goods).
Moreover, of the 20.8 per cent of total imports covered by quantitative
restrictions, only 7.6 per cent were reported by members as coming under
GATT rules (Winters, 1985). Another manifestation of the dissatisfaction with the GATT framework is the frequent criticism of its existing
rules and the call for changes in and extensions of these rules.

This paper reviews the major areas of dissatisfaction with existing
GATT rules and mechanisms and examines the pros and cons of various
proposals for changing them. There are four general areas of dissatisfaction.

1. The unconditional MFN principle, the cornerstone of the GATT, is
being honoured more in the breach than in the observance and should
either be changed or be reasserted.

---

* From Henryk Kierzkowski (ed.) (1987), *Protection and Competition in International
Trade: Essays in Honor of W. M. Corden*, Oxford: Basil Blackwell. A few paragraphs
dealing with a proposed negotiation on subsidies are omitted, since this subject is covered in
Chapter 15.

2. Existing GATT rules, especially those covering 'fair' trading practices, agriculture and textiles, are not stringent enough.
3. There is a need for the GATT rules and agreements to be extended to cover such matters as services trade, trade-related investment requirements and the protection of intellectual property rights.
4. Existing GATT mechanisms for settling disputes, reaching decisions and dealing with the developing countries are ineffective and unfair and should be revised.

## 2   THE MOST-FAVOURED NATION PRINCIPLE

Discussions about the appropriateness of the MFN principle and the permitted derogations under current GATT rules arise in considering such diverse matters as the safeguard provisions of Article XIX, the comparative openness of different country markets, customs unions and free-trade areas, and the Generalized System of Preferences (GSP). Those who believe that the GATT should be modified to permit the greater use of selectivity and the conditional MFN principle base their case on the perceived unfairness of the unconditional form of the principle and the regime-weakening actions that occur outside of the GATT framework because of this perception.

It is argued, for example, that when increased imports from one or a few countries cause serious injury to a domestic industry, it is unfair to impose tariffs or quotas on other suppliers of the product whose exports have not increased in an injury-causing manner. This view, according to the proponents of GATT changes in the principle, has led to the widespread use by governments of voluntary export restraints and orderly marketing agreements—measures that are taken outside of the GATT framework and that tend to weaken respect for other GATT rules. As Alan Wolff (1985) has argued, permitting the selective application of import restraints in safeguard cases is necessary if the GATT is to continue to play a central role in maintaining an open-trading framework. The unequal treatment among countries that already occurs under GATT-sanctioned customs union and free-trade arrangements and under the (GSP) is also cited as a reason why a shift to the selectivity principle in safeguard cases should not be regarded as too radical.

A similar argument for shifting to the conditional form of MFN is that the present GATT principle is tending to retard the pace of liberalization (Hufbauer, 1984). Countries now are reluctant to reduce trade barriers because of the free-rider problem associated with the unconditional MFN principle. Reciprocal bargaining works best, it is said, when free rides can be controlled, as under the conditional MFN approach. The claim that US markets are far more open than foreign markets is another frequently heard argument for shifting to this approach (Cline, 1983). According to this view, it is necessary to pursue an aggressive policy of selective retaliation in order to force other countries to open their markets to a comparable degree. Still another argument for conditional MFN that has come out of the recent literature on trade policy under imperfectly competitive conditions is that a country can secure a larger share of the international monopoly profits by varying the degree of trade restrictiveness (or export subsidization) among foreign suppliers (or export markets).

Those who favour the maintenance of the unconditional MFN principle and, in some cases, a tightening of its application so as to curtail the spread of preferential arrangements give the following reasons for their views. First, discrimination of the type that will increase under selectivity and the new notion of reciprocity will worsen international political relations. Second, conditional MFN and the bilateralism to which it leads result in a more inefficient use of world resources and a consequent reduction in world income and growth rates as low-cost producers are replaced by high-cost suppliers. Third, discrimination is often ineffective in achieving its intended purposes owing to shifts in supply sources. Fourth, acceptance of conditional MFN will open the way for the introduction of more trade restrictions, both directly and through retaliatory actions, and will further undermine the GATT. Finally, the administration of a conditional MFN system is cumbersome and costly because of the need to renegotiate all previous agreements when a new agreement is concluded that changes the old balance of concessions.

There clearly must be a subjective element in one's views about the relative merits of conditional versus unconditional MFN. If the international trading order will disintegrate even more unless the traditional MFN principle is given up, and if the trading world is so highly imperfect in a competitive sense that an active, aggressive trade policy position is needed to prevent exploitation, then the case for conditional MFN has merit. Unfortunately, we do not have enough historical experience on the first point or enough empirical evidence on the second to reach a firm judgement on this interpretation of the nature of the international trading regime. However, the potential political and economic costs appear to be so large, and the uncertainty about the policy's effectiveness so great, that it seems prudent to explore less radical changes in GATT rules before abandoning this cornerstone principle of the organization.

Since it is often said that the requirement to provide compensatory duty reductions (or else risk retaliation) has been an important reason why countries adopt safeguard measures outside of the GATT framework, dropping the compensation requirement (subject to a time-limited, degressive protective arrangement) seems a reasonable alternative to try first. Moreover, most of the instances in which unfairness is a major issue can be handled under existing GATT rules on fair trade that permit discriminatory protective responses.

## 3   REVISING EXISTING GATT RULES

One aspect of the current international trading regime about which public and private leaders in the United States often express great dissatisfaction is the manner in which existing GATT rules covering 'fair trade' operate. They point to the greater openness of markets in the United States compared with markets in Japan and the EC and the greater assistance provided by the governments of these and most other countries to their domestic industries. Because of these conditions, many US government and industry officials believe that, unless current GATT rules are somehow changed to provide 'a level playing field,' the United States should vigorously enforce its own fair trade laws or introduce subsidies itself.

US views on the fairness issue differ considerably from those of most other countries. In many European countries, for example, some traditionally export-oriented industries have suffered rapid losses in their foreign market shares as other countries have developed modern industrial capacity in these sectors. Since import restrictions are not an effective means of assisting an export industry, the governments of these countries feel justified in providing subsidies to these sectors to ease their adjustment problems.

Similarly, most developed countries other than the United States believe on infant-industry grounds that the state should assist the establishment of high-technology industries—not just with tariffs and other import barriers, but also by providing capital at below-commercial-market rates of interest. They maintain that their capital markets are not as large or do not function as well as those in the United States and thus there is a need for the government to step in. Furthermore, they point to the technological benefits received by US industries from the large defence and space expenditures of the US government. The developing countries also justify the use of government subsidies to speed up their industrial development on infant-industry grounds and because of imperfectly operating private domestic markets.

In justifying government subsidies, other countries point to such statements in the GATT subsidies code as: 'Signatories recognize that subsidies other than export subsidies are widely used as important instruments for the promotion of social and economic policy objectives and do not intend to restrict the right of signatories to use such subsidies to achieve these and other important policy objectives which they consider desirable'. In contrast, US officials point to another part of the code in which signatories agree to seek to avoid the use of subsidies that 'may cause or threaten to cause injury to a domestic industry of another signatory or seriously prejudice the interests of another signatory or may nullify or impair benefits accruing to another signatory under the General Agreement'. They believe other countries' subsidies are in fact causing material injury to many US industries.

Some movement toward reconciling these two divergent viewpoints is needed to avoid a potentially serious breakdown of international discipline on the fair trade issue. One step in this direction might be to try to distinguish better between domestic subsidies of the beggar-thy-neighbour type and those that either can be justified on the same adjustment grounds as protection introduced under Article XIX or that contribute to the efficient growth of the world economy. In particular, temporary and degressive subsidies could be permitted for export-oriented industries that are seriously injured by export competition in third markets. Delineating between subsidies that are justifiable from an economic viewpoint on infant-industry grounds and those that are aimed simply at shifting market shares at the expense of collective income in the trading community is more difficult, but a key feature of permissible subsidies is that they would be temporary, degressive, and carefully monitored by a GATT committee.

As noted earlier, a number of governments want the provisions of GATT covering agricultural products changed to prevent export subsidization in this sector. Likewise, a number of governments want to terminate the MFA and make the textile and apparel sectors subject to the usual GATT rules. These are important issues, but they will not be considered further here.

## 4 EXTENDING GATT RULES

In recent years the United States has pressed for the adoption of new rules to cover certain forms of trade not currently subject to the international discipline of the GATT. These include trade in services, trade-related investment requirements, counterfeiting and intellectual property rights. Most industrial countries have joined the United States in calling for negotiations on new codes covering services, counterfeiting and intellectual property rights, but a number of key developing countries have actively opposed bringing these issues before that body.

Support for efforts to limit investment-related performance requirements is lacking, even among some major developed countries.

The effort to bring trade in services within the GATT framework indicates a recognition that this form of trade is becoming increasingly important. Total recorded world receipts from exports of private business services were $366 billion in 1983, compared with only $91 billion in 1971 (US Department of Commerce, 1985). In both years these sums equalled about one-fifth of world merchandise exports.

The classification of services into four categories by Sampson and Snape (1985) is useful in bringing out the issues that arise in attempts to liberalize this type of trade. They divide traded services into: (1) transactions that occur without the international movement of either the factors producing the service or the receivers of the service; (2) transactions that take place as a consequence of the international movement of productive factors but not of the receivers of the service; (3) transactions that occur with the international movement of the receiver of the service but not the provider of the service; and (4) transactions involving the movement of both productive factors and the receivers of the service.

Such services as consulting, insurance, banking and the provision of technological information that are supplied through correspondence and other standard means of communication by productive factors located in the exporting country are examples of the first category. The provision of insurance, banking, transportation and construction services involving the movement of productive factors to the importing country illustrates the second category. Tourist and education services, in which the consumer of the service moves to the country where the service is produced, fit the third grouping. Transactions such as one country's ships or planes transporting people from another country to a third country belong in the last category.

As Sampson and Snape point out, under their classification all policies restricting international trade in services can be divided conveniently into restrictions on services transactions *per se*, restrictions on the movement of factors producing services, and restrictions on the movement of the receivers of services.

Services trade that fits in the first category is in principle no different from trade in goods, but it may be more difficult for officials in the importing country to know when such transactions have occurred, and thus to regulate them, than trade in goods. But this problem also arises with regard to some commodity trade. As Sampson and Snape note, freedom of trade in these services requires that there be no barriers on international contracting and on the transmission of information by mail, telegraph and electronic means.

It is the second category of services trade that seems to pose the most difficult problems for liberalization, since the provision of the service usually involves direct investment in the consuming country or movement of labour into the country. Most governments are ambivalent about direct investment and movements of labour into their countries. They welcome the employment opportunities provided by direct investment, but they are concerned about the control it gives foreigners over domestic economic activity. Many governments are, for example, reluctant to allow foreign firms to determine the rate at which exhaustible natural resources are exploited. Similarly, in such activities as banking and insurance, governments are concerned about protecting consumers from undue risk, preventing monopoly practices and controlling monetary and exchange-rate policy. These concerns also prompt them to regulate domestic firms supplying these services. In other fields, such as telecommunications, a desire to provide services to most citizens has brought about government ownership, involving the subsidization of some activities and monopoly pricing of others. Significant liberalization in this field will require deregulation and the ending of preferential domestic relationships. Obviously, the key issue in this category is the right of foreigners to establish affiliates in a country and to receive non-discriminatory national treatment, once established.

Most governments are also ambivalent toward the movement of foreign labour into their countries to help provide services consumed there. When there is a shortage of the type of labour required to produce the service, inflows of labour are welcomed, especially if the stay of workers is only temporary. But governments typically want local labour to be trained to fill all but a small proportion of the jobs generated by foreign firms, since increasing employment for their own citizens is a prime government objective.

The desire of governments to generate employment at home is also a reason why there are barriers to services trade in which the receiver of the service moves to the country producing the service. Limits are often imposed on the amount of funds that students and tourists can take out of a country to save foreign exchange and encourage domestic activity in the services they consume. In addition, there is concern that those educated abroad may not return to their home country to help in its development. The same factors influence governments when they impose barriers to the movement of their citizens to another country to consume services provided by a third country.

All observers agree that negotiations in the services area will be difficult, especially in fields such as banking, insurance and telecommunications, where there is extensive government control. Some writers, for example, Neu (1986), believe that the effort involved in negotiating in such fields as banking is not worth the disappointing results likely to emerge from such negotiations. Others are concerned that the time and resources required for negotiations in the services area will diminish the effort devoted to strengthening existing GATT rules, such as safeguards and subsidies, which in their view should be the prime concern of the next negotiation.

It is difficult, however, to justify leaving services trade outside of an international framework of 'good' behaviour such as the GATT. The rapid growth of this trade is another manifestation of the increasing interdependence of nations, and the problems related to this development are best dealt with as they arise. It may well be that it will be possible to frame only very general codes of good behaviour, such as the subsidies and government procurement codes agreed upon in the Tokyo Round. But this framework can retard the growth of barriers to trade in services and serve as a basis for subsequent detailed negotiations.

There is less international support for bringing trade-related investment requirements under GATT discipline than for traded services. However, because of the upsurge in recent years of trade-related performance requirements tied to direct investment in a country (Bale, 1984), trade officials are increasingly concerned that such requirements will seriously undermine the existing liberally oriented trading order. One survey found, for example, that local-content requirements are commonly imposed by governments of advanced developing countries such as Brazil, Mexico and India on companies investing in these countries (Bale, 1984). In about half of the cases, these local-content requirements significantly raised the cost of doing business in these countries. Requirements obliging investing firms to export a certain quantity or proportion of their output are also common. The Mexican government requires foreign companies investing in the auto industry to offset imports and other payments abroad by an equivalent value of exports. In addition, the minimum local-content requirement in this industry is 50 per cent.

In return for accepting trade-related performance requirements (as well as other requirements dealing with such matters as technology transfer, local equity participation and employment of host-country labour), foreign companies usually receive such benefits as tax holidays, rebates of duties on imported goods, infrastructure development and the exclusive right to produce a particular product. While these benefits may be sufficient to enable the foreign firm to earn a profit, the net effect of the various trade-related requirements and benefits is to restrict imports, artificially promote exports, and generally distort the use of world economic resources. Countries that impose performance requirements may reap short-run economic gains, but there is an abundance of development experience indicating that such distorting policies retard the growth process over the long run.

Existing GATT rules cover some trade-related investment requirements, but they have been ineffective in preventing the increased use of these measures. For example, in 1982 the United States initiated a GATT action against Canada's use of local-content and export requirements under its Foreign Investment Review Act on the grounds that they violated Articles III and XVII of the General Agreement. Article III states that imported products must be accorded treatment no less favourable than that accorded to like products of national origin in respect of all laws affecting their sale, purchase or use, while Article XVII requires GATT signatories to act solely in accordance with commercial considerations in imposing measures affecting imports or exports by private traders. The GATT panel appointed to consider the case agreed that Canada's local-content requirements were inconsistent with its obligations under Articles III and XVII but decided that GATT rules did not cover its export requirements.

A specific GATT code dealing with trade-related performance requirements imposed on foreign investors is very much needed to halt the spread of these trade-distorting regulations and to begin eliminating the existing ones. It would be desirable to link it with a general code on investment flows, but the strong disagreement among nations on the extent to which governments should interfere with inward or outward investment flows makes it unlikely that an investment code can be negotiated at this time. While not as strong, there is also considerable opposition, especially among the developing countries, to more explicit GATT rules aimed at preventing the imposition of trade-related performance requirements on the foreign firms permitted to invest in a country. Until a greater consensus can be reached, probably the best way to proceed is to continue to file GATT actions against these requirements (perhaps citing the 'unfair trade' provisions of the Agreement in the case of export requirements) and at the same time to attempt to negotiate bilateral agreements covering performance requirements. Unilateral actions are also likely to be needed to bring some countries to the bargaining table.

Providing greater protection for intellectual property rights and preventing the counterfeiting of trademarked commercial goods are other areas needing an extension of GATT rules. It has been estimated that in the United States alone the value of counterfeit imports is $6 billion annually (Aho and Aronson, 1985). The rapid expansion of trade in such items as computer software has increased the pressures from most of the technologically advanced countries for such rules. A code to prevent counterfeit trade in trademarked merchandise was tentatively agreed on in the Tokyo Round by the major trading nations, but it has not been put into effect because of the opposition of the developing countries, which still argue that the matter should be considered in the World Intellectual Property Organization rather than in the GATT. Whatever organization deals with the issue, the case for strengthening the rules against counterfeiting and the use of intellectual property without some payment to the owners is very strong and justifies the use of discriminatory unilateral actions against offending countries.


# 5   DISPUTE-SETTLEMENT PROCEDURES

Another area of general dissatisfaction with the present trading order is the dispute-settlement system of the GATT. It is alleged that the panels of experts appointed to render non-binding decisions in a dispute are influenced by political pressures from the disputants (particularly the major trading powers) and thus are not objective enough. Some countries have also blocked the adoption by the contracting parties as a whole of a panel's decision when the decision was unfavourable to them. Even when a decision has been adopted by the group, some countries have ignored it and continued the condemned practice.

An obvious drawback to current procedures is the appointment to dispute-settlement panels of officials representing the GATT governments that may later be involved in a dispute. There is a natural tendency for current decisions, or even the question of whether to bring an action against another country, to be influenced by possible decisions and actions on unrelated disputes in the future (Hudec, 1978). It is frequently suggested that the decision-making process would be improved by the establishment of a permanent roster of experts who are not currently representing any government and in whom members have confidence. In addition, it is sometimes proposed that the GATT Secretariat be permitted to initiate inquiries.

The 1982 ministerial agreement that no single nation would veto the dispute–settlement process may help to improve the manner in which panel decisions are handled, but more experience with this is needed before a firm conclusion can be drawn. It must be recognized, however, that, unless there is general acceptance of GATT rules, there is little chance of compliance with these rules, particularly by the large trading nations. The only way to make the dispute-settlement process effective is to restore confidence that the rules work to the advantage of all countries in the long term.

# 6 CONCLUSIONS

Although there is general dissatisfaction with how the international trading regime is operating, there seems to be no practical alternative but to try to improve upon the existing institutional framework. Attempts to replace the GATT with a new organization are, at best, likely to result in an even broader set of rules with a greater number of permitted exceptions than we now have, and, most likely, in no agreement at all. In attempting to modify the GATT to achieve greater conformity with a set of international rules of 'good' behaviour, the greatest danger may be yielding to short-run pressures for agreement at the long-run cost of harmonious international relations and world economic growth. Rule changes must not be made that go against political and economic principles that have proved their worth over many years of historical experience.

Much of the current dissatisfaction in the United States with the international trading order can be traced to US macroeconomic policies that have resulted in a very strong dollar and have put severe competitive pressures on both import-competing and export-oriented industries. No GATT rule changes will alleviate this problem; only changes in macroeconomic policies will do this. As the United States tries to adapt to the ending of its hegemonic position in the world economy, there is also a natural tendency to identify unfair practices of others as the cause of the relative decline in the US competitive position. But GATT rule changes are likely to have only a marginal effect on the US competitive position. Some changes can and should be made that will give the United States more time to adjust to its new role. But we must be careful not to create international trading rules that appear to help in the short term but work against the long-run interests of the United States and the rest of the trading world.

# REFERENCES

Aho, C. Michael and Jonathan D. Aronson (1985), *Trade Talks: America Better Listen!* New York: Council on Foreign Relations.

Bale, Harvey E., Jr (1984), Trade policy aspects of international direct investment policies. In *Recent Issues and Initiatives in US Trade Policy*, ed. Robert E. Baldwin, Cambridge, Mass.: National Bureau of Economic Research.

Cline, William R. (1983), 'Reciprocity': a new approach to world trade policy? In *Trade Policy in the 1980s*, ed. William R. Cline, Washington, DC: Institute for International Economics.

Hudec, Robert E. (1978), *Adjudication of International Trade Disputes*, Thames Essay no. 13, London: Trade Policy Research Centre.

Hufbauer, Gary C. (1984), The unconditional most-favoured-nation principle: Should it be revived, retired, or recast? Paper presented at a conference on international trade problems and policies, Melbourne, Australia, 13–14 February.

Neu, C. Richard (1986), International trade in banking services, Paper presented at the Centre for European Policy Studies/National Bureau of Economic Research Conference on Europe–United States Trade Relations, Brussels, 12–14 June.

Nogues, Julio J., Andrzej Olechowski and L. Alan Winters (1985), The extent of non-tariff barriers to industrial countries' imports. Washington, DC: World Bank.

Sampson, Gary P. and Richard H. Snape (1985), Identifying the issues in trade in services, *The World Economy* 8 : 171–81.

US Department of Commerce (1985), *United States Trade Performance in 1984 and Outlook*, Washington, DC: US Department of Commerce, International Trade Administration.

Winters, L. Alan (1985), Negotiating the removal of non-tariff barriers, Washington, DC: World Bank.

Wolff, Alan W. (1985), The need for new GATT rules to govern safeguard actions. In *Trade Policy in the 1980s*, ed. William R. Cline, Washington, DC: Institute for International Economics.

# 15 Alternative Liberalization Strategies*

## INTRODUCTION

All the major trading blocs have expressed dissatisfaction with the illiberality of the present international trading system. The United States complains that most other nations have failed to open their markets to the extent it has and that many nations artificially promote exports to the United States by unfair subsidization and dumping. Members of the EC contend that they are unable to penetrate the markets of Japan and many developing countries because of protectionist policies while at the same time Europe is being flooded with exports of manufactured goods from these same countries. In response, Japan maintains that its competitive ability is based on free-market forces and that, with few exceptions, its markets are as open as those of other major industrial nations. The smaller industrial nations also complain about the lack of open markets in many countries, and the land-abundant members of this group join the United States in strongly protesting against the protection given to agriculture in the EC and Japan. The developing countries object to the high barriers erected in the industrial nations against such labour-intensive manufactured goods as textiles and to the high effective rates of protection on many processed natural resource products.

This dissatisfaction with the existing trading system has led to a number of proposals for halting the protectionist trend of recent years and restoring a more liberal international trading regime. The proposals differ in three major ways: (1) the economic, political, and social factors deemed important in analysing the prospects of greater liberalization; (2) the degree of liberalization that their proponents seek; and (3) the extent to which they address the alleged causes of breakdown of the postwar

* From Herbert Giersch (ed.) (1987), *Free Trade in the World Economy: Toward An Opening of Markets*, Kiel: Institut für Weltwirtschaft an der Universität Kiel, pp. 579–604.

liberal trading order. It is the purpose of this paper to analyse and evaluate a selected number of these proposals.

The first section of the paper considers two broad analyses of trading regimes that emphasize different factors in understanding the prospects for a return to a more liberal trading order: one stresses the economic power relationships among trading nations and the second stresses the legal framework in which trade and other economic institutions operate. The second section discusses the importance of satisfactory domestic and international macroeconomic conditions. The next three sections focus on alternative strategies for moving toward a more liberal trading regime. The third section analyses proposals for utilizing a multilateral approach, and the fourth section sets forth the arguments for proceeding on a bilateral and regional basis toward more open trade. The fifth section considers a strategy of aggressive retaliation with discriminatory taxes and subsidies to force certain countries to abandon their beggar-thy-neighbour policies and accept a liberal multilateral trading order. The sixth section evaluates the three approaches by considering the likelihood of their being implemented and the extent to which, if adopted, they will serve to move the trading community toward multilateral liberalization. The last section puts forth another alternative, namely holding a negotiation on subsidies and other unfair trade practices to halt the spread of protectionism and set the stage for multilateral liberalization.

## 1   THE STRUCTURE OF NATIONAL ECONOMIC POWER, LEGAL RESTRAINTS ON TRADE POLICY-MAKING AND THE LIBERAL TRADING ORDER

According to the theory of hegemonic stability associated with such writers as Kindleberger (1973), Gilpin (1975), and Krasner (1976), when a nation emerges as the dominant and most economically efficient world power—as did the United Kingdom in the nineteenth century and the United States in the years following World War II—that nation finds it in its economic and political interest to promote the collective good of global stability through a liberal international trading and monetary regime. When the hegemon begins to lose its dominant position, as the United States has since the mid-1960s, the free rides given to smaller states by the hegemon's liberal trade policy, coupled with the MFN principle that this policy involves, are no longer politically tolerable to domestic economic interests. Consequently, the early versions of this theory predicted the inevitable collapse of the liberal postwar trading regime and a return to general protectionism.

When the initial dire predictions of the formulators of the hegemonic explanation of regime change failed to materialize, modifications in the theory appeared. Keohane (1984) argues, for example, that independent states have complementary self-interests that enable cooperation to take place within a non-hegemonic environment. Moreover, international institutions such as the GATT facilitate such cooperation. In his view, we are now in a period of transition between the hegemonic cooperation of the postwar period and a new state of affairs characterized either by the current discord or by posthegemonic cooperation. Whether discord or cooperation prevails in trade matters depends, according to Keohane, on how well governments take advantage of existing international institutions to make new agreements on trade matters and to ensure compliance with old ones. He points to the MFA, however, as evidence that the cooperative approach does not necessarily imply the choice of liberal trade policies.

Jan Tumlir also viewed the problem of achieving greater trade liberalization in broad political and legal terms. According to Tumlir (1984), the disintegration of the postwar liberal trading regime is due to legislatures' improper delegation of power to the executive branch of government, coupled with the lack of either international or domestic legal control over the executive's international economic policies. Tumlir criticized the diplomatic authors of the GATT on the grounds they misstated the case for a liberal trade regime by emphasizing that the benefits would stem from the 'concessions' of other countries rather than from the efficiency effects of lower import prices, and they conceived of the GATT as a universal organization in which the wishes of all members should be satisfied. In Tumlir's view, the need for continuing negotiation to keep members satisfied has eroded the basic rules of the organization.

Though Tumlir was pessimistic about the chances of returning to a truly liberal international trading order, he observed some offsetting tendencies to the excessive delegation of power to the executive branch, for example, the increasing use by private individuals of the courts to complain of the arbitrary and unreasonable exercise of trade-regulatory powers by national executives. He welcomed the US Supreme Court's decision in the Chadha case that declared the legislative veto to be inconsistent with the constitutional division of powers between the executive and legislative branches, seeing it as a step that would force Congress to use more care when it delegates powers to the executive branch.

## 2   MACROECONOMIC POLICIES AND LIBERALIZATION

When policy-oriented economists recognize the importance of the historic political and legal foundations of an international economic regime, most believe that significant steps can be taken toward a more liberal international trading order through practicable changes in existing economic institutions and policies. Many economists, such as Bhagwati (1983), Bergsten (1984), Donges (1984), Aho and Aronson (1985) and Hufbauer and Schott (1985), argue that there must not be changes only in the trade area. Because of the increasing interdependence of the world economy, the prospects for reducing protectionism depend not only on satisfactory international monetary and capital-transfer conditions but on domestic monetary, fiscal and regulatory conditions within the major trading nations.

Current protectionist pressures in the United States highlight the importance of the interrelationships between domestic macroeconomic policies and trade policy. The huge US trade deficit, which reached $140 billion in 1985, has sparked the introduction of some 200 trade bills in the US Congress, most of which their sponsors justify on the grounds that they will help reduce this deficit. One is the Trade Emergency and Export Promotion Act, introduced by members of Congress Richard Gephardt and Dan Rostenkowski, who chairs the Ways and Means Committee, the key House committee dealing with trade legislation. The purpose of the measure, according to its authors, is to 'reverse the enormous shortfall in our balance of trade', which they attribute to '(1) the overvalued US dollar, (2) the persistent growth of foreign unfair trade barriers, and (3) the lack of a coherent US trade policy' (Rostenkowski and Gephardt, 1985, p. 2). The bill mandates the imposition of a 25 per cent duty on any major US trading partner (defined as a country that has over $7 billion in annual trade with the United States) whose exports to the United States exceed its imports from the United States by 65 per cent or its exports to the world exceeded its imports from the world by 50 per cent, excluding oil trade. The Senate version of the bill also requires the US Trade Representative to apply counter-subsidies on exports of agricultural products when other countries are subsidizing their agricultural exports.

Unfortunately, the legislators' explanation of the causes of the US trade deficit is incomplete and flawed. What is worse, there is no reason to expect that the import-restricting and export-promoting actions mandated in the bill would reduce the US trade deficit. As economists have been pointing out for many years, trade deficits or surpluses are largely determined by macroeconomic conditions. The difference between a country's total exports and imports of goods and services represents its foreign investment, which, together with domestic investment, equals its aggregate investment. Aggregate investment, in turn, is by definition equal to aggregate saving, which is composed of private saving plus the difference between government taxes and government expenditures, in other words, government saving. The US trade deficit has its roots in a significant fall in aggregate saving brought about by the increase in federal government expenditures relative to tax collections. Since private saving has not increased to offset this decline in government saving, the effect of the increased government expenditures must be to crowd out either domestic investment or net foreign investment. The rise of interest rates as the government has bid for funds to finance its deficit in an environment of tight monetary policy has not only tended to discourage private investment but has led to a return of US funds previously invested abroad and an inflow of foreign capital. Consequently, the trade balance has turned significantly negative and the value of the dollar has risen substantially compared with the late 1970s as the international demand for dollars has increased. Fortunately, within the last year the dollar has depreciated significantly, a development that is likely to reduce the pressures for protection considerably once its trade-balance effects occur.

Unfair trade practices and the lack of a coherent US trade policy have had only a minimal effect on the US trade balance, since they have little effect on aggregate savings or investment. Unfair trade practices can, of course, cause trade balance deficits in particular product sectors. But under a flexible exchange-rate system, these deficits lead to a marginal depreciation of the dollar and thus to an offsetting of marginal increases in exports and decreases in imports in other sectors.

Similarly, the import surcharges required under the Rostenkowski–Gephardt bill are unlikely to have an appreciable effect on the US trade balance. The increased profits (and thus saving by import-competing industries that benefit from protection) will tend to be offset by lower profits and saving in export sectors that are harmed by the protection. Furthermore, most estimates of the revenue implications of proposals for import surcharges conclude that any favourable balance-of-trade effects will be offset by a further appreciation of the dollar. Retaliatory actions by other countries would also make the deficit problem worse.

While the US domestic policies that have brought about the trade deficit have benefited export industries in other countries, the outflow of capital from these countries represents funds that might otherwise have gone for domestic investment purposes. Furthermore, the high level of US interest rates has forced other countries to maintain high interest rates in order to control the capital outflow. This has depressed investment in such sectors as construction and further exacerbated their unemployment problem. In Europe and other areas where unemployment is a serious problem, it seems clear that better employment conditions are a political prerequisite to any significant trade liberalization.

A number of economists, besides stressing the need for better international coordination of domestic policies, argue that trade-liberalizing efforts must be linked to international monetary reform, to limit the risk of severe misalignment of the major countries' exchange rates, reduce the volatility of these rates and achieve a long-run solution to the debt problem of many developing countries. They welcome the recent coordinated efforts of the major trading nations to bring down the value of the dollar and reduce interest rates, but they advocate more formal arrangements. Bhagwati (1983) and others also believe that liberalization by the developing countries is unlikely unless larger financial resources are made available to them to ease their short-run debt-repayment pressures. Some suggest tying at least part of this increased financial assistance to trade-liberalizing actions by the recipients.

## 3    THE MULTILATERAL APPROACH TO TRADE LIBERALIZATION

Proponents of the multilateral approach to liberalization, including such recent articulators of this position as Donges (1984), the Scott Study Group of the Trade Policy Research Centre (Scott, 1984), Aho and Aronson (1985), Curzon and Price (1985), the GATT 'Wisemen's' Group (Leutwiler *et al.*, 1985) and Preeg (1985), believe that reductions in all forms of import barriers and export subsidies on a non-discriminatory basis across all commodities would create the most favourable conditions for high, sustained rates of income and employment growth throughout the world economy and for harmonious political relations among nations. They view the increased use of trade-distorting measures in recent years as a regrettable consequence of unwise macroeconomic policies and a reaction to political pressures from particular economically inefficient industries, and they maintain that only through a bold programme of liberalization in all trading sectors can the present creeping protectionism be reversed.

Proponents of multilateral liberalization would end voluntary export restraint agreements (VERs) and OMAs because they curtail trade on a selective country basis and involve the use of quantitative restrictions.

They would require all safeguard actions to be brought within the MFN framework of the GATT. Most also argue that the protection granted under such actions should only be in the form of tariffs, and any tariff increases should be temporary and degressive. There is general recognition that some modifications in safeguard procedures are needed to moderate the pressure to resort to selective protection. There is wide agreement that the country that increases protection under GATT safeguard provisions should no longer be required to compensate other countries with cuts in duties on other products, provided the protection is temporary and degressive. Retaliation would also be ruled out in these circumstances.

More effective measures to assist in the adjustment of workers and capital owners in import-injured industries are also advocated to ease the pressures for selective protection. At present, only the United States and Canada have special assistance programmes specifically aimed at import-injured industries, and recently a number of writers, including Schultz and Schumacher (1984), Mutti (1985), Lawrence and Litan (1986) and Hufbauer and Rosen (1986) have put forth proposals for making these more effective. A novel feature of some of these proposals is that the adjustment assistance to workers would be financed by converting existing quotas to tariffs or by auctioning off the quotas. To overcome the criticism that additional unemployment payments encourage displaced workers to remain unemployed for longer periods, Mutti (1985) and Lawrence and Litan (1986) propose that, in addition to extended unemployment insurance payments and job-retraining programmes, workers be given the incentive to take new jobs by partially compensating them if their earnings are lower in their new employment. The Reagan administration proposed in 1984 that displaced workers be given wage vouchers with which employers who hired them could claim a direct cash subsidy for a specified percentage of the wages paid to the workers. While more evidence on the effectiveness of this approach is needed, one American experiment with wage vouchers proved very disappointing (Burtless, 1985). In addition to special assistance to workers displaced by import competition, most proposals also include provisions, such as relaxed merger standards, to encourage the restructuring of the injured industry to enable it to become more efficient.

Supporters of multilateral liberalization regard the highly protected textile and apparel sector as a prime candidate for structural adjustment. They would use the occasion of the expiration of MFAIII in 1986 to set in place the procedures for bringing this industry back under normal GATT rules. World steel trade, which is increasingly subject to discriminatory quantitative restrictions, would be liberalized. In the agricultural sector, both domestic and international measures distort world trade to a significant degree, and advocates of general liberalization would progressively enlarge the scope for the interplay of market forces in trade in agriculture. An initial step would be to extend the GATT ban on export subsidies to agricultural products.

Advocates of a return to stricter enforcement of the unconditional MFN principle have some disagreement on the GSP. The GATT Wisemen's Group and the Scott Group believe that these tariff preferences have been of limited value to developing countries and, indeed, have acted to divert their efforts from reciprocal negotiations that would have yielded them greater benefits. Preeg and others are willing to 'graduate' the more advanced developing nations from tariff preference and other forms of special and differential treatment but are reluctant to eliminate such treatment entirely.

Clearly, multilateral liberalization cannot be effective without greater international consensus on the appropriate use of domestic subsidies. Most US officials and business leaders believe, for example, that many countries are unfairly subsidizing their industrial production, thereby causing disruptive import surges in US markets. These countries respond that they are using domestic aids for legitimate development or adjustment purposes.

Many see the new Subsidies Code negotiated in the Tokyo Round as too general to be useful in settling disputes that arise on this issue. Complaining about the subsidizing actions of other countries, the US points to the part of the code in which signatories agree to avoid the use of subsidies that 'may cause or threaten to cause injury to a domestic industry of another signatory or seriously prejudice the interests of another signatory or may nullify or impair benefits accruing to another signatory under the General Agreement' (US Congress, 1979, p. 280). Other nations, in support of the use of subsidies, cite another statement in the code: 'Signatories recognize that subsidies other than export subsidies are widely used as important instruments for the promotion of social and economic policy objectives and do not intend to restrict the right of signatories to use such subsidies to achieve these and other important policy objectives which they consider desirable' (US Congress, 1979, p. 279). As the GATT Wisemen's Group pointed out, there is a pressing need for revision and clarification of the GATT rules on subsidies to resolve these different views.

Besides calling for a strengthening of the Subsidies Code and other codes negotiated in the Tokyo Round, proponents of a revitalized multilateral approach to liberalization press for various institutional reforms in the GATT. Improved dispute-settlement procedures stand high on their list of needed reforms. Instead of the current practice of giving preference to government officials as members of dispute-settlement panels, it has been proposed that members be drawn from a list of non-governmental experts who, over time, would develop a harmonious body of case law covering various types of disputes, and that the countries involved in a dispute no longer have the right to veto the acceptance of a panel report by the members as a whole. In addition, speedier and more detailed reporting procedures have often been called for to increase confidence in this method of settling trade disputes.

Granting greater authority to the Director-General is frequently proposed for a better-functioning GATT. For example, the GATT Secretariat might be given the authority to collect information on the extent of protection, monitor trade policies for possible violations of GATT rules, and enter the negotiations over disputes at an early stage.

In addition to strengthening existing GATT rules, those pressing for a return to a more liberal multilateral approach generally favour broadening the scope of trade covered by GATT rules. Services trade is the most frequently mentioned area, but trade in intellectual property and high-technology items and trade-related investment issues are other fields proposed for greater coverage by GATT, with the objective of reducing the use of trade-distorting practices that have arisen in these areas and thereby widening the support for liberalization. Negotiating new codes of good conduct, as was done in the Tokyo Round for subsidies and governmental procurement policies, is the most frequently suggested technique for dealing with these subjects.


## 4 BILATERAL AND REGIONAL APPROACHES TO LIBERALIZATION

Hufbauer (1984) and Hufbauer and Schott (1985) and other observers of the trade policy scene believe that the multilateral approach would have little impact on the deeply embedded distortions existing in the present world trading system. In their view, bilateral and plurilateral initiatives should be welcomed on the grounds that they will eventually mature into multilateral liberalization. Aho and Aronson (1985) and others favour efforts to liberalize on a multilateral basis but are prepared to fall back to a bilateral and regional approach if multilateralism fails.

All recognize that there has been a significant increase in bilateralism and regionalism over the last forty years. The most important regional trading organization is, of course, the EC. Starting out with six member countries in 1957, it now includes, with the recent admission to membership of Portugal and Spain, twelve countries. Moreover, the Community has negotiated special free-trade arrangements with members of EFTA and with the former African, Caribbean and Pacific colonies of Community members. Various free-trade groupings of developing countries, such as the Association of Southeast Asian Nations (ASEAN) and the

Latin American Free Trade Area (LAFTA), have also been formed. Recently the United States has also moved in this direction with the Caribbean Basin Initiative (CBI), the free-trade arrangement with Israel and the launching of negotiations aimed at a free-trade agreement with Canada, as have Australia and New Zealand with their Closer Economic Relations Agreement. The extension of tariff preferences to the developing countries and the negotiation of NTB codes during the Tokyo Round that apply only to those members that are signatories to them are other illustrations of the abandonment of the multilateral approach in dealing with trade issues.

Advocates of the bilateral and regional approach, either as a first-best or second-best means of achieving liberalization, would build upon previous uses of this technique. For example, given the strong opposition of some countries to the inclusion of services trade and trade-related investment requirements on the agenda of the next GATT round, they suggest seeking selective agreements such as the Tokyo Round NTB codes or, if this path is blocked, negotiating bilaterally on these matters, using the threat of selective retaliation under national laws to bring about such negotiations. Agreements reached would be open-ended, in the sense that any country would gain the trade benefits of the liberalization that reduced its own barriers. The hope is that, as these benefits increase with increasing membership in an agreement, those reluctant to participate would find it in their interest to join, so that the liberalization eventually is multilateralized. Even if this does not come about, proponents of the regional approach maintain that it would produce greater liberalization than would efforts to pursue multilateral liberalization directly.

## 5   THE AGGRESSIVE APPROACH TO LIBERALIZATION

Critics of the bilateral and regional approach to liberalization fear that it encourages further breakdowns in the multilateral system and the politicization of world trade. Citing, for example, the resistance of the developing countries to multilateral tariff reductions that gradually erode the diversionary value of their tariff preferences, they point out that vested interests quickly emerge to protect the economic inefficiencies implicit in bilateral and regional arrangements, making it difficult to turn such agreements into liberal multilateral arrangements. They further argue that some of the countries taking advantage of the present lack of reciprocity in the trading system will choose to remain outside of bilateral and regional agreements that require them to open their markets to a greater extent.

An aggressive approach to liberalization is therefore proposed, and

Democratic and Republican leaders in the US Congress are its most vocal proponents, as Ahearn and Reifman (1986) point out. The Rostenkowski–Gephardt Bill outlined in section 2 illustrates this aggressive approach. Congressional leaders and, in fact, most members of Congress believe that the only way to restore open markets is, first, to threaten retaliation against countries that do not provide access to their markets that is substantially equivalent to that offered by the United States, and then to carry through with the retaliation if they do not respond in an appropriate manner. The retaliation would take the form of discriminatory increases in US protection.

A substantial trade deficit with another country or the failure of exports and imports to grow at approximately the same rate from a particular base period is regarded as sufficient evidence that the other country is not providing equivalent market access. As Cline (1983) points out, this new notion of reciprocity is unilateral in nature and means scrapping trade commitments agreed on in previous negotiations.

Another important element in the aggressive approach to liberalization is vigorous retaliation against unfair trade practices. For example, although GATT rules do not presently regard subsidizing agricultural exports as unfair, most members of Congress favour matching the EC's subsidies of agricultural exports with subsidies for US agricultural products. Various forms of assistance to domestic sectors, such as subsidies to high-technology industries or financial aid to depressed firms, would be met either by equivalent subsidies to US manufacturers of the same goods or by discriminatory protection that denies US markets for the products of these sectors.

The premise behind the aggressive approach to liberalization is that making it impossible for countries to increase their export markets by engaging in unfair trade practices will eventually eliminate such 'beggarthy-neighbour' activities, since the instigators will have nothing to gain by these actions. At that point, each country will come to see that only through a policy of open and reciprocal trade is it possible to obtain the income and employment benefits of trade. Defenders of the aggressive approach maintain that the enforcement of current GATT rules is now so lax and the rules so vague that it pays some countries to try to avoid granting full reciprocity and to undertake unfair trade practices.

# 6 AN EVALUATION OF ALTERNATIVE APPROACHES TO LIBERALIZATION

The majority of economists in the industrialized nations and many in the developing countries strongly favour significant trade liberalization on a multilateral basis. In their view, historical experience and economic analysis clearly indicate that multilateral liberalization promotes world economic prosperity and growth whereas restrictionism is associated with sluggish economic performance and periodic balance-of-payments crises. How then do we explain the existence of so much protectionism and discrimination?

Economists frequently attribute it to the lack of political will on the part of governments, that while governments may know that liberal trade policies are best for promoting long-run economic welfare, they lack the resolve to forego the political support of narrow special-interest groups who may lose in the short run from liberalization. Although this explanation has merit, the matter is considerably more complex. It is usually put forth with a finality that discourages further research into the political decision-making process and it may delude economists into believing the solution to thwarting protectionism is easier than is in fact the case. On the basis of the political-will hypothesis, one tends to conclude that greater efforts to educate public officials and the public generally on the advantages of liberal trade policies are the best way to restore multilateral liberalism. Empirical work in the political economy of trade policy, such as that of Cheh (1974), Caves (1976), Lavergne (1983), Baldwin (1985) and Anderson and Baldwin (1987), supports the view that public officials support protectionism not only because of political pressures from special groups but also out of concern for equity and the adjustment problems workers face as a result of industry-injuring shocks, perceived unfair trade practices by other countries, and the need to maintain a strong domestic industrial base. Consequently, to understand better how liberal trade policies can be implemented, economists must analyse the economic and political forces that shape the pressures for protection.

The protectionism that currently threatens the international trading regime has its roots in the structural changes in world production that have brought about a decline in the dominant position of the United States, a concomitant rise of the EC and Japan to international prominence and the emergence of a highly competitive group of NICs. After World War II, the trading regime that was expected to develop involved a sharing of responsibility by the major economic powers for maintaining open and stable trading conditions, but the unexpected magnitude of the immediate postwar economic and political problems thrust the United States into a hegemonic role. US economic dominance manifested itself in the trade, finance and energy fields, and enabled American producers to establish predominant export and investment positions abroad. Then, by facilitating the reconstruction and development of Western Europe and Japan and the industrialization of some of the developing countries, US hegemonic behaviour led eventually to a large increase in import competition in both labour-intensive sectors and certain oligopolistically organized industries and a marked decline in the American share of world exports. These developments significantly diminished the leadership authority of the United States.

When some of their economic sectors suffered with the shifts in comparative advantage, most governments in Western Europe responded by providing injured manufacturing industries with subsidies and injured agricultural sectors with greater import protection and export subsidies. Such behaviour was consistent with the active role these governments played in promoting reconstruction and development.

For the United States, where government intervention to assist injured industries was not accepted policy, the adjustment process has been difficult. When the pressures for adjustment first became noticeable in the late 1950s and early 1960s, it was thought they could be handled by pressing for greater liberalization to reduce the trade-diversionary impact of the formation of the EC and also to open markets in Japan and the developing countries. But this provided only temporary relief from problems that actually signalled the need for major restructuring. After US macroeconomic policies led to a substantial appreciation of the dollar, government, business, labour and agricultural leaders began to express the now-prevalent view that unfair trade practices are a major cause of US competitive problems. By urging more vigorous enforcement of US statutes and GATT rules on unfair trade, they are able to press for import protection and still claim support for the open trading regime the United States did much to establish after World War II. It is clear, however, that the US government is not now prepared to begin the process of dismantling protection in such key sectors as textiles and apparel or in steel. There is pressure for reform in agriculture but this will be politically difficult to carry out. It is not even evident what the US position on selectivity will be.

Nor can much in the way of real pressure for multilateral liberalization be expected from the Community. Most members face severe structural adjustment and unemployment problems, and a strong ideological commitment to free-market policies is lacking in all but a few countries. This means that chances are very slim that the Community will agree to significant changes in the GATT rules on agriculture. Reductions in Community subsidies for depressed industries and for the development of high-technology sectors also appear unlikely in the foreseeable future.

The way the Community is organized works against the development of any major initiative on liberalization. Although its members negotiate as a group through the European Economic Commission, the real power remains in the hands of the individual states, any one of which can block major change in trade policy. Given the highly divergent political, social and economic conditions of the member countries, particularly with the addition of Greece and now Portugal and Spain, it is almost impossible for the Community to take the lead in restoring multilateral liberalism or, indeed, to support this initiative.

Japan is likely to support significant liberalization but not to initiate a move in this direction. Like the United States in the 1920s, it is performing as a major trading power on the export side but not on the import side. Conventional barriers are reasonably low, but the existence of large companies that cover a wide variety of industries and the tradition of consumer loyalty to these companies make it difficult to break into the Japanese industrial market. Attitudes of 'Buy Japanese' that stem from efforts of this natural resource-poor country to become a major industrial power, an apparent aversion to unfamiliar products, especially foreign goods, and language and cultural differences further contribute to the difficulty in penetrating Japan's markets for manufactured goods. Thus, it is not clear that traditional liberalization measures will, in fact, do much to open Japanese markets.

The developing countries are still unwilling to undertake significant liberalization themselves. They are more likely to continue to push for further 'special and differential treatment' rather than for major liberalizing actions by the developed countries. The strong opposition of the developing nations to efforts to liberalize trade in services or reduce trade-related investment requirements will also limit the scope of any agreements on these issues in the next GATT negotiating round.

These positions of the major trading blocs make it unlikely that we will see significant liberalization in the foreseeable future. To expect that, under present international economic relationships, countries will somehow find the 'political will' to undertake liberalization seems to be wishful thinking. Another round of GATT negotiations has begun, but other than extending GATT rules to services trade, counterfeiting and intellectual property and introducing some changes in the dispute-settlement procedures, the main benefit from the negotiations may be simply to hold back further protectionism.

At the same time GATT-sponsored multilateral negotiations are proceeding, there are likely to be additional bilateral and regional agreements negotiated. The greater use of bilateral negotiation to settle disputes seems to be a positive step in reducing trade tensions. The GATT dispute-settlement procedures have proved too cumbersome to deal with the dozens of disputes on non-tariff issues that exist at any one time and mainly concern only a few countries. Some countries seem to take advantage of this fact, engaging in clearly unfair trade practices in the hope that the injured countries will be discouraged from utilizing the time-consuming and costly GATT procedures. Responding on a bilateral level to such actions and threatening retaliation unless the dispute is settled quickly have proved useful in dealing with this problem.

The efficacy of bilateral and regional agreements as a means of promoting liberalization is more problematical. In my view, they are not to be welcomed as a step toward multilateral liberalization. The motivation for bilateral or regional agreements is usually not to achieve mutual economic gains but to strengthen political ties through greater trade, a way for nations to band together to achieve greater collective political and economic power. There seems to be a strong desire to increase the size of regional groupings to display greater strength *vis-à-vis* other powers, but there is resistance to merging the major groupings to achieve multilateral liberalization because this would undermine the political identities that are the reason for the creation of the trading blocs. Thus, in the end, these agreements may act as a barrier to multilateral liberalization.

Pursuit of the aggressive trade policy approach also involves considerable risk for achieving an open trading system. This is most apparent in attempts of the large trading blocs to effect change in each other's behaviour by threatening retaliation. To make the threat credible, it is usually necessary to publicize the alleged unfairness of the other's actions. In turn, the other trading power, to deter the retaliation, may publicize the threatened action and its unfairness. Typically, the news media tend to give wide and sympathetic circulation to their own country's viewpoint and the dispute quickly becomes a matter of national pride. It then is very difficult politically for the government of a major trading power to accept retaliation and discontinue the practices that provoked it. Counter-retaliation is the most likely response. While a retaliatory war may not necessarily result, the outcome is almost surely not greater liberalization; an equilibrium with greater distortion of world trade is more likely.

The retaliatory approach may be effective for a large trading power when it is used against a small country. A small country is generally unable to cause economic injury by retaliating against a large trading nation, but can itself be badly hurt by a large power's aggressive actions. The difficulty with such aggressive action is that, while it may force a small country to stop certain practices, it is at the cost of worsening political relations with the small countries, which see it as exploitation. Large countries are often reluctant to pay this political price since they rely on the support of small countries in their power struggle against other large powers.

## 6   A NEGOTIATION ON SUBSIDIES AND OTHER UNFAIR TRADE PRACTICES

The preceding evaluation of the main proposals for achieving multilateral liberalization leads one to conclude that the most likely scenario for the rest of the 1980s is a continued drift toward further distortions of world trade and greater use of discriminatory measures. The main reason for pessimism is that the United States—the traditional leader of the push for multilateral trade liberalization—is in danger of abandoning this role and concentrating on bilateral and plurilateral agreements coupled with an aggressive trade policy stance toward outsiders. Given the unlikelihood that the EC, Japan or the developing countries will provide any real leadership for multilateral liberalization, the trading world will probably be divided into large trading blocs supported by special (often distortionary) relationships, with trade between these blocs regulated to a considerable degree.

As I have suggested elsewhere (Baldwin, 1985), a strategy that might prevent this outcome is to channel the dissatisfaction of the United States and other countries with the present regime into a multilateral negotiation that deals directly with the sources of this dissatisfaction. This would involve a comprehensive negotiation covering subsidies and other unfair practices, such as those dealing with technical barriers to trade and government procurement policies, that would be conducted in a manner similar to the item-by-item technique formerly used in tariff negotiations and in the determination of items to be covered by the government procurement code. In the crucial area of subsidies, the objective would be to phase out particular subsidies gradually, bind their level for specified periods of time, or perhaps introduce export taxes (where permitted) to offset the export-subsidizing element in domestic subsidies. The incentives for a country to engage in such negotiations would be the prospect of reductions in others' subsidies in return for its willingness to reduce its own subsidies, and the threat that others will carry out the countervailing-duty actions permitted by GATT rules.

Each country would undertake a comprehensive evaluation of all the subsidizing and other unfair practices of other countries that it believes are causing material injury to any of its industries, seriously prejudicing its interests, or nullifying or impairing its GATT benefits. Each participant would then make specific requests of other countries on the reduction or offset of these practices. At the same time, each would announce the countervailing-duty and other actions it was prepared to initiate if bilateral or multilateral negotiations were not successful. If past experience is any guide, most countries would be willing to enter into serious negotiations given the possibility that many others may take restrictive actions against their exports.

The negotiations would begin with the 'confrontation and justification' procedure used in the Kennedy Round for claiming exceptions to the 50 per cent linear-cut rule. Countries that thought, for example, that another's subsidy was inconsistent with GATT rules would present their evidence in a GATT meeting. The subsidizing country would be asked to explain the purpose of the subsidy, any government plans to phase it out or modify it and why it believed the subsidy was consistent with the rules. After any changes in request lists or plans for retaliation resulting from the confrontation and justification procedure, the negotiating process would begin with an exchange of offer lists specifying what, if anything, countries were willing to do to phase out particular subsidies, bind other subsidies, impose export taxes to offset their injury-causing effects or take other appropriate action to respond to the concerns of other participants. At this stage, either a 'confronter' or 'justifier' on a particular subsidy could also call for the formation of a GATT panel of experts to render a non-binding decision on whether the subsidy was consistent with GATT rules.

The negotiation would then proceed on both a multilateral and a bilateral basis, with any participant having the right to request a meeting with other participants to discuss a particular subsidy or other allegedly unfair trade practice. In some instances, several countries would meet with a particular country to seek its agreement to phase out, reduce or otherwise modify an allegedly unfair practice to meet the concerns of the others. In other circumstances, bilateral meetings may be more appropriate, even if the impact of the practice extends to more than one country. The GATT Secretariat would play an active role in coordinating the negotiations and ensuring that all promising lines of agreement were explored.

After these negotiations, each country would decide the extent to which it was prepared to modify its own subsidizing and other allegedly unfair practices and whether it would proceed with countervailing-duty and other retaliatory actions against others. For example, even if two countries believed that their subsidies on certain products were consistent with GATT rules, they might both be willing to phase out their subsidy in return for the phasing out of the subsidy by the other country. For the United States, any such agreements reached would be submitted by the president to Congress for approval and would include the necessary domestic implementing legislation. Industries covered by the agreements would be precluded from seeking countervailing duties during the time period covered by the agreements, just as industries covered by the reciprocal tariff agreements negotiated in the 1930s were not subject to the provision of the 1930 Tariff Act that required the president to set tariffs that equalized the cost of production of US and foreign producers. The escape-clause provisions of Article XIX would still apply, however. When countervailing duties are imposed, they would be presented as technical adjustments consistent with GATT rules rather than as political actions involving matters of national pride.

A greater consensus on the proper role of subsidies may emerge from the negotiating process that would lead to modifications in the Subsidies Code. In particular, a clearer distinction is needed between domestic subsidies of the beggar-thy-neighbour type and those that contribute to the efficient growth of the world economy or can be justified for export-oriented industries on the same adjustment grounds as protection for import-competing industries under Article XIX. Temporary and degressive subsidies should be considered for export-oriented industries that are seriously injured by export competition in third markets. A more difficult problem is distinguishing between subsidies justifiable from an economic viewpoint on infant-industry grounds and those aimed simply at shifting market shares at the expense of collective income in the trading community. Most trade officials would require that any permissible subsidies in this group be temporary, degressive and carefully monitored by the GATT Subsidies Committee. The negotiations may also lead to improvements in the Standards and Government Procurement Codes and to agreement on a new Safeguards Code strengthening Article XIX.

In conclusion, there are several reasons for considering a GATT-sponsored negotiation on subsidies and other unfair trade practices. Most important, such a negotiation could channel the present dissatisfaction of most countries with the existing trading regime in a constructive direction that leads to multilateral efforts to reform the system and away from the destructive, go-it-alone direction in which many countries seem to be headed. The United States would at last get the opportunity to deal directly and comprehensively with the fundamental issue that most concerns many officials. The executive branch is continually bombarded with complaints from members of Congress and the business and labour communities about the unfair trade practices of other countries but, in many instances, has a difficult time coming up with specifics that permit actions under GATT rules. Such a negotiation would enable it to deal with these pressures in a systematic fashion.

Japan and the EC, which believe that most of the other countries' complaints are unfounded, could confront the complainants before the international trading community and force them to come up with substantive objections instead of vague rhetoric. The power of the other

GATT members to force both the US and the EC to modify what these other countries regarded as unacceptably selfish positions was clearly demonstrated in the Tokyo Round negotiations on the tariff-reducing rule. The developing countries and the smaller industrial countries should welcome such a negotiation since it will give them an opportunity to band together as a group to try to modify certain market-contracting subsidizing practices of the large trading powers. The increasing use of bilateral negotiations by the large trading blocs has put the developing countries in a very weak negotiating position. As a group, they will be better able to defend their own subsidizing practices.

There are, however, significant risks in undertaking a negotiation on subsidies and other unfair trade practices. Failure to reach agreements that meet the main concerns of the participants on the fairness issue could touch off a series of countervailing and retaliatory actions that produce a trading regime less satisfactory to all than the present one. The possibility of this outcome should be weighed not only against the chances for a successful negotiation but against the prospects for the trading system if no such action is taken.

# REFERENCES

Ahearn, Raymond, J. and Alfred Reifman (1986), US trade policy: Congress sends a message, In *Current US Trade Policy: Analysis, Agenda, and Administration*, eds Robert E. Baldwin and J. David Richardson, Cambridge, Mass., National Bureau of Economic Research. pp. 103–26.

Aho, C. Michael and Jonathan D. Aronson (1985), Trade Talks: America Better Listen! New York: Council on Foreign Relations.

Anderson, Kym and Robert E. Baldwin (1987), The political market for protection in industrial countries, In *Protection, Cooperation, Integration and Development: Essays in Honour of Professor Hiroshi Kitamura*, ed. Ali M. El-Agraa, London: Macmillan.

Baldwin, Robert E. (1985), *The Political Economy of US Import Policy*, Cambridge, Mass: MIT Press.

Bergsten, C. Fred (1984), An agenda for the London Summit, Statement before the Joint Economic Committee of the United States Congress, 14 May, Washington, DC.

Bhagwati, Jagdish N. (1983), Rethinking global negotiations, In *Rethinking Global Negotiations: A Statement on North–South Economic Strategy*, International Economics Research Center, Current Policy Papers 1, New York, pp. 11–20.

Burtless, Gary (1985), Are targeted wage subsidies harmful? Evidence from a voucher experiment, *Industrial and Labor Relations Review* 39: 105–14.

Caves, Richard E. (1976), Economic models of political choice: Canada's tariff structure, *The Canadian Journal of Economics* 9: 278–300.

Cheh, John H. (1974), United States concessions in the Kennedy Round and short-run labor adjustment costs, *Journal of International Economics* 4: 323–40.

Cline, William R. (1983), Reciprocity: a new approach to world trade policy, In *Trade Policy in the 1980s*, ed. William R. Cline, Washington, DC: Institute for International Economics, pp. 121–58.

Curzon, Gerard and Victoria Price (1985), Is protection inevitable?, *Ordo* 35: 121–36.

Donges, Juergen B. (1984), *The International Trading Order at the Crossroads*, Working Papers, 199, Kiel: Institut für Weltwirtschaft.

Gilpin, Robert (1975), *US Power and the Multinational Corporation: The Political Economy of Foreign Direct Investment*, New York: Basic Books.

Hufbauer, Gary C. (1984), The unconditional most-favored-nation principle: should it be revived, retired or recast? Paper presented at a conference on international trade problems and policies at Melbourne, Australia, 13–14 February.

——. and Jeffrey J. Schott (1985), *Trading for Growth: The Next Round of Trade Negotiations*. Policy Analyses in International Economics, 11, Washington, DC: Institute for International Economics.

——. and Howard Rosen (1986), *Trade Policy for Troubled Industries*. Policy Analyses in International Economics, 15, Washington, DC: Institute for International Economics.

Keohane, Robert O. (1984), *After Hegemony: Cooperation and Discord in the World Political Economy*, Princeton, NJ: Princeton University Press.

Kindleberger, Charles P. (1973), *The World in Depression, 1929–1939*, Berkeley: University of California Press.

Krasner, Stephen (1976), State power and the structure of international trade, *World Politics* 28: 317–47.

Lavergne, Real P. (1983), *The Political Economy of US Tariffs: An Empirical Analysis*, New York: Academic Press.

Lawrence, Robert E. and Robert E. Litan (1986), *Pragmatic Approaches for Preserving Trade*, Washington, DC: Brookings Institution.

Leutwiler, Fritz *et al.* (1985), *Trade Policies for a Better Future: Proposals for Action*, Geneva: General Agreement on Tariffs and Trade.

Mutti, John (1985), *US Adjustment Policies in Trade-Impacted Industries*, Washington, DC: National Planning Association.

Preeg, Ernest H. (1985), Overview: an agenda for US trade policy toward developing countries, In *Hard Bargaining Ahead: US Trade Policy and Developing Countries*, ed. Ernest Preeg, Washington, DC: Overseas Development Council.

Rostenkowski, Dan and Richard A. Gephardt (1985), Introduction of Trade Emergency and Export Expansion Act. Letter to Colleagues, Washington, DC, 14 July.

Schultz, Siegfried and Dieter Schumacher (1984), The re-liberalization of world trade, *Journal of World Trade* 18: 206–23.

Scott, Brian *et al.* (1984), *Has the Cavalry Arrived?* Special Reports, 6, London: Trade Policy Research Centre.

Tumlir, Jan (1984), International trade regimes and private property rights, mimeo.

US Congress (1979), 96th Congress, 1st Session, Agreements reached in the Tokyo Round of multilateral trade negotiations, House Document no. 96–153, Part I, Washington, DC.

# Index